MY LIFE WITH
JOHN STEINBECK

By Gwyn Conger Steinbeck
As told to Douglas Brown

Copyright

Contents

Prologue – Gwyn Steinbeck

If you write a book, you have to have something to say. Long after we are gone, John Steinbeck will be studied, and his works read. His genius as a writer is undisputed, but what of the man?

I do not know of anyone who has discovered the real key to him, but from this story we may find it.

He was a man of complexities, and of a unique nature. At times of anger at himself, he knew he was hurting other people, yet he was helpless to control his anger because of his selfishness.

He was, of course, a literary giant. He was also a man of many lives. I know; I lived with him and shared his agonies, his struggles, his hatreds and jealousies of people and things. I shared his happiness and his joys.

John Steinbeck was not a hero. He was only a tremendously complex man who could be very beautiful one moment and then change into something very unbeautiful.

A tremendous love existed between us. No words can ever express the feelings of this love. Sometimes, love made us better than we were; it does that with everyone. My love for John was such that I had no hesitation in giving up everything I had for him, which I did. That was a mistake. Although our relationship brought us happiness, it also brought unhappiness. At one point, I became the Indian woman...walking three paces behind the master.

When John flirted with other women, he hurt me terribly, but I forgave him as I believed he did not know what pain he was causing. By the end of our marriage, I had lost all of my identity.

Then it was too late. He made me a subservient thing, and I was helpless to change it. This story is a fragment of John's life, but one that I wish to tell. I don't believe that anyone knew him, not his family, but if anyone knew him even a fraction, it was me. I lived part of his life with him and I knew of his masochism, his kleptomania, his drinking, his womanizing and his sadism. John was known to be both gruff and dissident by nature, and he was antisocial. He was, in fact, a middle-aged hippy. He knew the social graces, yes, although he did not care to practice them.

I made him friendlier, pleasanter to other people, and during our relationship, he began to embrace life instead of being a dedicated machine to his work. I believe he had never enjoyed himself in a relationship before the one we shared. I idolized him, and made him laugh. 'I have very strong morals, but I change my morals to fit the situation,' he once told me, before we were married. John's 'truths' were part of his wonderful personality. If he lied about something and I confronted him with it he would simply answer, 'Gwyn, for the moment that is the truth.' John wanted terribly to be loved, but he didn't know how to love. His love was a love of suspicion that was a part of his overall complexity. He had the unhappy life of suffering revenge and jealousy. He tried hard to fight it, but he could not change. There have been and will continue to be books about John, but I hope that in some way this contribution will be a helpful one for the overall analysis. I loved John with a passion. I will until I die. I never stopped loving him or respecting him for his lasting contribution to American and world literature.

John struggled for what he received, and the rewards he

received. He could not stand criticism although he received plenty of it. He earned his success by sweat and struggle. I was blessed, being able to share his most productive years.

But there was much more. There were my love and complete submission in him. To me, he was everything, my whole life. I did not request to change him when I finally did recognize his faults. People in love believe in each other for what they are, and we did in the years we shared.

Gwyn Steinbeck, Palm Springs, California, August 1972

Prologue – Douglas G. Brown

This is the story of a woman's love for a man hailed by the world for his literary genius. It is the story of John Steinbeck, the man, as told for the first time by his second wife Gwyndolyn, the mother of his only children, John and Thom. In later years, she preferred the name Gwendoline, or Gwyn.

Gwyn Steinbeck tells of how John loved, drank, caroused and worked at a fantastic pace and hated with a passion. He was a man of many passions.

She tells of her husband, a man of his time, who became a giant, a legend through his pen…and the price he paid was one of pain through his torment of those who loved him.

Gwyn speaks of John the man, who she said 'was not a hero. He was only a tremendously complex man who could be very beautiful one moment and then change into something very unbeautiful. I not only loved him with a passion, but I forgot to love myself…I think he was in love with love, and such people are always going to be hurt and hurt those they love.'

Gwyn tells of their first meeting, their courtship, living together and their marriage. She speaks of the years as his wife, as the mother of his only two children and of the turbulent years that led to their divorce.

I first met Gwendoline Steinbeck when she had a small art gallery and lived in a modest, two-bedroom house in Palm Springs, California. She had many mementos of her time and travels with her husband, John Steinbeck. She later enjoyed a good social life, hosting receptions for prominent artists at her gallery. She wanted to tell the story of her meeting, love, marriage, and divorce with and from one of the great men of American literature. We had many interviews, from which I created this book. During this period, she suffered from terrible asthma, not eased by her constant smoking and periodic heavy drinking. In the last two years, she lived modestly and, as I understood it, on a low fixed income.

Gwendoline Steinbeck in her last years recalled with clear memory her life with John Steinbeck, the times of happiness that later became a tragedy for her. The story is, as she said, 'but a fragment of John's life.'

But there were times when the challenge of whirlwind days and nights were shared by the two of them and became a unique life experience.

Douglas G. Brown, Palm Springs, California

Preface – Jay Parini

John Steinbeck (1902-1968) was, with Hemingway, Faulkner, and Fitzgerald, among the small handful of American literary giants of the twentieth century; the author of such classic novels as *Of Mice and Men, The Grapes of Wrath, Tortilla Flat, Cannery Row* and *East of Eden*. His achievements were recognized with the Pulitzer Prize in 1940 and the Nobel Prize for Literature in 1962, among many other awards. When he accepted the Nobel in Stockholm, he declared with typical eloquence: 'The writer is delegated to declare and to celebrate man's proven capacity for greatness of heart and spirit—for gallantry in defeat, for courage, compassion, and love. In the endless war against weakness and despair, these are the bright rally flags of hope and of emulation. I hold that a writer who does not believe in the perfectibility of man has no dedication or any membership in literature.'

There is, of course, often a dramatic, even jarring, difference between a writer's art and his life, between what the writer puts on the page and how he conducts himself in human affairs. As a man, like most men, Steinbeck had inconsistencies of character, some of them glaring. He drank too much, often to the point of complete inebriation; he could be thin-skinned and spiteful, hated all forms of criticism and was (in his first two marriages) unfaithful in his relationships. These early marriages failed in part because of ways that he behaved, without much consideration for his spouses.

This self-centered behavior came naturally. Steinbeck grew up in a lovely outpost of American life, in Salinas, California, the only son of a prosperous, middle-class family; needless to say, his mother and three sisters – Elizabeth, Esther, and Mary – doted on him. Spoiled from an early age, the center of family attention, his needs were met by adoring women. (His father seems to have been a remote figure who played a minor role in his development.) The family circle was, for him, an entirely comfortable spot, which he sought to reproduce in his three marriages. To the end of his life, he expected that every wish would be met, and to a surprising degree this happened. He was a lucky man.

His first wife, Carol Henning, adored him. She was brilliant and, by many accounts, quite contrary and demanding herself. They met in Lake Tahoe in 1928, when Steinbeck was just beginning his career as a novelist, working on a forgettable novel about pirates! They married in 1930, and Carol stood shoulder to shoulder with her husband through his most productive years, often editing what he wrote. These were the years of his famous California stories and novels, the work for which he will be ever remembered. She was an eager sounding board and intellectual companion; indeed, she gave him the title of his best-known work, *The Grapes of Wrath*. But Steinbeck drank far too much, was often irascible, and he had a roving eye. In California, in 1938, he met a woman fourteen years younger: Gwen (or 'Gwyn') Conger. She was a singer at a club near Los Angeles, and Steinbeck fell for her at once, although he was shy by nature and it took some time for them to consummate this relationship.

Soon after Steinbeck's divorce from Carol, in 1943 he married Gwyn, and in the six years of their marriage they had two sons,

Thom and John, and moved around a great deal: it was always an awkward and unhappy connection, exacerbated by the shifting circumstances of their lives. They lived in Monterey for a time, or in New York City, often traveling to Mexico and elsewhere. Steinbeck was a restless man, and he seems never to have settled into the marriage with Gwyn, whom many of his friends disliked. As it was, his beloved sister, Beth, said of Gwyn: 'She was awful. You couldn't trust her one bit. I sure didn't. Nobody did, except John – and he learned the hard way about that girl.'

This latter quotation comes from an interview I did with Beth (Steinbeck) Ainsworth when I was writing my 1994 biography of Steinbeck. I had written that book at the invitation of Steinbeck's third wife, Elaine, whom Steinbeck met in 1949 (after his divorce from Gwyn) and married in 1950. John and Elaine soon left for the East Coast, leaving California for good. From this point forward, they moved between an apartment in New York City and a small, beautifully situated house at Sag Harbor, on Long Island. There Steinbeck wrote his last books in an octagonal 'summer house' with a view of the water. Theirs was a happy marriage that lasted until Steinbeck's death in 1968. (Elaine and I were great friends, and I often visited her in New York and once at Sag Harbor.)

To me, Elaine had no positive words for Gwyn, whom she often told me was unstable and alcoholic, an unstable mother to her sons, and someone whom John never trusted with the children. I found in writing my biography it was impossible to get a good take on Gwyn. Steinbeck had been wildly attracted to her: she was beautiful, tall, and willowy. She had a lot of energy and intelligence, or so I gathered from various accounts. But as she had passed away, it was impossible to know how she felt about her famous husband and what that marriage was really like. Did Steinbeck value her? Did he treat her well? Did they have much in common? Was he a consistent husband, someone she could trust? What sort of effect did she have on his writing life, and why did the quality of his writing often seem to waver in the forties, fifties, and sixties?

The little book before you, *My Life with John Steinbeck*, is a memoir of her marriage to Steinbeck by Gwyn that has just come to light. To a degree, it answers these questions, and it's a compelling story, with many biographical details, asides, and anecdotes that make it well worth the price of admission. Published here for the first time, it's a genuinely significant literary discovery. Her memoir sheds light on the part of Steinbeck's life that has been in shadow over half a century. As readers will discover, Gwyn's voice is passionate, radiant and clear, and it tells us a lot about why Steinbeck might have fallen in love with her.

What is no longer in doubt is that she loved him deeply and regretted the course their marriage took, although this love was complicated in many ways by his rudeness, his selfishness, his lack of concern for Gwyn, who herself strikes me as a difficult character. Near the end of this memoir, she writes that 'somewhere our love for each other was turned off, for a moment.' But she swears that it didn't die: 'I know that the love we shared with each other never really ended and it never will.'

Her words might seem like a piece of sentimentality, a late and somewhat fantastic flash of fondness by a former wife who found her marriage less than tolerable. Gwyn was the one who terminated it, as she firmly reminds us here. So what went wrong? Many things, it would appear. At one point, for instance, Gwyn comments on the fact that John was 'taking aphrodisiacs.' She writes: 'He would get drunk and take those pills and want to plunge into his conjugal rights and have heavy sex. It is common knowledge that a man who has a little too much to drink will not be exactly at his best when it comes to making love. John usually tried when he was in that condition, though there were times when he was half in that condition, and even when he was just a little merry.' She continues to say that she knew that 'unless there were some drastic changes in John's attitude,' the marriage would never last, and it didn't.

The affair began slowly enough, with notes passed back and forth between them, and casual meetings when Steinbeck would visit Los Angeles; in due course, they fell into bed. It was a rainy weekend, and they took to each other passionately. 'I gave myself to him, willingly. It seemed like years since our first meeting. I thought of nothing but him. In bed, he was strong,' she recalls: 'I was ready for him, and he for me. We wanted each other, and gave ourselves to each other, passionately.'

But the relationship had its ups and downs from the outset, as John was often moody and remote, restless, irritable and demanding. In one extraordinary moment described here, he brought Gwyn and Carol together and told them to fight it out. He would go with one or the other, and he seems not to have cared which of these women succeeded in the battle over his soul. Briefly, Carol had won the day, insisting that she must keep her husband. But soon that fell apart, for good, and Steinbeck married

Gwyn.

Her opinion of him darkened soon after the marriage, as his daily habits often appalled her. He had a rat for a pet, for instance, and by Gwyn's account he was naturally cruel: 'John was a sadistic man, of many emotions, but being sadistic was one of his private qualities.' He would let loose his pet rat to frighten visitors, especially women. And he seems to have enjoyed doing so. (The rat seems to have represented Steinbeck's 'shadow self,' to adopt a phrase from Carl Jung: he used the rat to embody a seamy and frightening aspect of himself.)

Gwyn's story is full of harsh moments, often turning on her sense of betrayal, as when he preferred to talk to Lady 'M' in New York than her. The implication that he was having an affair with her is strong. Steinbeck often traveled by himself, and Gwyn worried that he was lost in his world, drifting away from her, preferring the company of famous friends. As it happened, he was doing a great deal of film work in the forties, writing *Lifeboat* and *Medal for Benny*, and working on other scripts, including a documentary in Mexico. He moved among Hollywood stars, some of them close friends, such as Burgess Meredith. Steinbeck drank to excess and cursed critics who dared to challenge the greatness of his work. He sought adventures away from home, as when in the middle of the Second World War he suddenly (over Gwyn's objection) set off for North Africa and Italy as a war correspondent, nearly getting himself blown up in the Battle of Salerno. (His collection of reports from the front, *Once There Was a War*, remains one of my favorite Steinbeck books.)

Gwyn proves an able observer of Steinbeck, the writer. She

notes his almost fanatical dedication to his work: 'He began his same usual work schedule, the one he kept to whenever he wrote, no matter where we lived. He arose early and made his ranch coffee. He always wanted a good brand of coffee, and it was always ranch coffee. A little past daylight he began his day, and after our coffee and talk sessions John, with his pajama top and khakis, went into his nest, usually by seven or seven-thirty.' He took a brief break for lunch at noon, although he rarely said much to her during these meals, not wishing to disturb whatever was happening in his head: 'If he were going strong, he would only have more coffee. He never talked, never said a word and I would not speak to him. Usually, his average output in those days was anywhere from twenty-five hundred words to five thousand words a day.'

Gwyn felt excluded, unable to get into her husband's field of consciousness, watching him from a remote distance. In her view, he was not a good father and took little interest in Thom or John. She had eventually to sue him in family court for child support, which Steinbeck gave only reluctantly. There was nothing good about this marriage, it would seem, and yet – if we are to believe Gwyn, and I do – she loved him dearly, and was always glad to have been married to a passionate and creative man, however impossible he might be.

She had a ringside seat to his creativity and was there when he wrote *The Moon Is Down*, *Cannery Row*, *The Wayward Bus*, *The Pearl* and other works. She saw firsthand how he managed, with deliberate effort and almost inhuman concentration, to write in the midst of chaos; some of this arose because of their unhappy marriage, which probably should never have occurred, as it didn't do much for the couple and was undeniably harmful for the children.

This memoir should fascinate anyone who loves the work of Steinbeck, and who wants to know as much as possible about his world. What sort of man was he? How did he manage to write so much and so well? The answers that Gwyn gives to so many questions are not pleasant ones, and her bitterness shows through in these recollections. How could it not? But there is something authentic about her response to the man, John Steinbeck, whom she married, with whom she had two sons. Authenticity shines through these pages; that cannot be denied.

Jay Parini

Acknowledgements

The family of the late Douglas Brown and Lawson Publishing Ltd would like to thank the following for their help and guidance:

James (Jim) M. Dourgarian. Bookseller and Steinbeck Specialist. California, USA

Stephanie Hale, B.E.M. Writer. Oxford, UK

Hannah Hargrave. Publicist. Chester, UK

Joanna Lawson. For her great support. Montgomery, UK

Jane Needham. For her genealogical research. Shrewsbury, UK

Jay Parini. Poet and biographer. Vermont, USA

Pat Weaver. For her IT and secretarial wizardry. Montgomery, UK

Susan Weinstein. Writer and publicist. New York, USA

The photograph on the front cover, courtesy of Ron Seymour of Illinois, was taken by the late Maurice Seymour as a CBS publicity photograph in 1938.

Bruce Lawson. Lawson Publishing Ltd. August 2018

Some Words of John Steinbeck

'This is a time of great joy. It will never be so good again – never. A book finished, published, read – is always an anti-climax for me. The joy comes in the words going down, and the rhythms crowding in the chest, and pulsing to get out.'

John Steinbeck. Journal of a Novel. The East of Eden letters 1951

'I have never looked on myself as an author ……….. I don't think I have ever considered myself an author. I consider myself a writer, because that is what I do. I don't know what an author does.'

John Steinbeck. Sweden 1962

1 – CHICKEN SOUP

One night, in late 1938, I went to a room at the Aloha Arms in Los Angeles, carrying a pot of my own freshly made chicken soup. There, in a room that smelled of drink and tobacco, and lying in an old Murphy bed and obviously in great pain, was John Steinbeck. He looked at me with his cold blue eyes. 'Sit down,' he said. 'I really don't like chicken soup.'

Max Wagner, a long-time friend and then a public relations man, was with me that night. The Wagner brothers were all madcaps, but the most charming Irishmen you would ever want to know. Max had been an admirer and escort for months. Max told me his 'friend from Salinas' was in town and was very ill, in pain and hiding out. 'What do you want me to do about it?' I asked.

Max was what a friend should be; he cared. 'I told him you were the best cook in the world. He hasn't eaten anything. Will you make him some chicken noodle soup? I already told him you and your mother made the best chicken noodle soup in the world.' I said I would see his 'friend from Salinas' on my day off, but Max made me promise I wouldn't tell anyone that John was in town. At that time, I was a twenty-year-old singer. I was a staff singer with Columbia Broadcasting Studios, and also worked at a cocktail lounge and restaurant next door to the studios. Max picked me up in his funny little second-hand Buick, and we went to the hotel. I entered the room still holding my pot of soup, and I asked: 'Have

1

you had any food?' 'No, just coffee,' he answered. He had had more than that. Obviously, he had been drinking heavily. 'Did you bring my scotch, Max?' 'Yes.' 'Pour some and let's all have a drink.'

Max did, from a new bottle, and after John drank his scotch, I made him eat the soup. I washed and bathed him, rubbed his back and his legs. He was a man of magnificent physique, yet never in my life had I ever seen such varicose veins of the legs.

We started to talk, and conversation came easily for this man of words, and his newfound Florence Nightingale. He had just finished *Fight for Life*, and he was running from the world and a tiff with his wife, Carol. He was in fact, suffering from a nervous breakdown. His whole condition was heightened by his own sense of insecurity as to how *The Grapes of Wrath* would be received but, more than that, he was afraid people were using him. Later, I learned that he felt this way all his life.

As it does so often when we least expect it, life takes us into so many things that we never visualized – as it did that night I met John. I guess it was a night of complete chemistry, a beginning of years of a love that became great and, in its way, would be forever.

Before I left with Max, John said he would like to see me again. Two nights after the back-rubbing, the hours of talking and chicken soup, he did.

To my surprise, he walked into the club where I was singing, leaning on a blackthorn cane like a cripple, and sat down at a table and listened to me sing. During a break, I joined him, and we had a few drinks. He was quiet, somewhat reserved, yet he was inquisitive just like any man. 'What else do you do besides sing?' he asked. I said nothing and just sat and looked at my drink. 'Who are you? Where are you from?' Natural questions. 'I was born in Chicago,' I began. 'My ancestors came here in the late 1600s, and one part of me is American Indian, and the rest is Welsh and English.' So I told him of my heritage, and he listened, his eyes piercing my whole body, dissecting and undressing me. He stayed until I finished work and we went for coffee. Over coffee, he told me a little about himself, but it was obvious he wanted to talk. He did tell me why he did not like chicken soup. When he was a little kid, his mother used to make him kill chickens. He hated the job.

'I didn't know it, but my father had bought some fighting cocks, and my mother asked me to kill six chickens because we were expecting relatives to visit. I did. I killed my father's six fighting cocks! I really got whopped for it. From then on I just hated to wring a chicken's neck. I hate chickens,' he said. As I was to learn so well in later years, John Steinbeck could not only hate chickens; he could hate many things, especially people who crossed him and even people he did not even know. And when he hated, he hated with a passion.

In those early days of our relationship, I began to know John as a man with whom I was falling in love. When John looked at me with those cold blue eyes, there was that unexplainable feeling that took over my whole being. In the days that followed our first meeting, he began to be a regular customer at the club. If he did not appear in the evening, he visited my mother and I, in the afternoon. Then, I was living with my mother and my stepfather, who was in the produce business. Times were not easy then, for it was in the last years of the Great Depression. John admired how my mother and I could manage with the small amount of money available. Oddly enough, he always managed to arrive around supper time. 'It is just a casual call,' he would say, looking me straight in the eye with his Svengali eyes. After we had eaten dinner, he would usually say, 'I would like to take you out to dinner sometime.'

Basically, John was a very shy man. He did not ask me if I liked him, yet somehow I knew that I did. At the same time, to me, he was like a little stray dog, who needed help and I felt I was the one who could help him. Finally, I accepted his constant invitation to dinner. First, we enjoyed a few cocktails with my mother and my stepfather, and then we went to The Little Bit of Sweden on Sunset Boulevard. Throughout that first dinner together we talked in subdued tones. Again he asked me all kinds of questions. What did I do? Who was I in love with? What kind of books did I read? Again, I went into my background and then he suddenly said, 'You are an earth woman.' 'I guess I am,' I answered. Now how, at twenty years old, do you know if you are an 'earth woman'? You don't, but since the age of twelve, I had a thirty-six-inch bust – if that helps.

That night he began courting me like a Don Juan. He rubbed knees under the table, and he held my hand, yet, strangely, he kept covering his face with his hands because he was afraid to be recognized in the restaurant. Our dinner was a very pleasant affair, but the time came when I told him I had to go to work. He reached for his wallet and found he had no money! I paid the check. I never forgot that. Apparently, it was the last money he had for the whole week. Of course, John was polite and said he would pay me the next day.

John found himself without any money when we dined together

three times in a row!

Naturally, I wondered why such a man of means never had any cash on him. John explained that his wife, Carol, gave him an allowance of about $35 a week. He did not want to be bothered with money. I found this hard to believe, but apparently, it was true. Never in his life did John know how to balance a checking account, and when he was married to Carol, she took care of the finances. That was the way he wanted it.

We did not see each other after that for quite some time. John kept in touch and sent me little books and little gifts, mostly books, and each one with a short note tucked inside. He said he wanted me to have the books in case he never saw me again; everything between us, which was not much at this point, had to be kept secret, he said. He sent me such books as the *World Anthology of Poetry*, with 'Black Marigolds' dog-eared; all of George Burrows and all of Robert Louis Stevenson. Later, when he thought he was going back to Carol and would never see me again, he sent me the translation of *Synge Marking Petrarch's Death of Laura.* He continued to live with Carol in Los Gatos, and I kept working in Hollywood, singing at CBS and earning an extra dollar whenever I could by working as an extra. When I sang, I either worked with Freddy Garger or Matt Dennis, two very talented musicians.

That winter, I got a strep throat but continued to sing, which was a mistake, but a dollar was a dollar, and still is. I kept getting sicker and sicker until finally I was put in the hospital in Los Angeles. My doctor was Alfred Huenergardt, who was incidentally in Palm Springs where, in those days, Hollywood's stars were beginning to discover fun, relaxing and loving weekends. In the early 40s, Charlie Farrell's Racquet Club was the only place for tennis, drinking, lazing and trysts.

When you feel sick or horrible, all you want to do is get well, of course, but with my throat, it seemed as if I were heading for eternal rest. Doctor Huenergardt came into my room and quietly announced to my mother and stepfather that the infection had reached the lower lobes of my brain. I shall never forget it. 'I must be honest,' he said in a matter of fact voice, 'there is very little chance you will live. The infection has entered the mastoid.' That was far from encouraging, but at least he was honest. The only thing he could think of was to lance my eardrums and hope that some of the infection would come out.

While everything looked pretty bad for me, I remembered something that John had told me the night of our first meeting, something about when he had been doing *Fight for Life,* his story about saving a woman from her puerperal fever caused by filth. He had gone to a Chicago clinic where they had saved women's lives by using sulfa for all strep infections. Somehow I managed to get that out to the doctor.

'Send a wire to Doctor Harry Ben-Aaron, and he'll get it to you,' I managed to say.

More people than Doctor Harry were involved. Paul de Kruif entered the picture and contact was made with Chicago. But by this time I was getting ready for the beyond. Fortunately, Paul mailed the sulfa, yet when it did arrive Doc Huenergardt did not know how much dosage to give me. I was given plenty, and it saved my life. For a while, I climbed the walls and was seriously ill for several days. Gradually I returned to the land of the living, and when I was able to sit up, I asked for a mirror. Being a woman, I naturally wanted to have a look at myself, and to braid my beautiful hair. My request was refused. I couldn't understand why. After all, to a woman, a mirror often is as important as a husband. I finally persuaded a nurse to let me have one. When I looked at it, there was not the fairest maiden in all the land. Instead, I saw a woman who was blue, beautifully blue! Even the moons on my fingernails had turned blue. I did not get upset. I was alive. The sulfa had saved my life: I said a prayer of thanks. Better blue than dead.

It was a long time before I fully recovered. John called me a few times and said he would try to see me. About that time he had gone to Chicago to have an operation on his back. It turned out that it was not his back that was the trouble – it was his tonsils! So I had a strep throat, and he had his tonsils out.

Now I was out of work and running short of money. Bad news. The club had hired another singer. In those days, clubs did not hold jobs open for long. I turned on the female charm and got my job back with CBS through a dear man, Russell Johnson. I returned to the club and did the little afternoon show from the cocktail lounge. I still felt weak, but I had to work. You still have to pay those hospital bills. I was happy because I was singing again, and I still had a good voice. Then one day I received a letter from my father whom I had never seen during my life, except once when I was fifteen. He had remarried and was living in Tampa, Florida. My mother had written to him and told him I was ill. He replied that he and his faith were praying for me. He was a Christian Scientist. He sent me $50 and a ticket to come to Tampa. He said he wanted to get to know me better and I could learn to know him better. Isn't that amazing? After years of emptiness between us he suddenly wanted to know his daughter. Perhaps his conscience had begun to bother him. I don't know. Russell told me CBS had a station in Tampa and, if I wanted, I could work there. I thought about it and decided to go.

I wrote John care of Ed Ricketts at his marine laboratory in Monterey. Ricketts was a brilliant marine zoologist and John's great friend. Ricketts, when I came to know him better, was enamored by sex, which didn't stop him from his work with sea creatures. Anyway, John was still with Carol. I wasn't a pusher, and have never been one of those women who will go nuts if they don't get something they want badly. By now, I was very much in love with John, yet I respect marriage and I respected him. Somebody had to drop out, and I was the logical one. So, I went off to Florida and worked at the Tampa CBS Station for six months.

One day Russell called. The San Francisco State Fair had started, and he wanted me to join his staff in the Bay City. I had had enough of Florida. I packed my bags and headed back west. It was 1939, and I was soon caught up in the whirl and excitement of the Exposition. Once again I was doing what I loved, singing, but I worked hard and enjoyed myself.

San Francisco is a beautiful city; it is a great city, crazy but with plenty to occupy the mind. That year of the Exposition there was plenty to see and do. One night, I received a long-distance telephone call. It was the Lab in Monterey. John had heard me singing on the radio. 'I have to see you,' he said.

Fine, that will be nice, I answered. His call was unexpected, but then John always did the unexpected. As our relationship developed over the months, you never knew what John was going to do next. He was an extremely impulsive man, always restless, always searching for something, for life – but was I that life?

In those days John was taking flying lessons, and he flew to San Francisco in a chartered plane. We had a long talk over drinks at the Cliff House. 'Things aren't getting any better between Carol and me, and I can't get over you,' he said over his scotch and my vodka. 'I think I am very much in love with you. Will you wait for me?' His words came as a shock. By then, I already loved him, but I did not commit myself. All I remember saying was, 'I'll try.'

He went back to Carol, and I went back to my singing. Before the Fair ended, he was back in San Francisco to see me again. This time he asked me to meet him at the top of the Mark Hopkins Hotel. As people usually do in clubs, we sat at a low cocktail table. I happened to be short-sighted and had forgotten my glasses. He ordered Stingers. We had not been there long when John said 'Gwen, everybody is staring at you because you are so attractive.' I leaned over and patted his knee and happened to look down. 'Oh, you have a new keyring,' I said. He looked down to find something other than a keyring. Everyone had not been looking at me.

John had his fly open!

2 – MOTHER KNOWS BEST

Our feelings for each other developed slowly. We did not leap into bed. I knew that whatever was going to happen between us would need time. After the Exposition, I returned to Los Angeles, and John went back and forth to Mexico for his work on *The Forgotten Village.* He had a great affection for Mexico and its people. During this period he wrote letters and told me he had written 'some poems' for me, and he wrote about his love for me. He wrote twenty-five love poems to me, a suite. In his letters, there was an anxiousness although he urged me to wait for him, always to wait for him. Frankly, I was in no hurry to become his permanent acquisition; besides, I did not want to hurt his wife, Carol. Apparently, something was happening that was causing a rift in their marriage. What, I did not know and did not want to know. It was none of my business. I later found out that Carol did not know then, of his relationship and feelings toward me.

Life went on, and John continued to send me letters and little pieces of paper with messages scribbled on them. They were sad writings, secret and furtive little things. And then, during one of his trips he called and announced his arrival in Los Angeles. John's coming and going during this period was like predicting the tides in a universe without a moon!

'I have some presents for you, darling,' he said. He loved to give presents, especially crazy presents, and being a woman I naturally liked to receive them. When I could afford it, I also liked to give them. In those days, I could rarely afford it.

The presents he gave me were a voodoo bird in a coffin, a silver bracelet and a small book of love poems. I must admit that the voodoo bird gift surprised me, but later I found out that John enjoyed and delved into the mystical. Some people have denied it (and they still do) but while John was and may have been many things he was, too, a firm believer in the supernatural. He also had a habit of picking up pebbles from the ocean floor and, if it was a soft stone and had what he called a 'culture,' then he kept it in his pocket. As the Greeks have their worry beads and the Chinese keep jade in their sleeves, so John kept his stones in his pocket.

Another weekend, when he returned from Mexico, he again brought me presents. This time it was an opal ring. He bought it because he thought opal was my birthstone, yet I am a late October child. That was a beautiful thing about John, his love of surprising people. Whenever he gave a gift, he was as excited as a little boy at Christmastime. He told me the story of how he found the opal ring, and it was then I received my first insight into a man who, once he wanted something, never stopped until was his – no matter what means he had to take to get it. I have met some women who are like that, too.

John first saw the opal around the neck of Trini, a witch doctor. It had a bubble in it, and, according to Trini, the god of evil hairs lived there, and she used the opal to cure children of pneumonia by placing it on their chest. As I said, John was determined to have Trini's jewel for me. It was not easy for him to get it. The old woman at first refused to sell it, but John was not a man to give up, so he went to a nearby village and bought chairs for Trini. The chairs were a sign of stature, and she thanked him, took them, but still kept the opal! Again, John returned to the village and bought two more chairs which created an even bigger thrill among the people of Trini's village. Still he could not get the opal. By now, John was irritated. Back he went to the area, some 20 miles away, and found a cow that had just been freshened and was quite pregnant. He took the cow back to Trini. She gave him the opal.

Later, he took it to Mexico City and had it mounted by one of the primitive artists. The top of the ring represents two cow horns, and the space inside is lined with gold. It reads in Spanish, '*Yo te cuido*,' which means 'I protect you,' and one side has the initial 'J' and the other reads 'G.'

The weekend he gave me the opal ring, we made contact with Max (Wagner) and went on the town in Los Angeles drinking tequila and eating all kinds of Mexican foods. We had a ball. We ended up on Olvera Street. John liked good food, all kinds, and it's well known he liked a good drink. That was a wonderful night, one of many I was to have with him, but, as with all good things in this life of ours, it had to have its ending. None of us wanted the night to end, so as a remembrance I bought three little silver rings with clam shells on them, little bells, and we performed what was like a brotherhood ceremony; we each kept a ring.

Max, John and I had great times together, times when we laughed, joked, sang, raised constant hell in an almost childlike fashion. Oddly enough, in those early days of our relationship John and I were never alone, although when we were, John wanted to make love to me as any man would. He tried hard to get me into bed, but I resisted. I knew I was in love with him, but I was not ready to jump head first into a sex relationship. Besides, I was afraid of getting hurt, and my mother felt I was getting into a relationship that would break my heart. I thought she was being silly and being a worrying, overprotective mother. After all, I was twenty years old and knew that the world was no rose garden, even though there were roses in it. During our growing relationship, there was a great deal of zipping back and forth to Mexico. I never knew from one day to the next when John would appear. It was nothing for him to call in the middle of the night and say, 'I am coming.' When I did not want to see him, I had his letters and poems that drew me close to him, letters that always spoke of us being together again, somehow. Each of his letters told me, 'I need you; you give me comfort; wait for me.' I was young, full of life, pretty, not rich and not prepared to sit at home and wait for my knight to arrive. I had fun. Why not? I went with Max, went to parties and entertained my friends. I shared a deep and loving friendship with Max. Some of our friends felt that our relationship was more than that, but it was not. I was in love with John and Max knew that John was his friend since childhood. Max loved John, and I suppose that John's friendship with him was for Max a kind of claim to fame. If he had known John as I came to know him, would he have kept the same feelings as in those early days? Like so many, Max knew only one John Steinbeck – the hero. There were others.

After the weekend that ended up on Olvera Street, John said, quite casually, 'Why don't you and Max come up to Monterey some weekend? We'll have fun, all of us.' By that, he meant Ed Ricketts, his closest friend and confidant, and Carol, his wife. Max would be with me as a front. The only reason for the weekend was so John could see me again.

Max and I drove to Monterey, that beautiful place on the California coast, for what turned out to be a crazy weekend. My feelings for Monterey were simple – it was beautiful Steinbeck country and like its people, another world. Monterey has so many wonderful characteristics that John has revealed to millions. We stayed at an old hotel in Salinas and went on one long bar crawl. John liked bar crawls. We hit bar after bar, on foot, until I just could not walk anymore. We were in one bar – I don't remember which one as there were so many – and I told Ed Ricketts, 'I can't go on, I just can't.' Ed left the bar and came back after some time, smiling.

'Come on,' he said, 'I have solved the problem.' We all trooped outside, and there was this little red wagon. 'I have rented it from a kid from the flats for twenty-five cents, and we've got it for an hour.' Ed bowed to me. 'Your taxi service awaits.' We continued our barhopping with me riding in the little red wagon. In one bar I remember sitting on the piano and singing for them *Some Day I'll Find You* and *Just My Bill*. I remember a red-checkered tablecloth that I used *à la chanteuse* Helen Morgan. Nobody went to bed that night, and we ended up at Ed's laboratory where Ed cooked Wing Chong's home-cured bacon and scrambled eggs, topped off with pineapple pie and blue cheese. Chong was the Chinese grocer John immortalized in *Cannery Row*.

With that to fortify us, Max and I drove back to Los Angeles. On the way, we heard the news: 'War in Europe.' We pulled over to the side of the road and, for a few minutes, we cried. We both had the feeling that the future held a kind of horror, that the world had never seen before.

Things quietened down after that weekend, but not for long. John was on his ranch in Los Gatos, and I was back singing in Los Angeles. Not long after I had returned to work, John called. 'Must see you,' he said, sounding despondent. He was. Apparently, he and Carol had had another family tiff. John drove down and picked me up, and we went to Oceanside, a little town not far from Los Angeles. Not very romantic, however. We stayed in a small hotel by the sea, and I could see that John was mentally shaken up, but I did not ask why. It was easy to guess.

That weekend it rained. That weekend I went to bed with John Steinbeck for the first time. I gave myself to him, willingly. It seemed like years since our first meeting. I thought of nothing but him. My feelings were unexplainable. It was one of the most beautiful happenings. John was strong in bed. I was ready for him, and he for me. We wanted each other, and we gave ourselves to each other, passionately. But while that weekend of sex and passion was wonderful it was also bewildering. John became moody. He called Ed Ricketts all the time, always asking about Carol, and phoned his agents. I did not know what to do. There was nothing I could do so I accepted John's strange, brooding behavior because I was in love.

I wrote in my diary: 'He is wonderful. He is so beautiful, but I wish to God, he would stop trying to play God!'

During our life together John tried to play God many times. So many times he declared that no matter what he did or said – it was always right. He hated to be wrong; he wanted to be perfect, yet he was not, for he was only a man.

The weekend ended, and he drove me back to his ranch. I did not know when or if I would ever see him again. He did not even say goodbye. He merely said, 'I guess I'll see you around, honey,' and drove away. Once more for me, it was back to Los Angeles, yet I knew that whatever happened I would have one beautiful, beautiful memory.

That weekend in Oceanside became a storm after a rainbow. I discovered that I was pregnant. We took no precautions because John had a thing about using contraceptives. He didn't. He said they made him 'impotent.' I did not complain about my situation; it always takes two. I called Ed Ricketts and told him. He called John. When John called me he did not seem particularly upset or concerned, but then, that was his way, his manner. It was not his problem.

'I am sorry. Can I do anything?' Then he asked, 'Why don't you have the baby?'

'I can't. It's impossible. I don't want the baby. I don't have the money for it, either. Besides, I have a career,' I answered.

'Come and see me,' he said.

I flew to Monterey the next morning, and when we met, he said, 'Somehow we'll work things out.'

He forgot to say how, and nothing was worked out.

It was clear that John did not give a damn about me being pregnant. There was only one thing to do. I left and flew back to Los Angeles the same day. How does a young and pregnant and unmarried woman feel? I felt like crap. I felt entirely alone while

John was back in his cocoon of married life with Carol, secure. Our weekend of passion was seemingly nothing. I was mentally depressed and even thought of committing suicide. But then I turned to my mother and told her. My mother was a kind, yet robust woman, although John never liked her. Like many mothers, she had told her daughter many times, 'If ever you are in trouble, come to me.' Who else could I turn to? She took me to a doctor, and he gave me some medicine. Fortunately, I was not that too far along, and the medicine removed the pregnancy. I felt rotten.

Several months later John called. Casually, he asked: 'How are you?' How kind. Then he said, 'I am terribly upset. I have to see you. I need you.' He spoke the words in his usual quiet voice. It began to have a familiar melody. He sent me a plane ticket, and I joined him in Monterey. On the flight, my mind asked me: 'Why are you doing this? Are you being used?' I still loved him and had the feeling that our relationship was incomplete and some decision had to be made.

That weekend we talked a lot, and drank a lot, and spent the evenings with Ed Ricketts. By now, John was working on a prose outline of *Sea of Cortez* which became a journal of travel and research which he co-authored with Ed Ricketts. By then, too, *The Forgotten Village* had been edited and was almost ready for release.

That weekend in 1941 was a strange one. It seemed as if he was looking to his great friend Ed for support and silently looking to him for an answer to his relationship with me. I felt as if I was being inspected by Ed, but not unkindly. John drove me back to the hotel where I was staying, and on the way said that something would work out; all I had to do was hang on. He also said, 'Ed likes you very much.' With that remark, I felt as if I had passed the supreme test. I returned to Los Angeles but still did not know where I was going. I had to be content to let life show me the way. Sometimes, we all have to do that.

For a long time there was nothing, and then, from nowhere, a telephone call: 'I have to see you. Will you fly up? I will arrange everything.' John was back in Monterey. He and Carol had bought a house in Pacific Grove. Here we go again. What would it be this time? He met me at the airport.

'I have had some things brought down from the ranch,' he said as we drove from the airport. I knew John well by now, and knew he had not sent for me just to show me the house. 'I finally told Carol all about you. I have done all I can to make her happy. What more can I do? She says she's tired of living here. She says she is too lonely; the place is too remote. I don't understand. She wanted it so much.'

We arrived at the new house. It was dark and gloomy and surrounded by an eight-foot fence. It looked like something from one of those old horror movies. It was not helped by the fact that it was one of those grey Monterey days. Any moment I expected Boris Karloff to greet us. We went through a very narrow gate. It was a funny, ugly little old house and it smelled of age and decay. There were packing cases here and there. John and Carol had had a few drinks. I felt like a ninny as I sat down on a crate.

'Like a drink? Pink champagne?' asked John.

'Thanks.' I took it. I needed it although I was not in the mood for drinking as it was in the middle of the afternoon. Carol sat in a chair and John spread himself out on a funny-looking overstuffed couch. He quickly came to the point. 'I know you both love me,' he began, 'and I have been thinking. I want you two to talk this out. What do you women want to do about me?' This was a jolting statement, to say the least, and at least to me. I wasn't used to that kind of situation. I am sure that Carol felt the same. Then he said, 'Whichever of you ladies needs me the most and wants me the most, then that's the woman I'm going to have,' he added, smiling. I thought he was joking. He wasn't. This certainly revealed his ego.

Carol started to talk. With all due credit to her, she told me, 'You don't want him, and you don't love him. I love him, terribly, but he hasn't slept with me for three years. I have done a great deal for John, and we've done a great deal together...' John went into the kitchen, poured another drink, came back and said, 'I'm going for a walk, and you two argue it out. Whichever one wants me I guess gets me.' Just like that. He left the house, and the two of us were alone. I wasn't ready for that kind of shit. It was like a Nixon/Kennedy debate.

'You'll never be accepted by his family,' Carol warned. 'You won't because they're very possessive of him and extremely clannish.' There she proved to be right. 'And furthermore, he won't be faithful to you...' There again she was right. 'And he is a jealous, nasty man, and if you get him...' She paused and then said, 'I'm going to take him for every goddamned f***ing cent! I want him!'

She went on talking, telling me about the intimate details of their marriage. It only embarrassed me more, and I'm far from being a prude. What I heard from Carol that day I could not believe, but I know she was speaking the truth. She loved him, too;

no matter what might have happened in their married life; she loved him.

John returned a short time later and by this time Carol was pretty well along with her sipping. She asked me to follow her to the bathroom. I sat on the tub. She was a little unsteady on her feet. She pleaded, 'Give me a chance and get out of John's life.'

'If this is what you want, then I will,' I said. Carol continued with more intimate details of their life together, but it was just too much for me to take. We went back into the room and I finished my drink. The three of us had gone through three bottles of vintage pink champagne, that grey afternoon. And it was grey, inside and out.

'I am leaving,' I said.

'Please take me to a hotel, John.'

It was done without any drama. He suggested I stay with Barbara and Ellwood Graham, the artists, which I did. The next morning I flew home, and that was the last I heard from John for several weeks.

While Carol was experiencing an emotional upheaval I, too, was living traumatic days and nights. In was fact, I became very ill. Mother took me to a ranch in Cherry Valley, just outside of Palm Springs. It was raining and cold, and I was, in every sense of the word, physically and mentally exhausted. Now my mother's Welsh spirit was aroused over the protracted situation with John, and she called his attorney and then took a train to see him. It was a brief visit and to the point: 'What was John going to do? Was he going to break it off? Gwyn has to know so she can go back to work or do something,' Mother told the lawyer.

She returned two days later and told me the attorney's answer was, 'Well, I'll tell you, Bird Eyes, once upon a time Carol was a sweet girl and John made her into a monster, and if he gets Gwen, he will make her into a monster, too.' He said he would see what he could do.

Mother and I stayed at the Cherry Valley ranch a while longer and then went home to Los Angeles. A wire was there. All it said was 'Coming. John.'

A week later he was in Los Angeles.

'Carol's going to New York, and we have agreed. I love you, and I need you. Come back to Monterey with me,' he pleaded; yes, I swear, pleaded. Mother did not exactly approve.

But it was my life. It was no snap decision. Mother, John and I discussed it for several days, and then I made up my mind. I was going. Early one morning we set out for the old house at 425 Eardley Street in Pacific Grove. It began to rain hard. We stopped on the way in Andersonville and went into a dismal little restaurant. John knew the place and told me they had good split-pea soup.

Behind the counter was a pubescent, pimply-faced girl who paid no attention to us. She was bowed over a spiral notebook, writing. John leaned and read, upside down, what she was writing. She had written, 'Dear Clark Gable...' She stopped and served us. John never forgot that pimply-faced girl and stored her until he was ready to use her like he memorized so many people and things. He used her in *The Wayward Bus.*

As we sped towards Pacific Grove, I felt exhilarated for the first time in many months, although I felt apprehensive as to what the future would hold. There was little conversation. The swishing of the windshield wipers gave me no answer. I looked out into the rain.

3 – CRYING FOR BURGESS

From the outside, the house looked almost like nothing, but behind the high walls and the fence was a house that was unique. It was built like a string of freight cars, and the inside was almost all glass. It was the first house I had ever seen that was a 'His' and 'Hers' house. In the living room were two built-in desks; in the bathroom, two built-in medicine closets. In fact, there was a 'His' and 'Hers' of everything in that house. John was in the process of cleaning it up, although he was not a domestic man, not by any means.

He was intrigued by the house. He told me he had found all kinds of weird wiring and things for lighting, and concluded that the former owners, the Johansens, must have held seances. Besides, he had unearthed yards and yards of black velvet gauze in a closet.

He showed me around and begged me to stay with him and help him fix it up. 'I am very lonesome, and I am upset. I must work, and I need you,' he told me. John had chosen the house because of its seclusion. He always liked a secluded atmosphere. He did not like people looking in windows.

The dining room, immediately off the living room, was solid glass. It made you feel as if you were in a garden because the fernbrakes were as high as five and six feet.

A door led to several steps and a fishpond. Directly to the right of the dining room was a kitchen, then a small hallway and another door leading to the first bathroom. Next came a large room with narrow windows, very high-up windows. John turned that room into his library. As well as being almost fanatical, he was an avid reader. From the library, there was another passageway, again solid glass, with window seats. It was a quick passageway and this, too, led into the garden. It led into another bedroom, a pleasant room, again with high windows and a big bay window facing the garden. John wanted to turn this room into the master bedroom, which he did. Next to that was another, with a small kitchen. It was solid cement and only had one window, again facing the garden. The kitchen did, however, have its exit door, which led to an area where there were once rabbit hutches. Apparently, the people slaughtered their rabbits because there were hanging hooks and butchering tables. Everything had been left in a state of disrepair. Mother called this room 'Little Siberia.' Outside of this area was a large gate that led into a vacant lot, a lot so overgrown with mattress vine that we could barely open it. John left it that way.

We started work. We painted, and we scrubbed. We burned weeds and tore out things. John and I did most of the painting ourselves. Mother visited, and she helped a little. Then we began the task of furnishing. I handled that while John worked in the garden in the mornings.

He seemed at peace with himself during this time, although I know he was very restless. He knew I loved roses, so he went down to the Cannery and ordered a whole truckload of fish guts and had them turned into soil, spread everywhere. You do that, and you don't have to fertilize for another seven years. And he built me a rose garden outside the guest house, directly opposite the room he turned into his 'nest.' He hired a Japanese gardener named Frank. John had been brought up around Japanese, and he felt they were good people to have work for you, which they are. On the gate, John installed a big Mexican bell. The only way he would let anyone in was if they pulled the cord and rang the bell. It made a big noise.

We had a great sense of accomplishment cleaning up the house and painting it. It looked stunning in yellow and white. We bought furniture from Holman's store, and the house began to turn from an old brown shack into a lovely, warm home. As you might imagine, we were extremely proud of what we had done. We were together – but not alone. We found out that the house was haunted!

I say that because many things happened in that house at 425 Eardley Street; strange and weird happenings.

John was a mystic, as I said earlier, and he was interested in the unknown, and at the same time, he liked to scare people. He would get enjoyment out of sitting in the living room with guests, and suddenly the doorknob would turn, and the door would open. Everyone would get up and pour another drink. Furthermore, you could not keep that house locked up.

John did not believe in reincarnation, but he did acknowledge ghosts, and we certainly had them on Eardley Street. At night the place groaned and creaked, and nobody wanted to remain alone in that house. John would not stay alone there, either. Toby Street, John's lawyer, later tried to live in that house and said it drove him crazy. Lewis Milestone, the director who did the movie *Of Mice and*

Men, and who had come up to work on the script of *The Red Pony*, awoke in the middle of the night. He said afterward, 'John, I hate to say this and I know you won't believe it, but when I got up and looked out of the windows that garden was full of people!' John laughed and said, 'I believe you.'

I remember the time when a friend of John's, Ellwood Graham, had painted a very modern painting of boats in the Monterey harbor. John loved it and bought it and decided to hang it above the living room fireplace.

'Old Johansen won't like that,' I said.

'Oh yes he will,' he answered. We were having our morning coffee. John hung a big bulldog hook over the fireplace. I watched him as I sat on the hearthstone below. He hung the painting and stepped back to admire it. 'It looks very nice there, don't you think?' he said. With that, there was a loud noise, and the bulldog hook was torn out of the wall. The painting crashed down and missed my head by the umpteenth of an inch. John laughed.

'I'll fix that old sonofabitch,' he said. He went to the garage and came back with a spike a good four inches long, and drove it into the wall. 'He won't pull that out!' he said, and rehung the painting. We admired it again and left the room. Moments later, as we were in the kitchen, there was a terrible screeching noise. We rushed back into the living room. The nail had come out of the wall, and the painting was on the floor, its frame smashed.

Needless to say, John moved that painting to another part of the room. I simply believe the former owner did not want anything modern around.

There was another time when Mother was helping to clean up

the lawn in the yard, because it was so overgrown with weeds. She had gotten mud on her shoes and took them off and tapped them against the wall.

The wall tapped right back at her.

That's the way the house was: if you touched anything and rapped – it rapped right back!

Despite the ghosts, the noises, there was contentment in this house. The reason for that was because John was able to write again. His energy peak was usually from daylight onwards. When he worked, he worked damn hard. John was a man of great discipline, and he let nothing, absolutely nothing, interrupt him. His power of concentration was phenomenal.

Sometimes, after a morning's hard work, perhaps he would come in from his 'nest,' and decide that we would have a love scene, a little matinee. There is nothing unhealthy in that, I assure you. However, when we began to make love we often ran into a funny situation because of the folks next door. They were migrants from Texas who worked in Cannery. No sooner would we start making love when they would put on a record, full force, and we would be lying in bed naked, listening to *Roll Out the Barrel*. We invariably broke up, and even if we were in bed at night, there it would go again, rolling out that damned barrel! All we could do would be to roll on our backs and kill ourselves laughing! But there were of course quiet, loving times when we shared each other's body, like any couple in love, as we were.

While we were living in the haunted house, we found our famous rat – Burgess.

One day John came home with a baby white rat. 'I thought you might like this, darling, and at least save it from the guillotine and the snake pen for twenty-four hours,' he said. 'A boy came running into the lab and yelled to Ed that his mother told him to sell it because it bites everyone.'

It was a beautiful little rat, three months old. I took it in my hands. 'Why, it's darling,' I said, 'and looks like Burgess.' I meant Burgess Meredith, that actor. So we named him Burgess. I don't think Burgess ever forgave me for that.

The weekend we acquired the rat, Eli and Mollie Kazan visited us. They also decided the rat looked like Burgess. Loving animals is part of me, and it was something that John loved about me, too. Animals are very precious to me, as all life is precious. John had a special feeling for animals, too, especially dogs, as the world found out later in his *Travels with Charley: In Search of America.*

He doted on Burgess; that rat loved him, and he loved the rat. Whenever we took a drive Burgess would perch on John's shoulder. In the evening we would go down to the sea and see the sundown, and little Burgess would be with us. He would scramble out of the car and run down to the sea. John would say, 'Come here, Burgess.' Burgess would come. It was not, as some people might think, weird having a rat as a pet. It was fascinating.

But then sometimes John would do peculiar things with Burgess. John was a sadistic man, of many emotions, but being sadistic was one of his unattractive qualities. He would let people in and set Burgess loose and gain a great sense of enjoyment, watching women scream and pull up their legs. Once, he wanted to amputate Burgess's tail because he felt that the reason people disliked rats was because of their raw tails. But I would not allow him to experiment. That was one time he let me have my own way. When we drove down to Los Angeles to visit mother and my stepfather, Burgess would ride all the way in the 'funny box' as John called the glove compartment. We checked into a hotel and John would do some kookie things like deliberately return to our room and let Burgess out of his cage and then go down the hall and wait for the maid to go into the room and listen to her scream. I, I might add, would run and hide!

The story of our pet rat Burgess does not end there. Months later, after we had been to New York, we returned to California. My mother and stepfather had taken care of Burgess while we were gone. One day they went fishing in Malibu to get John some fresh herring for breakfast. That day it rained, but Burgess remained on the porch in his cage. He was about four years old then, which is old for a rat, yet he was healthy as hell. But he caught pneumonia and the next day he began coughing blood, so Mother called a vet.

'Lady,' the vet said, 'you've gotta be drunk. Your rat has pneumonia?'

'But it's John Steinbeck's rat,' she persisted...

'Yeah, yeah, goodbye lady.'

Mother called us at two in the morning and informed us, 'I think Burgess is dying, and it's our fault. We can't get a vet.'

We got up and went to look at Burgess. John looked at our pet and said, 'You poor little shit, I loved you so.' He took Burgess and put it in Mother's oven and put it to sleep. Then he sat there and cried. 'There goes the last pure thing I ever loved,' he said.

That was the only time in my life I ever saw John Steinbeck cry. He never cried for me. He never cried for his sons. He never cried for anybody.

But he cried for a rat called Burgess.

He came home, and he wept, and he wept, and he said again, 'That poor little shit, that poor little shit.'

He was a brilliant man, but a strange man.

Then there was the incident of the bird, which happened while we were living in the haunted house. We had cleaned the house up, and the birds were coming into the garden to nest. One day, out of the blue, a mangy old cat appeared – an aged black cat with an ulcer on the side of its face. It began to kill the birds (animal instinct), and John became angry. He decided to trap the cat and give it to Ed Ricketts for the laboratory. I found him in the garden whittling away on several sticks of wood.

'What are you doing?'

'Haven't you ever seen a figure-four trap, you old nature lover?' he snapped back.

'Yes, I have.'

'Well, that's how I'm going to catch that damned cat.'

'What will you use for bait?'

'I'm going to the Cannery for a big fish head.' He did. He came back with a fish head a good eight inches or more, and solid meat, too. He laid the trap on the lawn. It held up a galvanized tub. When he had it fixed, he tried it; it was a like a hair trigger. It was tough balancing the fish head, but he did it. Just before daylight, I awoke with John shaking me.

'Call Ed and tell him to get here fast with the burlap sack.' I did.

Ed staggered out of bed and came to the house. The three of us stood by the tub listening to a helluva lot of noise and scratching.

'Now Ed, you know how to catch him,' said John.

'You hold the sack, and I'll lift from this side. Gwyn, you stand on the other side.' It was quite a production, an MGM job. Next step, John raised the tub, and nothing happened. He lifted it a little further. Ed stood ready with the gunny sack open, and I crouched on the other side. One of us had to get him. Then, from out under the rise of about two and a half inches off the ground, popped a baby robin, all of two and a half inches, not even a fledgling. 'Cheep! Cheep!' It went, madder than hell. Ed and I began to laugh. Ed fell over on the lawn with the empty sack, and he and I convulsed in laughter. John's reaction was different.

'I don't think it's funny,' he said, and stomped into the house. He was mad as hell, too, and when John was angry, he was angry. He did not speak to either Ed or me for a few days. Still, he did catch the cat. It was a battle, and in the process he was thoroughly scratched up. At the height of his successful cat-catching escapade, he pointed at me in one of his rages and said, 'I told you! I told you I would catch that cat! I did!'

That was the way it always was with John. If something funny happened to him, or perhaps he had been the cause of it, or it was against him, he did not like it. If his friends or I fell, he became hysterical.

Life with John was never dull.

We lived in the haunted house four months, and then John's usual restlessness came back to life. He wanted me to go back east, to New York. He did not tell me, but he had found out – also unbeknown to me – that his old friends, except Ed Ricketts, were not his friends anymore; they resented his success. They should have welcomed it, been happy for him. Such is jealousy. I did not know this until many years later. He also found out that Carol was moving back to the west coast, so we packed up and went to New York. John directed my mother and stepfather to sell the haunted house in Pacific Grove. Mother did, although John's lawyers said it would not sell because it was too haunted. My mother did not care. She finally swelled enough courage and, standing in the house alone, said out loud, 'Now listen here, Johansen, if you don't behave I am going to burn your house down!' From that time on there was no trouble, and the house was sold in seventy-two hours to an army captain.

John and I flew to New York, and we moved into a double suite at the Bedford Hotel. It faced the river. John liked that because he could stare at the river and it reminded him of the ocean at Monterey. Mother did not exactly approve of my going to New York with John, but she knew how much I was in love. And I was. She loved me, and whatever I wanted, she wanted.

We had not been in New York long when, one morning over breakfast, the news came over the radio: Pearl Harbor was under attack. John shot out of his chair. He was in complete horror. He wanted to go to war right then. 'I told you we would have to get in it sometime. I told you!' he blurted.

By this time, John had finished *Sea of Cortez* with Ed. Ed was a great influence on John until World War II ended. As I said earlier, they had this unique bond of friendship and respect between each other. And before Pearl Harbor, John had been living out the war in Europe. He ate, slept and dreamed it. The radio was never turned off. The idea of *The Moon Is Down* had been forming in his mind all during this period. So life at the Bedford went on as we were at war with Japan. But there were moments when the war did not exist. One of those involved our dear, dear friend Burgess Meredith, the actor. Burgess was a lieutenant, a liaison officer, and had a terrible crush on a young, beautiful singer at the St. Regis, where he billeted.

John and Burgess decided they would have a night on the town, which was alright with me because I never stopped John from having his night out with the boys before or while we were married. Men had to do that at times, even though they loved their wife, girlfriend or mistress madly. No woman should stop her man from having a night out with the boys. I never knew about John's nights out with the girls. And he had them. But what I didn't know, I didn't have to worry about. Burgess wanted to see his friend when she finished work, about one in the morning. He took John to her dressing room, and they invited her out to Reuben's Restaurant for a sandwich. John, of course, was taking a back seat. After they had eaten, she said, 'Let's go to my apartment,' which they did. She made them drinks, and Burgess naturally tried to make points with the Junoesque girl, who was somewhat on the tall side. She enjoyed the attention Burgess gave her, and besides, she was damned good looking.

Suddenly, the key turned in the lock and in walked a portly gentleman. As John explained to me later, it was clear that the singer was kept. Burgess's mouth fell. After all, any man who has a crush on a girl thinks he's the only one – and he is not.

'I think we should leave,' John said.

'No, no, don't go, finish your drink,' implored the man.

They told me they had another scotch and soda, which the man made while they sat looking on, saying nothing. They finished their drink and thanked the man. John said he was pleasant, but his face was cold, like ice. John and Burgess left but began to feel ill. They brushed it off as having too much to drink, so they started walking back to the Bedford.

Just before daylight, I was met with two of the sickest-looking men you have ever seen. The 'gentleman' had given each a Mickey Finn!

All I could think of was Mutt and Jeff. John, six foot tall, and Burgess a foot smaller, looking smaller than ever.

In they came and it was a fight to get to the bathroom. Of course, I had to mop up. I ran out to a nearby drugstore to get baking soda. Now how do you go to a drugstore first thing in the morning and say, 'I'd like something to counteract a Mickey Finn?' A Mickey makes you vomit, and you have diarrhea. The only thing I could also think of was to get a hen and boil it, and I made some strong chicken broth. Burgess was laid out on the couch, and John lay groaning in bed. Burgess had ruined the front of his uniform. I sponged it down and even washed their underwear. It was quite a scene.

John admired Burgess for he had a great sense of humor, and held his liquor well – which John could too – and the two of them raised hell together.

Life with John Steinbeck was quite a combination of heaven and hell – I never knew where one started and the other left off.

I was never, ever bored with John; angry, yes, but how could you be bored with a man who always, always had something exciting to say, even if he made it up with his immense imagination – and often he did.

After the Mickey Finn episode with Burgess, John once again began to grow restless and moody, but I was used to that by now. I did not mind his moods; our lovemaking was passionate, morning, afternoon or night; John was a man of much strength, not only in his mind, but in his body.

He decided we ought to rent a house at Snedens Landing, overlooking the Hudson River. It was an upscale area, and one of our neighbors was Burl Ives. It was twelve miles from Manhattan and 'the action,' as he said. We moved into our retreat, as John liked to think of it. With us was our Willie, our sheepdog, who was just a puppy. Once more he had moved, and like everywhere else we lived, John had to have his personal 'nest,' and it had to be away from the house and the telephone. He did not like his nest to have a beautiful view.

Many times John wrote in articles that he hated the idea, because he found himself staring out of the window and not concentrating on his work. His nest at Snedens Landing was in the woodshed.

'I'm going to clean it out and move in,' he said. He got a chair and a writing board, a place for his coffee cups, his pipes and his ashtrays. John always used an outsized writing board as his desk. He also liked directors' chairs, camp chairs. He bought one from the army and navy store, and then he was ready to go to work.

Usually, he had six or eight pipes, which he took good care of; he preferred one as a change from cigarettes. Whenever he bought anything, it was always the finest. He also bought a new record player and beautiful records. He loved classical music. His favorite composers were Beethoven, Bach, Monteverdi, some Ravel and quite a lot of Debussy and Stravinsky. Oddly enough, he also liked Prokofiev and Schoenberg. Sometimes, during a work week, he would listen to a symphony, stretch out, close his eyes and that would refresh him.

There is a particular story attached to the nest at Snedens Landing – skunks. A family of skunks moved in on John. One morning he came flying out of his nest yelling, 'MY GOD! WHERE IS THE SKUNK?' His face was an indescribable blue.

Our house was then more or less in the woods. I didn't know where the hell the skunk was until one morning when up at dawn. I looked out of the kitchen window, and there they were, Momma and Poppa Skunk with five baby skunks out for an early morning walk. When they finished, they went right back under the woodshed. I called John but he didn't believe me. 'Alright, let's set the alarm for five-thirty tomorrow, you'll see.' We did. Out trotted the skunk family. He killed himself laughing.

John thought he had an answer to that problem. He built a feed pen hoping the skunks would stay out while he worked. They did not. When the baby skunks were old enough they left, but by that time the heat and humidity rising from the Hudson River was too much, and John moved his nest into the guest room. He wasn't mad about that situation; he wouldn't have harmed the skunks for anything, and neither would I.

That period of my life with John was a pleasant one, the only way to describe it. During the shad season, we would take an afternoon walk and watch the fishermen on the shad run. John would wave at them with a handkerchief, and they would stop, and he would get his shad, so he could have his shad roe, which he adored. John's friends then became my friends. There were wonderful people living nearby. They included Maxwell Anderson, the playwright, and his wife, Marg, and Burgess, who by then was wooing Paulette Goddard, the actress. Also close by were Henry Varnum Poor, the ceramicist and painter, and Kurt Weill, the songwriter, and wife, Lenya. Other neighbors we had then were Sally Lorentz, Pare's wife, and Jack Radcliffe, who wrote for Readers Digest. Living next door to the Weills was another great actress, Helen Hayes.

There were plenty of dinner parties and barbeques, and show business and literary talk, and talk of the war in Europe and the Pacific. But John became restless and discontented as the summer progressed, and the humidity increased. John felt that the war would end before he had a chance to get in it.

After dinner together, when we figured it had digested, we used to walk down the stone steps into our octagon-shaped pool, and we would sit there until we were chilled to the bone and then run like hell for bed before we started to sweat again. John never thrived well in humidity. Does anyone?

Every evening, he sat and removed the mildew from his beautiful handmade Mexican boots, cursing the summer weather. By August he had become angry at Snedens Landing. 'I want to go back to California,' he said one day, without warning. When John made up his mind, that was it, believe me. It was packing time again.

4 – JOHN, ED RICKETTS AND ME

Millions of words have been penned and spoken of John and Ed Ricketts, some true and some false. I do not profess to know all, but I know much, since I was there and lived through an important part of their lives. Ed Ricketts was possibly one of the finest marine zoologists the world has ever seen, or will see, and his untimely death in an accident was a tragedy. He was one of the most benign men I have ever met, and he became the best friend I ever had. Ed was one of those people who give you strength while they lack that for their own emotional problems, their own involvement with others, both men and women.

John and Ed had a tremendous bond of friendship between them. I never experienced anything from Ed except sheer goodness. He opened my mind to philosophy which I had never skirmished with since school days. To me, Ed was a kind of Jesus. I believe John thought that way, too. Ed wore a beard, this man of middle stature. Everything he did had the essence of kindness in it. If he did not really like you Ed would not display it with unkind words or temper; he just looked at you, smiled and said, 'Oh yes, really.' He did not say, 'Get out of my life, you're a pain.' He said, 'It's nice meeting you.'

He had this great essence for life, and you could not help but admire it, whatever his faults. He was, in a way, enamored by sex, which perhaps isn't too bad a fault. John loved Ed's love of life;

perhaps it was the qualities that Ed displayed all the time that John wished to have but could not show, or would not allow himself to have. With Ed, they were built in, solid.

In our correspondence Ed would write: 'My dear girl – never be ashamed of using the word "good." There is much behind that, if you think on it. There is "good" everywhere; sometimes it takes people months, even years to discover it through mistakes, and God knows I have made them, and, anyway, who hasn't?' Ed used to say, 'Don't bother about hyperbole; simply say you like it – because it is good.' It was that simple; beauty in that simplicity.

Ed was simple, too, in that he never cared about material things. Life was his work, and music too. He would listen from the moment he got up (if he was alone, he went around the house naked), and throughout the day while he dissected a starfish or anemone, or when he cooked. He would try to cook anything and was a gourmet. Once he said, 'You can eat from the world if you know how to preserve.'

Ed Ricketts never wavered in his loyalties – John didn't, either – and would never show jealousy. Even when some of the women he loved and who loved him left him, Ed continued to be their friend. Many times he saved their life.

There was a special magic about Ed Ricketts; in many ways he was John's offspring, the source of the Steinbeck Nile.

It is a well-known fact that Ed and John's correspondence was one of the most prolific between friends other than writers. Whenever John discussed anything with him, Ed had a way of saying something was not right without saying it, and that is an art. At such times he would sip a beer and look to the ceiling and say, 'Hmm, hmm, John, but that's not quite right.' Never did he say, 'No, don't quit.'

For John, sharing moments with Ed – and they shared many – was like going to an analyst. Afterwards John would tell me, 'I'm all right.' There was not any problem that he ever took to Ed that he could not solve, where John was at a loss.

I first met Ed in the early forties. John wanted me to meet him to see whether Ed approved of his 'choice.'

Ed Ricketts watched all life go by, everything. There was nothing in the passing parade that escaped his eye or he could not laugh or cackle about. He was a slow speaker, exceedingly slow; every word he spoke was a saga. The way he spoke was like a Max Beerbohm drawing.

Another side of Ed was that you never knew what you were going to eat at his house. God knows, John loved good food. One day, while the rain poured a monsoon, Ed called and asked us over for chicken soup. It was one of those cold, raw Monterey days. We went, and he served the soup in vast bowls, complete with his homemade bread. The soup was delicious, and I know how to make chicken soup. But Ed's 'chicken soup' was made out of sea cucumbers, which are part of the slug and worm family. He had collected his 'chicken' that day, and chopped it up. 'I simply wanted to try it,' he said nonchalantly. It was delicious. 'You can always live off the land or the sea,' he said, smiling.

'Goddam it, Ed, I wouldn't be surprised if you went and made a ground-up clam milk shake!' said John.

'Wait a minute, I have to write that down and try it,' teased Ed.

'With malt in it,' added John.

'What else?' Ed replied.

Ed should have published a recipe book from the sea and elsewhere. It would have made a fortune.

No matter what you said to Ed Ricketts you could not shock him. Take the time he told us about a woman he had picked up some place (and there were many women) when he had been drinking his usual rum or beer. Ed always drank rum or beer. He had been in no hurry. Ed said he felt the woman had been suffering all her life, and he helped her. John and I listened to him, unmoved. Ed always expressed himself freely about his sex life. 'Yes,' he said, 'we made love and if it hadn't been for me, she would have never discovered that she had a double vagina.' 'What?' said John. 'Yes, after the first time, I discovered it,' he said in a very low tone of voice, but yet completely natural.

In a way, Ed was over-idolized, but maybe John made him that way.

There is a story a professor told me, that John and Ed treated each other like Greek sisters, and I think in a way they did, if walking arm in arm on a beach makes you a Greek sister.

They had this so-called gypsy pact, and they were brothers. Anyone can do that – if they're rotten drunk.

It is open to conjecture, but I believe that although John, with his own brilliant mind, gave so much to Ed, in turn Ed was a father figure to John.

The three of us had many good times together, and you always came out of them learning something from two great minds. In my eyes, Ed was nine feet tall, although he was only five-foot-six. But he had this aura. When he entered the room everyone stopped, turned their head, and asked, 'Who is that?' John once told me Ed would make one hell of a politician because he went around patting babies' heads. He listened to everyone. Ed wanted to know what everyone else was thinking.

About a year after I first met Ed he had been carrying out research and, since he lived on Cannery Row, he said to me, 'You know, before I die the Cannery will be dead, and we'll fish out our waters. Every day we're going out farther, and I've studied the waves, tides and fish schools. Every year when I go down to the wharf, the fishermen tell me they had to go out six miles while the year before it was five.' He predicted the canneries would die and we would fish out 'the beautiful waters,' as Ed always called them.

The Cannery was dead before he died.

When John and I were married Ed wrote us that the canneries were closing because we had taken so much from the sea and had given nothing back. He felt about the sea as Jacques Cousteau feels, although Ed pre-empted Cousteau by twenty years.

It was an experience to be with a man who took us out in a dune buggy and said, casually, 'Oh, there's a paleolithic rock over there and we'll find some seashells.' We would look at the rock and he would turn, saying, 'All this was under the sea once.' There wasn't anything you could discuss with Ed Ricketts that he did not know about; he had an understanding of archaeology and geology as well, but his particular knowledge was of marine biology and the sea.

Ed cared little for money. John financed him. Ed's laboratory did become a sagging enterprise. He did not have the driving desire for fame that John had; he was a philosopher and a scholar, and there was not one single thing that passed him by that Ed did not study.

In his makeup he did not have time to stop and fight. Occasionally he might get tight and then would say, if it were a lady, 'Lady, you're full of shit!' When he spoke it was as if Jesus had said it.

Ed was happy for John and me, although he never visited us in New York. Once, he felt let down because John was not allowed, on medical grounds, to go with him on an excursion to the Aleutian chain.

I do believe that John was, unbeknown to himself, highly possessive, and this sometimes showed in his relationship with Ed. In many ways, Ed was a man's man as well as a woman's man. I never saw him without a drink, yet only saw him drunk twice. From the moment he arose and started the day, he started on beer, and by two in the afternoon he was on rum. John liked that about him. Sometimes for breakfast, Ed used to go across the street from the Lab to Wing Chong's and get six cans of beer, a large hunk of cheese and a pineapple pie. Some breakfast!

Ed was what he was, and my life was vastly enriched for knowing him. He never spoke much about his family. Ed loved animals, although he put them to sleep and cut them up; that was his living. 'You can't make anybody like you who doesn't like you,' he once said. How true.

He told John and me the story of when he was a young boy and he had a cat that liked to jump on the mantelpiece in his home in Chicago. His father didn't like the cat, and it knew it. His father had a high wing chair with a lamp beside it, and would there sit and read the evening paper. Each night the cat would get up, turn around and wet all over his father.

'Every night my father would say he was going to kill that cat tomorrow. I used to hide the cat. He didn't kill it. You see,' said Ed, 'if you give bad feeling you're going to get it back."

If something went wrong and someone tried to start a fight when the three of us were together, Ed would simply look up to the ceiling and say, 'Well, I guess the cat's about to piss.' That was the signal – don't fight, just get out.

But Ed had problems always with women or his love life, his wife or his children. He knew how to solve others' emotional problems, but not his own. He watched the world go by. Ed read constantly, and I have never seen such a magnificent library as his. He had a constant desire and thirst for knowledge.

I am proud that once he said he liked me, because when he was talking about something I didn't know about, I would say, 'I honestly, don't know what you are talking about.' Said Ed, 'Most people say, "Oh yes, uh-huh, I think I know what you're talking about." Gwyn never does.' That was a great compliment coming from a man I so admired. He was never condescending. If I would tire, or be busy he would politely ask forgiveness; never would he say, 'Get lost, you bother me.' Sometimes he got angry, but I never saw such control in a man, and he always refused to argue; Ed always wanted to debate a problem. 'You have your point of view, and I have mine,' he used to say.

When Ed died a horrible death from injuries after being hit and dragged by a train, John went to pieces. He flew from New York to Monterey. After the funeral, he went to Ed's house and destroyed diaries and letters, including their letters. Why? I believe John thought there is a beauty in the world you just don't want others to pore over.

Ed Ricketts, John and I shared a special relationship, the kind that comes along once in a lifetime. John left a legacy of great writings to the world. His beloved friend Ed left himself.

5 – MEN CANNOT READ MAPS

Throughout his life, John continually showed me that he was a man with a drive and energy that was remarkable and a determination that was unbelievable. Anyone who succeeds in life has to have a complete focus as well as talent. John was a powerhouse of single-mindedness.

The summer of 1942 we prepared to leave a hot and humid New York for good old California. We ended the lease on the house at Snedens Landing. John decided he wanted to take everything with us, including our fine record collection and all our china, and pack it all into his grey-blue 1941 Packard convertible, which he called 'Baby.' He called all his cars 'Baby.'

'Why don't we store the china?' I asked. 'We'll take it. We might be living in California, and we'll need it,' he replied. Even then he was not sure what he wanted to do, but his mind was made up about California, and when John made up his mind, that was it, nothing changed it.

He built up the back of the car and fixed it so that Willie, our sheepdog, could ride high up and see out; he made it so Willie could be level with our heads, sitting right behind us. I packed all his files and his clothes, and he stacked the car. We had a heated discussion over how to deal with the records, some five hundred dollars' worth. He packed them all one way, and I told him he should alternate, a hard end one side and then a hard end the other side. He became angry. When anyone argued with John, it was like talking to a brick wall. He was so adamant that I left him to it. He piled the records on the floor and our luggage on top, and the rug on top of that for dear Willie.

The unfortunate thing was that he had the clothes we were going to use from night to night packed in the trunk! 'How are we going to have fresh underwear and other necessities?' I asked. We had a few words over that: very choice.

'To hell with it,' he blasted at me. 'You can last with what you have on until we get to Wake Robin!'

That was that! Wake Robin is in Michigan, and it was the home of Paul and Rhea de Kruif, his friends. Why argue, I told myself, it won't do any good. I grabbed an overnight bag, opened two suitcases, and pulled out two pairs of socks and shorts, a couple of clean shirts and a sweater and put them in the bag.

We started out for California early one morning. It was such a beautiful day as we headed out through the country. After a while, we came to an 'Apples for Sale' sign, and he wanted to buy some. He came back with two great big bags of apples, plus a gallon of hard cider. He was as bad as a woman at a white sale!

'We won't stop for breakfast, we'll eat the apples,' he said.

We ate apples all morning. By noon John was feeling sleepy, but we kept going, and we stopped at some motel in Pennsylvania. In those days, in the early forties, they weren't quite as lenient about taking pets, so poor Willie had to stay in the car all night. That upset us, and we didn't sleep very well. And the apples worked on both of us all night long, too. It was a restless night. I would get up, throw on some slacks and take Willie for a walk, then bring him back to the car and go back to bed after the bathroom. We didn't get much sleep. Believe it or not, John found some ice and chilled the cider. That was our breakfast.

The next day John really pushed the car, and we arrived at Wake Robin exhausted. I had suspected that I was pregnant, but the ride removed that problem, and by the time we reached Wake Robin it was all over. John was much relieved, and so was I.

Wake Robin is a pretty place, and we spent four glorious days and nights there, cooking and drinking with Rhea and Paul, and John and I melted into each other's bodies. John also cleaned some guns he had bought. He had not told me about them. Throughout our relationship and then our married life John always had to have loaded guns around the house. He had this maniacal attraction for possessing all kinds of firearms. Why I don't know. Guns create violence, yet in John's writing, there was such a strong bond with his fellow human, a feeling that was rich for the land, the sea and its people. There was no specific emphasis on violence, just human failings, and emotions.

Autumn was on its way and we repacked the car (thanks to Rhea's support), and again headed west. John kept pushing that car; he was anxious to get to his beloved California where we would stay with my mother and stepfather until we found our own house. I did not drive because I am nearsighted. Besides, anyone else driving always made John nervous. Oh, I would relieve him for a while in some of those remote parts of the desert so he could put his head back. After all, we were pounding out some ten hours a day on the highways. Nothing was going to stop him from getting to Los Angeles as fast as he could.

After we arrived in Albuquerque, New Mexico, he began to complain about his back; he did have a problem with his spine and legs. We decided to relax. 'I've never been to Santa Fe,' he said. 'Let's go.' Now I loved the Southwest and traveled through it a lot when I was a kid. We stayed in some motel and John poked around the museum. He had a tremendous interest in anything historical; in fact, he was quite a historian. He went to all the Indian art stores and in one found an Indian blanket he liked and bought. That went piling into the car. The weight of 'Baby' was something, what with the records, luggage, a ninety-pound sheepdog and the two of us. When we hit bumps, and we hit many, we sure did know it! I felt then at any moment the transmission would go. Fortunately, it did not.

In Santa Fe, John asked me about Taos. 'Did you like to hang around that place? How far is it from here?'

'About seventy miles.'

'Let's go.' It was as simple as that. So off we went to Taos, a place steeped in history, the resting place of the legendary Western hero, Kit Carson, and a place where there are many reminders of the Old American West, plus an iconic Spanish restaurant that had been there since I was a child. Taos also has, among other things, a beautiful gorge where the Colorado River begins. John was intrigued with this town. We dined at the Spanish restaurant where they still made sopaipillas; John had been raised on that kind of food, and he ate six for lunch and six more with dinner. John never ran short of an appetite for solids or liquids.

We spent a perfectly wonderful time in Taos. We spent a night in a little hotel off the Plaza where people admired Willie. They had never seen an Old English Sheepdog, so Willie had a ball, too, with all the Mexican dogs. Dogs are such gentle animals, often human-thinking, and kinder and more loving than many a man or woman. We played around and were the typical tourists for two days, and then John was his restless self again and anxious to get to Los Angeles.

The only way to get back on Route 66 from Taos is through Santa Fe. We piled into the car and off again we went. John drove like Barney Oldfield, the race driver, at the wheel, staring ahead as we moved along sixty or seventy miles an hour. If he wanted a cigarette, he just leaned over and patted me on the knee, which meant, 'Light me a cigarette.' There was no conversation; that was his signal. Perhaps we might sing together to the radio with me carrying the harmony. After a brief stop in Santa Fe for gas, we headed towards Route 66. We had been traveling for some time when I said, quietly, 'John, I hate to say this, but I think we took a wrong turn.'

'No, we haven't. I studied the map this morning, and we're going to hit Las Vegas.'

'Las Vegas?' I said, with surprise.

'Yes, I'd like to look it over, see what it's like,' he went on.

Politely I said, 'Well, I've been looking over the land, and it doesn't look familiar to me.'

'Well, I studied the map, and it says Las Vegas 150 miles, and it isn't wrong.'

How could Las Vegas, Nevada, be 150 miles from Santa Fe, I asked myself? I shrugged my shoulders. There wasn't any point in further comment. By this time, Willie was drooling over my neck and pawing me. 'I think we'll have to stop for Willie, darling.'

'He'll have to wait. I want to be in Las Vegas for lunch.'

I kept quiet, although by now I knew it wasn't the right road. John asked me to reach in the funny box, the glove compartment, and get his dark glasses. I did and put them on him. 'John dear, if we're heading west, why is the sun in our face and it's already eight in the morning?'

'For God's sake, I don't care how many times you've gone over this country with your family – I looked at the map!' was his retort.

By now, we had already gone some ninety-nine miles due east!

'I don't think you know as much about this country as you say you do,' he said.

'Want to stop the car and we'll get out your compass, dear?'

He laughed, but he was mad and drove on. We began to come across funny little towns and then, suddenly there was a sign that read, 'Las Vegas 25 miles.'

'That's impossible! We've only been on the road two hours, and if we're going due west, how the hell can the sun be in our eyes?' I said.

With that, he slammed his hands on the wheel and said, 'Goddammit! I'm doing the driving.'

'All right, all right,' I said and lapsed into silence. Soon we came into something as well populated as Los Alamos bombing field – a few shacks and a sign that read, 'Welcome to Las Vegas.'

There was never any arguing with John. He was right, and I and everyone else were wrong. That was all there was to it. We came to this little town and spotted a kind of cantina. 'It must be the outskirts,' he said. By now I gave up, and he gunned the motor to a short rise. Over the top we found some men doing some construction work, a rough-looking bunch. 'Lock your door,' John snapped. I pushed the lock button. 'Get the gun out,' he said. I did. Suddenly, there was no road, and we hit bottom. We were stuck because the car was so damned heavy.

I realized that John was quite frightened. We sat there as the wheels spun. 'We're going to have to get these men to help us, dear,' I said.

'Let me do it my way,' he answered. Always, it had to be his way, the Steinbeck way; never anyone else's, because he said that was the right way. The men began to walk toward us. Whenever John was nervous or angry, he broke out in sweat which ran down his face. The men came over, three of them, and one said in a heavy Spanish accent, 'I theenk you're going to need some help, Meester.'

'I think I am,' John said through a window open about two inches. Right beside him, he had a cocked thirty-eight. The men had brought some planks and pushed the car, and we got out of the sand.

'Isn't this Las Vegas?' John asked, much relieved and very grateful.

'*Si*,' answered the man. '*Si*, Las Vegas.'

'Nevada?'

'No, New Mexico.'

The rest of the day John did not utter a single word to me, and we never did reach Las Vegas, Nevada. He went back on Route 66. He still did not speak to me. I did not dare ask him to stop and let Willie out, and he did not ask me if I wanted to go to the bathroom, either. I knew that whenever he was in that kind of mood the only thing to do was shut up and be quiet.

We drove something like five hours in total silence. Finally, we stopped at a diner as John said he wanted coffee. It came as a relief to me, not to mention dear Willie. I took Willie for some exercise and wrung his tights, as they say. We took off again, and still, John didn't talk to me. The radio was on, and, except for the purr of the engine, there was total silence. Nothing to break the ice. In a way, I was frightened. I was afraid that if we stopped for gas, he might go off and leave me: that's how angry he was over making a mistake. Nearing twilight and the sun again in our eyes, I broke the silence. 'Where do you want to stop for the night?'

'I'm going right through to Los Angeles.'

We arrived in Los Angeles the following morning, and he had done nothing but pound that highway. It was almost daylight when we woke up my mother and stepfather. They were not expecting us until the following day. John was unnecessarily exhausted, and I wasn't feeling any better. Even poor Willie was shaking. John had a stiff scotch and mother made a pot of coffee. I don't remember what John did, but I know I slept for twelve hours. It had taken us less than five days to get to Los Angeles from New York.

I don't blame John for his frustration. He had goofed, badly. I do not believe any of us want to make a mistake, even though of course we do. And of course, that time he did.

John decided to rent a house. He found one, furnished, in the San Fernando Valley. By this time he was involved in the filming of *The Moon Is Down*, the story of the Resistance in World War II. That book sold over a million copies and Twentieth Century Fox bought the film rights. The motion picture was released in 1943.

Anyway, John arranged for the Haitian woman who had worked for us at Snedens Landing to join us. Her voodoo intrigued him, and besides, he loved the way she fried fish. She would not fly, so she came by train. She stayed with us the whole time we lived in that house in the valley.

John returned to a calm state of communication with the world around him, and his life once more was pleasant. We spent Thanksgiving and Christmas in the valley with Mother, my stepfather, and numerous friends. There was plenty of party action, but John still worked. He worked Monday through Friday on the script of *The Moon Is Down*, but when the weekend arrived, we saw friends and the corks popped. We had some great times with the Merediths and the Milestones. We went to most of the Hollywood restaurants and usually ran into people we knew, maybe at Mike Romanoff's or Dave Chasen's, both movie star and celebrity hangouts. The Wagner boys were around, and we often had dinner with them.

While we were in the valley, Jack Wagner approached John with an idea for an original story, which he could not write. John did. I have the original outline of that story, which John typed. It was *A Medal for Benny*, that on screen starred Arturo de Córdova and Dorothy Lamour.

The first part of January 1943, we headed back to New York. John decided he did not like Los Angeles anymore, nor did he like living in Southern California either. It lacked privacy, he said. Being on the move again did not matter to me. We were together.

6 – THE BEAR OF ALL TIME

John sold 'Baby' in Los Angeles, and we traveled back to New York by train. We had a stateroom, and we would not have dear Willie with us at the beginning because of the law about pets walking on trains. John and my stepfather hunted around and found a cage; the largest they could find was adequate for a miniature poodle but not for a ninety-pound sheepdog! Four days before we left, we taught Willie how to back into his cage. Poor Willie went to the luggage car, but when we were moving John had the porter bring Willie to our room. He wasn't about to make his dog's life uncomfortable. The journey was without any of the incidents that followed John, and we arrived back in New York. His agent, Elizabeth Otis, suggested an apartment hotel on the East Side facing the Hudson River. We moved in. It had a small kitchen where John could make his morning coffee without having to get dressed. In that apartment, John started on *Lifeboat*, the story of survivors from a torpedoed ship.

Lifeboat was the result of World War I pilot-hero Eddie Rickenbacker's experience of being shot down and spending three weeks in a life raft in the Pacific Ocean, before his rescue in November 1942. John was absolutely intrigued by the story. After the rescue, he interviewed Eddie Rickenbacker and another survivor, Hans Christian Adamson, in hospital. The more John thought about it, the more he wanted to write something about it.

His first thought was to write an article, for a magazine, but the idea grew and grew in his mind until he decided he would tell the story as a piece of literature. He did, but was dissatisfied with it. It wasn't full enough for him. He discussed it with Annie Laurie Williams, his trusted theatrical agent who took care of all his movie and play sales. From his discussions with Annie there evolved the idea for the film, *Lifeboat*. Once that was decided John could, as a fictionalist, insert various characters and build the story.

Alfred Hitchcock heard about it and came to see John. They discussed the idea of a movie; the outcome was to be a joint venture. John enjoyed working alone all his life, and he found it very difficult to write a movie script with another person. John had his ideas, and they were quite definite ones. He was a determined man, while Alfred Hitchcock was a powerful man, in his way. They made quite a combination. John did like the casting of the film, yet they were far from comfortable days to live with him. I used to get out of the apartment and walk Willie or visit a friend, or just do something, anything, because the tension between John and Hitchcock was great. At the end of a workday, John was depleted, nervous and usually very, very cranky.

During the writing of the *Lifeboat* script, John decided he wanted to live in New York City again, and told me to start looking for a more spacious apartment. While out walking Willie I saw a 'For Rent' sign not too far from the actress Katharine Cornell's house, and near William Shirer's, the author of *Berlin Diary*. John liked to visit Shirer when he wasn't working. The apartment I found was two blocks from our apartment hotel; it was a duplex with a garden. It was quite run down, but I took John to see it. 'I love it. Let's do it all over; take it, and when I get through work I can fix up the garden so it will be beautiful,' he said. We took the apartment at 330 East 51st Street, and I began furnishing it while John continued with Hitchcock and *Lifeboat.*

When the script was finished, there was no problem in placing it, and *Lifeboat* was filmed in North Hollywood, California. John did fly out to see part of the shooting, but, according to John, Hitchcock had taken out his little pen and began rewriting. John was madder than hell; it turned him into the bear of all time. He would not go to see the film and didn't attend the premiere. I saw *Lifeboat* and liked it, but in my time I don't believe John saw it.

John was very impressed with John Hodiak; *Lifeboat* was the movie that made him. In casting, John wanted Constance Bennett to play the part that Tallulah Bankhead did. He wanted the woman to be hard and sophisticated, and he thought Constance was the answer. I thought Tallulah did a fantastic job. John later saw Tallulah and told her he'd seen some of the rushes, and he praised her for her performance. *Lifeboat* received mixed reviews, but as time went on, of course, it has become a classic. For it's time, in the early forties, it was a successful motion picture. Now it's one of those late, late shows on television, badly cut up so that it doesn't resemble the *Lifeboat* John wrote and I saw. It could be Doris Day up the river for what was done with it.

John didn't particularly like writing for movies. He did enjoy working with Elia Kazan on *Viva Zapata!*, which was after we divorced. For John, the only thing that ever really came close to what he had in mind on the screen was *Of Mice and Men* with

Burgess Meredith, his friend, and Lon Chaney Jr., and he liked *A Medal for Benny* too.

He did not go to the opening of another of his classics, *Tortilla Flat*, but when he finally did see it, he told me had to get up and walk out. This was when he saw the scene with Akim Tamiroff down on his knees in the forest, with the heavenly shafts of light coming through the trees. He told me, 'I had to leave or else I would have thrown up!' That was what he disliked about writing for the movies – people changing his creativity, pulling out all the stops and releasing the doves. That was one of the reasons he delayed for so long before he gave his permission to Raoul Lévy to do *Cannery Row* in France in 1954. It was never made in his lifetime. So many people approached John to film *Cannery Row*, but he always turned them down. 'I can't go through the same thing again,' he told me, 'I know what they'll do with the frog hunt, they'll wreck it!'

However, John did like *Grapes of Wrath*. He had huge respect for Henry Fonda as an actor and thought he did such a magnificent job in the film, which of course he did. Nobody could read Steinbeck the way Fonda did. He read him with such feeling, beautifully.

It drove John absolutely crazy when people took his work and sliced it up. He just could not stand it. John worked so hard, so damned hard; everything he had in him poured into his work in progress at the time, and when he finished he was mentally, physically and emotionally depleted because he worked like a thundering machine.

7– A WEDDING BLAST

Every wedding has its special feeling, its brand of nuptial magic.

John and I had all that and much more the day we were married, 29 March, 1943. It was only a few days after his divorce from Carol had become final, and the month the film *The Moon Is Down* came out. I do not believe there was or ever will be a wedding quite like it.

Carol had finally agreed to give John a divorce, and, after a couple of days, we were talking in our New York apartment. John casually informed me, 'Well, Carol has finally made up her mind; she's going to get a divorce, so I presume some day we will be married.' Apparently, he had known for some time but had decided not to tell me until then. In March, in the duplex at 330 East 51st Street, John asked me to marry him. He was staring at the fire, with a drink in his hand. Suddenly, he said, 'Honey, I guess now we can get married.'

A few of John's friends, including the Howard Hunters, decided the wedding would be at the home of novelist Lyle Saxon in New Orleans's French and Spanish Quarter. Lyle's place was in an old Spanish army barracks. He had broken them up into two-story apartments centered around a courtyard. He wasn't a friend per se of John's, just an acquaintance, you might say. Howard and Marge Hunter lived in one of the largest apartments. Howard was then undersecretary to Howard Hopkins.

And so the wedding day was set for 29 March, 1943. I was deliriously happy; so was Mother. All our friends were happy, and so was John. We picked out wedding rings at Tiffany's. John wanted an antique ring, an old-fashioned ring. We settled on two semi-round twenty-two-carat gold rings. They would have made a fine set of brass knuckles! But that was what John wanted, and when he wanted something, he got it.

I went to New Orleans a few days ahead of John and was a houseguest of Roark and Mary Rose Bradford. Roark was a well-known American writer. He did *The Green Pastures* with Marc Connolly, and used to write the 'Little B Plantation' in the old *Collier's* magazine. I stayed with them for my so-called 'brideship.' Meanwhile, Jed Harris, the producer-director, had latched onto John and was trying to get a piece of property for him to do a play. John called me every day from New York, usually around seven at night. He would be stinking drunk with Jed. 'Well, we're on our way!' The next evening I would get the same call and the same message.

Lyle (Saxon) wrote John and told him that in the State of Louisiana a man had to be tested for a venereal disease to get married. A woman does not. John was insulted. 'It's only women who have venereal diseases,' he told Lyle. He resented the test and demanded that if he had to have one, then I did, too. His macho character again.

Anyway, after a whole week of bachelor dinners with Jed, John arrived, hung over but sober. He flew down after obtaining a special permit through President Roosevelt, because in those days you were bumped off a plane for the army, air force or navy. John arrived in New Orleans and then it was just one big party after another. Everyone entertained us. It was quite fantastic.

At that time, Higgins, the boat builder, was involved in making landing craft for American troops. Part of my wedding present was driving the bayous in one of those boats. We crowded into one and had a ball; it was one of many pre-wedding parties.

Every party I went to I started out with a beautiful dinner dress, usually a full-length and low-necked dress and with slippers to match. At one of the first, at the Sheflins (John's friends), no sooner had I entered the house than a drunk came over and poured a whole glass of scotch down the front of me. As I sat in a chair, someone else came over and dumped champagne on me, vintage at that. The next party, I forget where, someone spilled a dish of shrimp jambalaya on my lap – all that shrimp and tomatoes and beans and rice. Yuk!

It seemed like everyone was giving us a party; it was one round of moving from house to house, and everywhere somebody spilled something on me: champagne, shrimp jambalaya, scotch, gin, all kinds of drinks, all kinds of food. Personally, I do not take to champagne very well – always been a vodka martini fiend – and I was allergic to seafood, and I am not particularly fond of Crêpes Suzette. My dresses got them all, and everywhere we partied we got roaring drunk. John did pretty well for himself, too. When John drank, he drank. And he sure could hold his liquor.

At one party I remember he sat down in a place of honor reserved for me, the blushing bride-to-be (blushing?) and, hell, if it didn't happen again. This time, someone spilled a whole plate of Crêpes Suzette into my lap. My poor dress was a mess. We kept going, we kept drinking and eating, which was fine since it was a pre-wedding party, although a rather long one. We ended up on Bourbon Street, then a great place back in the forties, full of so much life. We hit a bar, and I got on the piano, high up behind the bar, and sang with a bunch of colored people. They were wonderful. My dear dress continued to get sloshed with drink; all I seemed to do was to have my damned dress mopped up!

Naturally, all that eating, drinking and partying took its toll on the human body. 'I've got to go home, John, I don't feel well,' I finally said. An understatement. We headed back to the Bradfords' house on Toulouse Street in the old French Quarter. That was another haunted house; yes, haunted. Like all Southern houses in New Orleans, you have to reach it through an alleyway that's very small. We were staggering down the alleyway, and I began to feel faint. When you're going to be sick, you get a certain feeling. I did.

'My God, John, I'm going to be sick.' I managed to stumble out the words.

'For God's sake, let's go, kid,' he said.

'What, and get stuff over the front of my dress!'

He broke up. 'You gotta be kidding,' he laughed. We both stood there, laughing, and then I started to faint. He carried me the rest of the way into the house, and I let go in the courtyard fountain. That was an event in itself, a wild climax to the night before our wedding day.

8 – ENTRANCE OF THE GLADIATORS

The day of my marriage to John Steinbeck arrived. It was a foggy, chilly morning when I awoke. I had a crashing hangover, as did most of our friends. My mother – Bird Eyes, as John called her – arrived in New Orleans and we moved into the old Monteleone Hotel. We had taken a double suite, Mother and I in one room, John in the other. It was old-fashioned, having a double suite, but it was going to be an old-fashioned marriage.

The groomsmen arrived for John about six-forty-five and started feeding him Ramos fizzes. John went to the bar with his pals Paul de Kruif, Clark Salmon and Howard Hunter, and they duly revived their spirits. In fact, they were overserved. About ten-thirty, John came to my room as I was trying to do my hair. Mother had my clothes laid out on the bed, including my trousseau, a simple little brown-and-white dress. 'You better take care of things,' he said and put two ring boxes on the edge of the bed. I took them and put them in my purse. I was very nervous and shaking; why I don't know. John went back to the bar. After he left, Mother snapped at me, 'For God's sake stop crying and being nervous. You'll get used to these marriages. I'm on my third!' I still cried. Maybe I cried because I was just so happy, as brides are supposed to be.

We took a taxi to a department store to pick up the wedding cake, and then we bought a record of Wagner's *Lohengrin*, the wedding march. Mother and Marge Hunter did the picking up; I stayed in the cab. We continued to Lyle Saxon's home where twenty or so guests were waiting, absolutely pie-eyed. John was stoned, too. By now, the judge arrived (he was tipsy) and I went to Marge's bedroom to retouch my makeup. John came in and said, 'You better give me the rings.' I opened my purse. His ring was there. Mine was gone.

'Oh my God!' I exclaimed and went into hysterics. During my outburst and gushing of tears John remarked, 'Well, I guess we weren't supposed to be married.' The judge said he could still marry us; we would use just one ring. John would put it on my finger, and then I would take it off and put it on his. I was so nervous and upset that I sat on the toilet crying my heart out. My great day had finally arrived – and I had lost the ring.

Time for the ceremony. I didn't want a bouquet, but mother insisted, and so I carried a bouquet of yellow Calla lilies. After the 'tragedy' of the rings came the comedy of the wedding march. Joe, the colored butler shared by the Hunters and Saxons, was supposed to play the *Lohengrin* record when John and I entered the courtyard where the wedding took place. We made our entrance. Poor Joe put the record on Marge's beautiful record player, the finest money could buy in those days. We did not hear the *Lohengrin* march but heard the other side, twenty-eight bars of 'The Entrance of the Gladiators.' That's the music used in circuses. It was quite some scene. The guests sure straightened up as we walked to the makeshift altar. John broke up.

The music went through twenty-eight bars before Marge Hunter left my side and turned the record over. But then the damned needle broke! She dashed back, terribly embarrassed, and changed the needle.

Our first ceremony was in French, yet before the dear judge stopped to pause, I burst forth with, '*Oui.*' The second was in English. Finally, after it seemed like ages had passed, the judge pronounced us man and wife. We kissed. I was now, legally, Mrs. John Steinbeck on 29 March, 1943.

The press was then allowed to join us. They asked me my age in between the picture-taking. I said I was twenty-seven. Mother was upset at that. So what? I said I was twenty-seven because I was trying to look older. You see, John had this phobia about our ages. He never said it outright, but I knew it. I was just trying to protect him because I knew many people thought, 'Oh, for Christ's sake, what the hell, the old man marrying the young chick.' I didn't care. John was then forty-one. Age was nothing to me because I was so in love with the man, not his years. Age should never mean anything.

The ceremony over, the drinking resumed. It was a very drunken wedding. John and I were in the middle of cutting the cake when there was a loud banging. All heads turned. What the hell was that? In burst several squads of police. They rushed over to John and handed him a summons for statutory rape! He God near fainted! He took it seriously. He turned deathly pale and began to splutter. That should have given me some indication as to his past! I think everyone has a little extracurricular experience in their life at some time or other, well, perhaps many do. I knew John had. We recovered from the scare of the summons and continued to serve drinks. The gag was well timed. Paul de Kruif and Howard Hunter, witnesses to our marriage, had arranged that little piece through an old school pal of Howard's – the sheriff.

By now, John was plastered and mad at me for losing the ring. I could understand that, but I had forgotten about it and thought the rape charge incident was hilarious.

Around four in the afternoon, everyone was just one side of passing out, all the photographs taken, and we were supposed to freshen up and have a siesta before the wedding dinner party at Antoine's. However, Mother and I were stone-cold sober; me because I had only had a couple of glasses of champagne. I subconsciously guess I was still in a state of shock over losing the ring. John was by now in a sulking mood (he could get that way sometimes), and when we were back in our hotel he went to his room, and Mother and I went to ours. I took off my wedding dress and those awful war rayon stockings and took a bath. I lay down on the bed and cried my heart out. Suddenly, I said, 'Mother, get Marge on the 'phone. I know where my wedding ring is.'

'Marge, I know where my ring is. Go out the door, take five paces left and look in the gutter. That's where it is.'

'Hang on,' she said. 'You're drunk.' She went, and when she came back on the line, she said, 'I have your ring.'

In those days whenever there was any celebration in New Orleans, especially in the Old Quarter, there were always dozens of picaninnies around. The streets were unwashed and the gutters were dirty. When I had paid the cab driver on our shopping trip, the ring had fallen from my purse. The box had sprung open, and my ring had fallen in the gutter. Call it what you will, but I did have a vision of my ring lying in the gutter.

So, my wedding day nightmare turned into sunny that beautiful spring day and John allowed me to sleep with him that night. I had been forgiven by the Great One – and he was.

That night, we continued the celebration at Antoine's, where the de Kruifs gave us a dinner party. It was supposed to be a wedding supper, but, again, it turned out to be nothing but Crêpes Suzette and champagne. I just cannot eat that kind of food. All manner of toasts were made. It's a Southern custom at a wedding that you buy a drink for anyone who comes in off the street. We had one of Antoine's private back rooms, but people kept coming in, and we kept giving them drinks. It just went on and on, and Marge kept telling the story of how I found my ring. Finally, it ended. John and I were back at our hotel around eleven o'clock.

We had hardly climbed into bed when the telephone rang. It was Lady 'M' calling from New York. John talked to her for an hour and a half. Lady 'M' was a part of the office force of McIntosh and Otis, his agents. Seemingly he knew her very well. After we moved back to New York, I think John and Lady 'M' had a 'matinee' about three times a week, and I was still his wife. Let's put it this way: they were 'cousiney.' His conversation with Lady 'M' finally ended, and we made love. It is common knowledge that a man who has been drinking too much is not exactly the best thing in bed, and if I did not respond joyfully that night, it was not my fault. And that night it wasn't. But, other nights and days we were passionate as a couple could be, and, as I had learned before my marriage, John did what he wanted to do.

We stayed in New Orleans for seven days, then went back to

begin married life in New York. John, Mother and I went back to New York by train. John insisted that my mother come with us; why, I didn't know at the time since he didn't like her.

And so, my wedding day was one to remember. It might not have appeared the ideal wedding a girl dreams about, but I accepted it. At that time of my life, I was a very mild person, and I was so in love with John, and he was in love with me. Everything was perfect as the three of us walked into the apartment on East 51st Street, but I did not know then that soon there would be packing again – only this time I would be left behind.

9 – AWAY TO WAR

We were back in New York a week after we married. John, as I said, had asked Mother to come with us. Although he did not particularly care for her, he did like her wacky sense of humor. John liked people who had a sense of humor and could laugh. There was no reason for Mother to be home, as by this time my stepfather was in the army. And, unknown to me, John too, was thinking of becoming involved in the war in some way. One of the reasons for Mother's presence was because she would soften the blow when he told me he was going off to war.

It was satisfying to be back in our apartment on East 51st Street, in vibrant New York. I think New York is like an action capital of the world. Oddly enough, we did not receive too many wedding gifts, and what we had seemed mostly for me. But we were off and running, attending one party after another in our honor in the weeks that followed. Life was one big party. Sometimes, if things didn't go John's way, he would become slightly sadistic. He loved his women to be very beautiful and to be dressed up. One night, we were going out, and it was snowing, and Mother and I wore furs, beautiful dresses, and velvet slippers.

'Will you call a cab, please, John?' Mother politely asked.

'No! We're going to walk.'

Why he said that I don't know, and so we walked, in the snow to The Chambord, one of New York's most exclusive restaurants. We arrived sopping wet. Mother and I looked like drowned rats while John had a big grin on his face. He had a way of downing other people, and he enjoyed seeing us in that state. I shall never know why John liked to sometimes act in the manner of putting down a person. But then, he was a creative giant but an impenetrable person, behind his greatness.

Mother stayed with us for two weeks and then went back to Los Angeles. I settled down to everyday life as Mrs. John Steinbeck. John liked antiques, and gradually we began to acquire some very nice things.

Many New York duplexes are old brownstone houses remodeled, and ours was one of them. John liked to putter about in the garden and, as spring came along, he bought six perfectly huge tubs, planted tomato plants in them, and decided he would begin his victory garden. He hung the pots on the fences, and when he took a break from his writing, he sometimes would take a paint brush and try to fertilize the blossoms *à la* bee. He was unsuccessful, and we had no tomatoes. I believe the plants came up, took one look at the filth in New York City, and went right back into the ground.

One nice happening came from those early days of our marriage. John was out walking Willie when he met George Frazier, and then George's wife, Mimsi. They, too, had a sheepdog. John brought them home for dinner, and we became great friends.

In those early days, John kept talking about the war. 'I've got to get into it. I've got to do something,' he kept saying. 'I have got to be part of my time!' He was his old restless self again, in the same category as Hemingway. He hated it when nothing was happening, and, although he loved to putter in the garden, he knew life was not exactly thrilling him, trying to grow tomatoes! Finally, John made an appointment with Mrs. Ogden Reid at the *Herald Tribune*. She was the wife of Ogden Reid, the owner, and had a great deal to do with the running of that then great newspaper. 'I'd like to be a war correspondent,' he told her. She thought it was a great idea. John told her he could do a better job than John Gunther, the war correspondent. He said he could give a different point of view on the war than the usual. But there was one slight problem: John did not have a passport. It had been taken away from him after he and Carol had returned from visiting Russia in the thirties, and after he had given iodine to Spain. Apparently, the lady who signed the passports in those days 'hated my guts,' he told me. 'She didn't like *The Grapes of Wrath*, and thinks I'm a Communist.' For my money, I thought he had no hope of getting a passport, but I should have known better.

John felt the war was going to last a long time and he wanted to be in the European theater. Why? Before we were married, Harold Guinzberg, the president of Viking Press, went to England, and when he returned he managed to get John involved with the O.W.I., the Overseas War Institute. From that, John got his brainstorm that he wanted to be a war correspondent.

The O.W.I. was like the Red Cross then; everyone sat around and talked about the 'good war,' but nobody did anything. I have to give John credit; he was the kind of man who said, 'Hell, if we've got a bucket of crap, let's shovel it out, not just stare at it!'

Well, he did not tell Mrs. Reid he had no passport. He said he had 'overlooked' it. The Reids invited us to dinner. She was a marvelous woman, vastly intelligent, always immaculate, but, above all, one hell of a businesswoman. Over dinner we discussed John covering the war in Europe for the *Tribune*. It was all agreed, and then John dropped his bomb. 'Well, you'll have to help me get a passport. I don't have one anymore,' he said, in a quiet tone.

After that initial shock wore off, Mrs. Reid broke the silence. 'I'll take care of that,' she said, and we returned to our meal.

Back in our apartment, John said, 'Honey, I hope you don't mind.' He always called me 'Honey' whenever he figured he might be in the wrong or was going to blast out with something that might or would terrify me.

'No, of course not, but do you have to go?'

'Yes I do, it's something in me. I must get into this war somehow.'

I did not say anything. I did not particularly care for John going to war. We had only just married, legally, that is. But I knew full well that once John made up his mind, only an act of God would stop him.

The following days he went to lunch with his agent or a friend, so he told me. What he was doing was working on his passport and with the *Tribune* to get overseas. John always was a secretive man; another part of his nature. And then one day he came home and said, in his usual soft-toned voice, 'I think it's going to work out, darling.' He was somewhat vague. 'What is, darling?' I asked.

'Mrs. Reid will be able to work something for me.' He did not say what. Shortly afterward, when he was out on one of his afternoon meetings, he called me.

'What do we have for dinner?'

'Baked beans, Boston style.'

'Good, I'm bringing a guest,' he said, but did not say who.

John adored Boston baked beans, especially the way my mother made them, which is the way I also made them. That's where they boil for one whole day, and you bake them for two days. John had no trouble eating a quart of them. That night, he brought home a charming man, Sam Spewack, the playwright, and we had a Boston baked bean dinner. John said nothing about going to war. The next morning he arose early and left. Again, he did not tell me where he was going. By seven John was in downtown New York. At eleven he called and asked me to dig out his birth certificate. I still did not know what was happening. Three o'clock that afternoon he and Sam Spewack came home. He was in a great mood.

'I've made it! I've had my physical. Let's have a celebration,' he said with pride.

He poured several large scotches: Cutty Sark, which was hard to get in those days. We drank them, on the rocks, and they sat around making small talk about how terrible army nurses were. John and Sam compared their physicals. Suddenly, John grew quite pale and went to the bathroom. The next thing was what sounded like a series of machine-gun shots, then another, then the toilet flushing. John had thrown up the beans! Sam and I tore up the stairs and found him out cold on the bathroom floor. We got him onto the bed and undressed him. His right arm was swollen, and his upper arm was as big as his thigh! He was allergic to tetanus.

It took two days for him to get over that reaction. He was in a kind of semi-coma and a great deal of pain. I kept his arm in ice packs, and he could not hold down any food. By the fourth day,

John had recovered. It was daylight, and I heard him moving. He was packing. 'I'm leaving,' he said, just like that, completely out of the blue. He had secretly bought a navy flyer's bag and hidden it in a closet. He was packing bare necessities. I was in that usual wake-up daze, but I asked if he wanted any coffee.

'I don't have time,' he said.

I jumped out of bed and put on a robe. John finished packing and went downstairs. He said nothing. I did not know what was happening. Then he said, 'I'm on my way. I must be part of my time. You'll hear from me.' That was that. No explanation, no kisses, no nothing. He opened the front door and left. I went into a state of shock and started to cry and beat the door with my fists. All day long I walked about in a daze. I called his agents, and they said, 'Isn't that wonderful.' Great for him, but hell for me. Still, I should have known being Mrs. John Steinbeck was going to be a daily adventure. And, despite what some of his friends thought, I wished his happiness as much as I wanted mine.

Anyway, at two the next morning the telephone rang. Marie Arnstein, my neighbor and friend, told me she saw John while she was working at the Red Cross. 'He told me to tell you goodbye, and you'll hear from him as soon as possible,' she said. What could I do? Simply nothing. There I was, a bride of a few weeks and my husband had packed and left to go to war – without so much as an explanation as to where he was going, and not even a goodbye kiss! Just like that. But that was John Steinbeck, creative genius, very secretive, often impetuous and impenetrable.

I did not hear from John for six weeks but knew what was happening because I read the *Tribune*. The paper called me and said he had landed in London, but I still had no idea where he was! Then, six weeks later, and after reading his copy from London, I received a letter. How nice of him! He told me how much he missed me and how sorry he was, leaving me the way he did. Letters were frequent after that. Naturally, I was relieved that he was still alive and still loved me. I loved him.

'I love you very much…I miss you so much…' he wrote me. In one letter, my husband told me a fortune teller had said we would have four children. In each letter, John expressed his love for me with great nostalgia. At first, I admit I was not only shocked but scared every minute that he might be killed.

John went to France, then Africa, then Salerno, through Italy, and I lived on in New York, always anxious for the mail, just like so many women whose men were at the front. In one letter, he related funny stories about capturing a German. In another, he told of meeting Douglas Fairbanks Jr. 'I always thought he was such an aesthetic snob, but I have discovered Fairbanks was quite a nice guy,' he wrote me. In fact, he often partied with Fairbanks, then a ranking officer in the British navy, and with other reporters like Quentin Reynolds.

John always sent me presents, usually via his mail and delivery service – men of the armed forces. My doorbell would ring, and perhaps a naval commander would be there with a golf bag. And at the bottom of the bag would be some package or other, an antique bottle, a scarf, pieces of silver, or some gadget. Another time, in one of his letters, John said we must get Willie a wife. He had been in England and had seen some beautiful sheepdogs. I must say that John's letters were highly connubial. He wanted everyone to have a wife, for everyone to be mated.

That long, lonely summer of 1943, Mimi Frazier and I went to Connecticut and bought a sheepdog, a high-quality one, and duly introduced her to Willie. Willie hated her, and we had to get rid of a very expensive dog.

The months rolled on, and John's letters reflected that he was now bored with the war and thought it was 'stupid.' It annoyed him, he wrote. Meantime, he sent me Ernie Pyle, legendary correspondent loved by the fighting men. Ernie arrived in the middle of summer, in his winter uniform! And New York in the summer is one blisteringly hot city. Ernie was always physically cold. He had on his long underwear, too, but sat shivering in the apartment, drinking straight scotch.

It didn't take Ernie and I long to become friends, for he was such an easy-going man to get along with; he was a real human being. His presence turned the dullness of summer into a time of continuous interest. President Roosevelt had asked Ernie to go to Washington and receive an award, and Ernie was terrified. He was a quiet, humble and shy man, and he did not know quite what to do about that kind of honor. He asked me to go with him, and I did. We went by train, and I tried to get Ernie to dress up for the event. He would not. Ernie refused to take off his dog-toed shoes and met the President in one of those old army winter uniforms. Ernie later told me he had trembled through the whole presentation and was embarrassed about it. After the White House ceremony, Ernie and I went back to New York and spent some enjoyable evenings with friends, talking about John, the war, and the hope for peace. I became a hostess for Ernie's gatherings, which were never dull, and I could never hear enough about John from Ernie.

John arrived back in New York in mid-October 1943. He had written to me that he wanted to be home for Christmas. He had been in England working on an army propaganda film with his pal Burgess Meredith, who wanted him to stay. So did the *Herald Tribune*, because his columns were so prolific and popular. I had no warning about John's return. He hated greeting people as much as he hated goodbyes. I shall never know why he did not tell me when he was coming back, but he was always one for surprises.

He flew back to New York from England with his friend little Charlie Lytle. His luggage was lots of boxes and packages, but, most of all, he had with him six quarts of Gordon's English gin, and two quarts of Fernet-Branca.

I was at home, alone, when the doorbell rang. He had a key of his own, naturally, but this time he was loaded down with packages, his kit, portfolio, attaché case, and the briefcase with the liquor. It was early that October morning, and quite chilly when I opened the door and saw him standing there. I almost died. He wasn't exactly sober, but he looked understandably, desperately tired; in fact, he was quite weak. But he had had a good time drinking on the plane. I flung myself into his arms and started to cry. He gave me a big kiss and a hug and said, 'I want a hot bath and ice, lots of ice.' And came in.

I was so excited I did not know what I was doing. I threw on a coat and ran to the delicatessen, and bought ice. We sat and drank and talked – for forty-eight hours solid. Amazingly, neither of us became drunk. Happy, yes. 'The war won't last much longer, but if it goes on another eight months that means it will go on for another two years,' John said, in between scotch and gin. As history proved, it did last another two years, until 1945. Finally, after this forty-eight-hour talk marathon, we went to bed. It was beautiful. He was alive. And how!

It took him, naturally, a few days to unwind, and then we began to see everybody. It was back to the parties, parties all the time. John Steinbeck had come back to New York.

All John wanted to eat was raw onion sandwiches and drink...milk! He ate dozens of raw onion sandwiches and drank quarts of milk. And a few scotches in between. I did not care what he ate or drank. He was home, alive – and mine, all mine.

Two weeks after he came home a delayed reaction set in, and he did not feel well. He became depressed, and he kept turning his head and rubbing his neck. I asked him what was wrong, but he did not know. John wasn't the kind of man who would willingly discuss his health. I managed to drag a story out of him, and that in itself I knew was quite an accomplishment as he never, ever particularly cared to talk about himself.

He tried to make light of the story. 'I was in Salerno and going behind a guy in a minefield. I don't think I made a good soldier because the guy told me he had a minesweeper, and once he turned and said, "Mr. Steinbeck, I think you'll cut a more military figure if you put your helmet on right." I had it on backward.

'Then those babies started coming. Boom! Boom! Everybody dove into a foxhole. I went for one, and as I landed got hit on the back of the head with an oil can. It sure stunned me. Ever since then my head and neck have bothered me.'

'You better see a doctor.'

John was terrified of doctors. I don't think he ever believed in them, but he went, after a struggle. An X-ray of his neck showed that he had an arthritic spur and a cracked bone at the base of the neck. John went through big shots of vitamins. He was down, really down, very depleted, and said he felt 'very old.' He was still a young man – forty-one. The doctors told him that he was exhausted and needed male testosterone. They started to shoot him full of male hormones. He did feel better after that treatment, and then he went to an osteopath for his neck. Again, his old restlessness came alive, and he was getting excited because Christmas was coming. John was a big sentimentalist about Christmas, and that attitude probably went back to his childhood. He loved Christmas for it meant parties, and John did love parties.

That first Christmas as Mrs. John Steinbeck was a sensational one, day and especially the nights. We were both quite passionate. During this festive holiday season – and Christmas and the New Year is always somehow special in New York with excitement, and snow – we went to one celebration that was out of this world. Mildred Bailey and her husband, Red Norvo, the great musician, threw a party. What a blast! I shall never forget it, nor, I imagine, did anyone who was there. Everybody in show business was there. In the crowd were Humphrey Bogart, Virginia Mayo, Burl Ives, the Robert Ruarks, George and Mimsi Frazier, the great pantomimist Jimmy Savo, and all of Red Norvo's band. Hazel Scott was there, too. She later married Adam Clayton Powell. Perhaps I may have been ahead of the times in those days: we did not care about color, just friendships, and talent.

It was a huge party, and every singer, entertainer, and great jazz musicians performed. Mildred had invited a whole group from Harlem, including the great negro keyman, Eddie Heywood. Mildred was working at Café Society then, so naturally, she got up and sang. That evening was the first time, too, that I met Robert Capa, who was John's partner when they did *A Russian Journal.* John adored those kinds of parties. If you loved life, music, good friends, who wouldn't?

In our home, of course, we had a traditional Christmas tree, and John was like a child with it, prancing about, decorating the tree with tinsel, bells, and lights. We put a red stocking cap and ribbon on dear Willie. Secretly, we had bought each other presents, and John had bought me several gifts from England and had them stored away for Christmas, including some beautiful Georgian silver.

For three days I cooked for our open house, and all kinds of people came to us Christmas Eve and Christmas Day. John Mealy, of *Life* magazine, took photographs, and we just had a great big party, with everyone getting royally toodled. The partying went on for hours, and when it ended, John and I and Willie took a long walk in the snow. These were such precious moments in my life.

It was such a marvelous Christmas. Life then was a heaven, a world of two people very much in love and so very happy.

And I was pregnant with our first son, Thom.

10 – HAM SANDWICHES

January came with its thick snows that turned into slush. People put on their winter clothes in preparation for the rushing madness of day-to-day life in New York City. John had no thoughts of working because he was still exhausted from his war experience. We usually spent the evenings at home; occasionally we went to the theater, and John saw many people he had not seen for a long time. He was moody, mean to many; there wasn't that Steinbeck sense of humor anymore. The war had changed him.

Our New Year's celebration was considerably quieter that year of 1944. We went to the 21 Club, a great hangout for the who's who of New York and show business people, then did a bar crawl and went home. Early in the new year, John suddenly said to me, 'I've got to get out of here. I can't stand New York. I can't stand still. Let's go to Mexico.'

If that's what he wanted to do, then that was what I wanted.

'What will we do about Willie?' I asked.

'Call your mother to come here and take care of him. Your stepfather's in the army, and she loves New York. I'll pay for it. We'll only be gone two or three months.'

Mother came, and she brought her dog. New York was still blacked out because of the war, and Mother felt she needed that extra protection. Willie was the kind of darling dog who would have shown any prowler exactly where to find the silver; he would have been most courteous and, in his direct way, would probably have said 'Ha! At last, I have a new friend.' Willie had a habit of always barking at the wrong things.

We were packing for Mexico, Mother had been with us a week, and one morning she said, 'Gwyn, you're going to have a baby, aren't you?'

'Not that I know of,' I said, surprised.

'Oh yes, you are. I know, because John has been throwing up every morning.'

'Don't be ridiculous, that's because of his medicine.'

'You're going to have a baby!' She was right. I was pregnant, but the trip was still on. Air travel was out; even with priority you could get bumped off from New York to Newark. We decided to take the train to New Orleans then to Corpus Christi and on to Brownsville, Texas. From there, we were assured we would have no trouble getting a flight into Mexico.

Before we went, John and our friends, Miguel and Rosa Covarrubias, led me on about Mexico during one of their high teas. I had never been to the heart of Mexico, and so did not know what to expect. John, Rosa, and Miguel kidded me with such remarks as, 'Wait until you've had the octopus cooked in its own ink,' or, 'You'll love the *gusanos*, fried worms...' They only did that because I was pregnant and had a squeamish stomach. Several friends, including Rosa and Miguel, saw us off at the station. There was more drinking. John was loaded – on B_{12} and B_1 pills and male hormones, all on doctor's orders.

Food was scarce on the train, so we took a wicker basket filled with food and drink. Those wartime days, you did not know if you would eat on the train, because troops had priority and fed first.

Besides, John was well fortified with some of the London gin that Charlie Lytle had given him in England. He had all the gin to himself. I couldn't drink in my condition, of course. In fact, I could hardly say I enjoyed the so-called cocktail hour in our stuffy stateroom, what with the ham and cheese sandwiches, the rocky-road bed and the large Mexican briefcase with the gin. That case had its unique odor. It kind of stank. An adoring Mexican fan had given it to John, and it was large and highly decorated with a Mexican calendar seal, and it had three large locks. But it had been cured in Mexican fashion – in bull manure! John delighted in carrying it when he had an appointment with someone he did not like because the effect in a warm room on a rainy day was quite overpowering.

When we arrived in Chicago, the de Kruifs met us. We went to the Drake Hotel and dined on delicious red snapper soup. That was the only real food we had time for before we caught the train for New Orleans. The de Kruifs had sandwiches made for us at the Drake. We went to the train and on to New Orleans where we were met by Marge and Howard Hunter. It was nostalgic to see New Orleans again, a city of so much spirit and life, and music. We pulled into the station on a beautiful afternoon; we had tickets to leave the same day, but we had them changed to the next day. John was tired, and his legs were bothering him. Besides, he did not like trains that much anyway. When we left New Orleans there was, in addition to our wicker food basket, five bottles of Five Star Metaxa brandy, a parting gift from Howard. 'You'll need it, the train you're going on has no berths, no sleepers, no anything,' Howard informed us, encouragingly. The train did take us to Corpus

Christi. Howard was right; we did need the brandy.

We were both in a spirit of high adventure leaving New Orleans. John told me about Mexico City and places where we would go as the train clickety-clicked along the tracks. We talked about taking a few side trips with our friends the Covarrubiases, probably to Mitla. 'Of course, I don't think they've finished the roads to Mitla, but we can always take the train,' said John, smiling.

I looked at him, and he burst out laughing. 'Do you want to get on a train that soon again?' I asked. We both broke up and laughed. Late that evening and about halfway to Corpus Christi our train stopped and pulled into a siding. It was pitch dark, and John and I decided to walk to the end of the car and investigate. Half an hour later it was apparent that our halt was for the military. Out of the darkness came shouts and the semi-abbreviated conversation known best to the army when something is about to happen. Then we heard screeching wheels. It was an army troop train. The night was hot and humid; you could smell the sea, and the June bugs were thick. The doors were completely open, and I was driven back into the car by the mad desire of the bugs to reach the lights. I went back to our room, and shortly afterward John returned.

'It's a big sonofabitch, forty cars of kids,' he said. 'If you don't mind, honey, I'll go back and talk to some of the boys. I might get an idea for an article.' He left. I kicked off my shoes, rolled up his raincoat for a pillow, and settled back. Ninety minutes later, John came back. 'Honey, they're the saddest bunch of kids. I'm going to take back a bottle or two and give some of the kids a snort.' He said the cars were open like cattle cars, but were screened and had bunks. 'Frankly, those cars aren't any cooler than where we are, but at least if we get up to twenty-five miles an hour, there's a little breeze. Come back with me and meet some of the kids,' he said, grabbing another bottle of gin and a brandy bottle. Off he went, and I followed.

We arrived in Corpus Christi around daybreak. The smell of the sea was strong, and all kinds of insects clung to the screening so you could hardly see out. When we stopped, we said goodbye to the young troops and returned to our car. In that hot and sticky town, our train moved forward, and then back, forward and back. This shunting went on for half an hour, then a conductor came in and politely informed us that our diner (if you could call it that) was about to be removed. He suggested we have coffee in the Corpus Christi station, then held up two tickets and told us that from there to Brownsville we would be eating at an army diner.

There were three army diners. We were given a timetable: midday meal at one, dinner at four. The conductor went on to tell us that we had better be prompt for our meals. We would be eating straight army chow. In case we were too late, he said, they were attaching a bar to our part of the train, and there would be an open grill where we could get sandwiches and coffee. 'What kind of sandwiches?' John asked. With John, you always had to be specific. 'Fried ham,' the conductor replied.

'My God, I bet they slaughtered every pig west of Kentucky to put on this train! Let's go and see what the thing looks like,' John said. We left the car, walked the length of six cars, and arrived at what John called the 'Elite Bar and Grille.' The conductor had been right; it certainly smelled of ham, years of it. The air was blue with ham fat; a few officers clung to the bar, nursing swiveled barrel chairs, with beaten-up ashtrays on stands. The lights were still on, even though morning sunlight was breaking in. All the windows were closed. I felt ghastly and sat down on a chair next to the bar.

'How does that go for breakfast?' John asked an officer pointing to his beer. The officer next to him said, 'I think you could drink a gallon of it and not feel it. You sweat it out in two minutes.'

John turned and said to me, 'Do you want a beer, honey?'

'No thanks, I'll try the coffee.'

He raised an eyebrow in his inimitable way (and he had such ways), and said, 'And a fried ham sandwich?'

'Why not, I'm game.' We began to laugh. All the food we'd had since New Orleans had been ham sandwiches!

'What's the joke,' the young officer asked. John told him about our solid diet of ham sandwiches and then he, too, laughed. 'Well,' he began, 'why don't you and your wife be our guests, we have chicken and dumplings.'

As I have related, John was not a lover of chicken in any form, but the thought of a change in diet made his eyes light up. 'I'd like you to meet my wife,' he said. As the officer leaned over to shake my hand, he hesitated. The briefcase odor was working due to the humidity. I began to laugh to myself for I knew what he must have been thinking, but he was polite enough to continue. 'Have a midday meal with me,' he said.

'We'll be glad to, but I have a feeling that the chicken is going to taste like ham,' said John. He showed the officer our food cards with the hours stamped on them.

'Well, this doesn't coincide with my time, but I'll fix it so we can eat together. Let's meet at the diner door around one-thirty, and

I'll take you in,' he said.

We went back to our bedroom, and by now John was looking a little bleary-eyed, and I was exhausted. No sleep and all the heat, plus John's Metaxa brandy, were beginning to show on his eyelids. We decided to get some sleep, but that was impossible. There was no air conditioning in those days, and the windows were sealed. We both collapsed in our beds, inhaling the same air over and over again. For whatever it was worth – and that was almost nothing – our inhalations were whirled back to us by a tiny electric fan. Of course, that was not all; there was this darling briefcase; its odor went around the little fan, too. We gave up, wiped each other off with cold, wet Pullman towels, freshened ourselves as best we could and prepared for our chicken dumpling luncheon. We gradually pulled back on our soiled clothing, which somehow the little fan had managed to dry out. John suggested we walk back to the 'Elite Bar and Grille,' just for the exercise and to kill time. As we began to walk, the rocky roadbed made it seem as if we were traveling much faster, but we were not. We were going at about thirty-five miles an hour. We shouldered our way into the bar, and John asked the man in charge, 'What time do we get to Brownsville?'

The man answered. 'Don' know exaklee, suh, but I does know, we'se goin' to stop someplace midway and drop some cars.'

'Lord, not another delay,' John said, in one of his 'Oh shit!' tones.

'It won' be long, suh, they'se jus goin' to drop some o' de troop train and we shud get into Brownsville aroun' nine tonight.'

'Good Lord, do you have enough ham to last?' John asked.

'Yus, suh,' was the very serious reply.

That was too much for us, and we both started laughing again; John had a beer, and he asked me for a cigarette. We both smoked too much all our lives. I only had two left, which we shared, and then he asked the bartender, 'Do you have any cigarettes?'

'No suh, sorry.'

'You mean there are no cigarettes on this train?'

'No suh, but I'll get you some of my Luckys, and when we stop midway there's a little stand with newspapers and the like, and you can get some there.'

'How many do you have left?' John asked the man.

'Don' know, but I'll look.' He produced a crumpled pack of Lucky Strikes from his jacket. There were four left. John gave him twenty-five cents for them, then went back to wearily nurse his beer. I smoked. John kept looking at his watch. Finally, he said, 'We'd better start for the diner.' He paid for the beer, and we jostled, painfully, back to the diner. John went ahead, opening the doors chivalrously for me, then letting go so I received them, full force! This was unintentional, but it was the way of the roadbed. John could show chivalry as well as his meanness, but then, so can any man or woman. We arrived, no officer. We waited ten minutes in the vestibule, but still no officer. John went to the diner and looked around. A young military policeman demanded to see John's card. He showed it, and when the MP saw the time, he said, 'You are too late.' John's disposition flew apart like a July Fourth pinwheel when anyone spoke to him with that kind of authority, especially when John felt he was in the right. He was too overtired and hungry to be polite to a uniform. Under ordinary circumstances, John always had the greatest respect for anything in uniform; even had a little fear of a uniform. But this was too much for him. Usually, John was a soft-spoken man and seldom raised his voice, but by now he was in high C and informed the MP that we had been invited to dine by an officer. Sorry, no luck. Finally, he drew up his best resources and informed the young man, 'Look here, my wife is standing in the vestibule, she's pregnant, and has had nothing but HAM for thirty hours, and if she doesn't get something decent to eat she will get constipated! I WON'T HAVE IT! YOU HEAR? SHE HAS GOT TO COME IN AND SIT DOWN!'

Complete silence coincided with his utterance of the word 'constipated.' Because of his wrath (and it was) he had not heard the train come to a complete halt, and beautiful silence collaborated with 'constipated.' The next few moments were somewhat of a blur. John flopped his arms like a duck in winter, and his one eyebrow was practically up to his hairline, yet somehow and quickly the door opened, and I was ushered in and seated at a table, the first one on the right of the door. By now, John was mumbling, and he pushed my chair up to the table neatly and with the most utmost politeness (he could be so polite when he wanted to be) and placed the briefcase at my feet. All the uniforms were to my back, but I could tell instantly that the men were finishing their meal. Finally, I understood what John was saying to me. 'I'm going to get off here, honey, and get some cigarettes.'

'If we're not going to get into Brownsville until nine, and considering the way we both feel now, I think you'd better double our quota,' I said.

'Right!' John answered, and began to mumble again. By then it was obvious that we were both tired out and dirty, and one of us was very hungover. Furthermore, for some reason I was embarrassed by the whole thing – why, I shall never know – but I was, and filled with a bleak feeling. I just wanted to get back to my berth. John kept mumbling and said, 'Do you have any money, honey? I've only got twenties.'

'I think you'd better hurry, darling; remember the man said we'd only be here a few minutes.' With that, I received a very snappish retort. 'Well, if it's anything like the rest of this trip we'll still be here and won't get to Brownsville until tomorrow!' John was angry with everyone, including me. I had the good instinct not to reply, but placed my napkin on my lap and stared straight ahead. 'Himself' opened the diner door and his feet clomped down the metal steps as I sat waiting patiently for my army fare: my first thrilling experience and, I hoped at that moment, my last. I sat for some time, staring toward the diner door when suddenly I was aware that there was daylight between the diner vestibule and the forward car. My first thought, naturally, was that I was moving, too. Somehow through my tiredness (my overtired body seemed to be moving) I realized that the car and I were standing stock still! I jerked my head around to find I was all alone. Behind me, at the end of the car, there was daylight. I jumped from the table, opened the door and glanced down into the familiar face of our conductor. The same instant, he saw me. 'Lady, what the hell are you doing here? We're taking off after the army diner.'

'But my husband,' I cried out.

'Can't wait,' he said, and leaped up the steps, grabbed me around the waist, I grabbed my full- length Beaver coat and the briefcase, and we both jumped. We landed surefooted on the moving vestibule of the car. I screamed again, 'BUT MY HUSBAND, HE'S GETTING CIGARETTES!'

'Can't stop now, lady.'

I interjected, 'But we're supposed to have lunch.'

'Can't help it, we take this car off here and pick up another one at six o'clock.'

For some stupid reason, I looked at him and said, 'But we were supposed to have dinner at four.'

Somehow I managed to get back to our carriage, and there was no John. My husband had disappeared. I first thought that he had forgotten about me and was up in the bar car again. Yes, I said to myself, that's what he did, he saw the train moving and went to the bar. I pulled myself together, straightened my hair and began the six-car trek forward. I staggered into the 'Elite' – no husband. 'Have you seen my husband?' I asked the bartender. 'No, ma'am.'

We were not traveling very fast, and suddenly we came to a quick halt. There was the sudden noise of joining couplings and, again, we were moving. I sat in a swivel chair waiting for John, aware that we were gaining speed. I was, I admit, frantic. I got up, staggered all over the bar and asked the steward, 'If my husband missed this train, where can I catch up with him? Is there another train going through?' 'Don't know, ma'am, but I know one thing: he ain't been in here.'

I sat down again, and then I recognized the first signs of maternity. I became quite ill, yet I held it inside. It was not the usual morning sickness, it was a rage that kept growing. I had already lost a child, and somehow this rage and fear kept building.

I was beside myself with anger and tiredness. By now, we were moving at a good twenty miles an hour. A kind of bitterness grew, yet I tried to control it. I got up again and went to the bar. 'What did we hitch onto?' I asked the bartender.

'Well, I guess they hitched up to the troop train again, ma'am.'

By then, my anger was complete. I thought John must have known about the diner. He must have tried to make the train. I know where he is, the 'sonofagun,' I said to myself, he's bought a case of beer and is whooping it up with the troops. I had reached such a point of anger where the thought of desertion entered my mind – cruelty and the nobody-loves-me feeling. Then it happened. Heavy panting. I looked up to see six feet of very disheveled man, covered with road soot, knees out of both trouser legs, shoulder pads awry, one slipped halfway off, and one cheek embedded with cinders. I hung onto the side of the chair, looked up and said, 'Did you get the cigarettes?'

11 – A MEXICAN ADVENTURE

We finally made it to Brownsville from Corpus Christi and arrived two very, very exhausted travelers. John had managed to stay on the train because of his determination to catch it after it had pulled away from Corpus Christi. He said he had been waiting for a little Mexican boy to return with beer, then saw the train start to pull away, so he dropped everything and ran. The troops urged him on, and, after a great effort, they hauled him aboard. He did not get the cigarettes. Such is life.

Brownsville, Texas, is a small town and is like all Mexican border towns: dingy, atmospheric and full of little buildings and railroad shacks. We checked into a hotel that you could see for miles because it was five stories and everything was like an adobe jacal. All we had to do was get off the train, walk across six sets of railroad tracks and we were in the hotel lobby. We checked in and washed up. John was an absolute wreck, still covered with cinders and bruises. Through a contact of the Covarrubiases, Pedro Chapus, we were able to get a plane and fly into Mexico City. We made quite a couple, a wreck of a man and a very weary, slightly pregnant woman. We had had little food, and both of us were constipated! We were ending our first year of marriage on a somewhat unpleasant note – not with each other, no – but with our bodily functions.

We arrived in Mexico City without any problems. We took a taxi to the Hotel Nacionale, then the largest hotel in the city. We checked in, and there was almost a fight over who got to use the bathtub first. After all, when you've traveled on a train for five days and nights and not had a bath or a shower, you do not feel very clean. I won the tub race, and John even took photographs of me in the tub. He was not much of a photographer, but he liked to take pictures.

That tub was sheer heaven, and while I was in it, John said a national food anyone can have in Mexico is the hot bread that arrived fresh every day. He told me he was quite proficient in Spanish, and, according to him, my Spanish was only 'kitchen Spanish.' Well, there we were in this hotel, I'm in the bath, about seven in the morning, and we were starving! I heard him call room service and – this I shall never forget – gave his order in Spanish. He wanted two pots of coffee (at least we could get real coffee) and then I quite distinctly heard him order, '*Café con leche, los quartos bosillos*,' instead of '*Los dos*, and *quartos muy caliente*' – he ordered pillows and a hot roll! I laughed like crazy.

'What are you laughing about?' he asked.

'You must still love me because you just ordered four hot pillows!'

That was one of the many times when I discovered that John, who had such a great sense of humor, could never take a joke on himself. He insisted that he had not ordered four hot pillows, but did add that the maître d' had laughed. Mexicans are very polite, not like the French. If you make a mistake in grammar, a Mexican will smile and say, 'Si, Si – let it go.' The French say, 'You did not pronounce that right monsieur, madame,' and tell you that you did so-and-so – but not the Mexicans. They try to help. The man who ran the hotel was called Bloomenthal, known to the world as 'Bloomy,' and was at one time married to Peggy Greer. In no time we had a basket of flowers and a basket of fruit in our room and were invited to dinner. It was a memorable dinner, especially after the ham on the train. We listened to the music of Everett Hoagland for a while, even danced, and then we went to bed – for thirteen hours. When we awoke, we made love. John loved the feel of my large breasts, and I made him feel like the man he was.

The next day, John telephoned his friends, and he also called the Covarrubiases. Then he began to show me Mexico City. We had guest cards to all the country clubs, but the first thing he wanted to get me was a dozen pairs of silk stockings. The Mexicans still had pure silk even though the war was on and it was 1944. We went sightseeing and shopping, just like two typical tourists. It was wonderful. We were happy. If anyone knows anything about Mexico and its high altitude, then they would understand that with my pregnancy I could not walk very far. The baby was due in August. I would huff and puff and have to sit on one of the benches on Cinco de Mayo. There are benches everyplace in Mexico City. We shopped, and John bought me more silk stockings. The Covarrubiases took us to dinner, to a Cantonese restaurant. Plenty of alcohol flowed: champagne, scotch, liquor hard to get in the United States because of the war. John kept saying he did not feel anything, but did pretty well. He took pride in showing his new bride to his friends. I met so many new people, including Ilya Ehrenburg (who had written the score to *The Forgotten Village*, made in Mexico and released in 1941), the artist Diego Rivera,

Orozco, Montoya (another Mexican muralist) – so many wonderfully talented and artistic people. John knew many of them, but even more, they knew John. It was a great and fun time for me, and John enjoyed it.

We stayed in Mexico a little over two months. John was feeling better and, while he was not looking toward work, he was, however, quite excited over my pregnancy. He was quite the expectant father, ever concerned, protective. While we were in Mexico City, we were invited to celebrate the anniversary of the Russian Revolution at the Russian Embassy. We went. It was one of those unforgettable afternoons. Madame Osmanski, wife of the Russian ambassador, met us in the door of the receiving line wearing an apron! She was physically a little along the same lines as Bess Truman.

Madame Osmanski supervised the whole celebration, despite the servants running around. She wiped her hands on her apron and said, 'You will have to excuse me, I am making pirozhki.' I had never met an ambassador's wife who came straight from the kitchen to stand in a receiving line as though she were a cook! But this little woman was making pirozhki, which is a little bread stuffed with meat and served with soup. It is delicious, and tastes like spiced meat. When you first see it, it looks like a fritter, but when you bite into it, it tastes like yeasty dough, and inside is very spicy meat.

That afternoon was colorful, and we enjoyed it. The Osmanski home was a little palace, and they had the finest in champagne, caviar, and naturally, Russian vodka. I danced with several Russian officers. The United States was well represented. John said, 'Madame Osmanski, it's been such a pleasant afternoon; the caviar, and everything is fine, but you don't seem to have many representatives here, while we have more than a hundred.'

She replied, wiping her hands on her apron, 'I know, isn't it unfortunate that all our men are out fighting...' She turned to me and said, 'You must excuse me, I must go and see how things are in the kitchen. Would you like to come?'

'Certainly, thank you,' I replied.

Madame Osmanski was making all the hors-d'oeuvres herself because she did not speak any Spanish. I had had two glasses of vintage champagne and suddenly began teetering back and forth. 'Forgive me, Madame Osmanski, I'm feeling very ill.'

'Ah, the altitude and the baby.' She dragged me upstairs and put me to bed, in her bed. I thought I was going to pass out. 'From now on, you drink nothing but the herbs, crème de menthe, or Campari,' she said. 'You must not drink the wine or the American liquors.'

'I won't,' I said. It was so sweet how Madame worried about me. She put cold towels on my head and let me rest awhile. I shall never forget that kind little Russian woman. She and her husband died in a plane crash, and John and I knew that they were murdered.

Not long after May Day, John had heard that the highway was open from Mexico City to Oaxaca, and he decided we should go there. As usual, John had picked up what I call a couple of 'bearers.' He always picked up some flunkies along the line, who waited on him or did his shopping. They would not be valets. In Mexico City, he came home with Bill and Hans. He had met them in a bar. It was in the middle of the night when he woke me up and introduced me to them.

'They're going to drive us to Oaxaca,' he said. 'I hear the road's open, and I want to take you there and go see the ruins.'

Within two weeks he had the whole thing arranged. We were to go in this Hans's broken-down old Buick that hailed from the year one. It still had a running board, which indicates its condition. When we started out, I did not feel very well. The way we took curves did not exactly help my body any. On the way, John, who considered himself an authority on the history of Mexico, decided that on the way we would stop and visit all the church fortresses, which the Spanish explorer Cortez had built during his conquest. We had traveled about two hundred and fifty miles south of Mexico City when we ran into no twentieth-century highway at all. The map was an illusion. There was nothing but deserted roads. We stopped at little towns and all the fortress monasteries. In those days we did not have air conditioning, and we also had one flat tire after another. Our trip was interspersed with interminable waits, standing by the side of the road while Bill and Hans took turns changing the tires.

'For God's sake, help them with the tire, John,' said a very irritable me.

'NO!' was his usual answer, followed by a grunt of sympathy. He wasn't about to do it; after all, he had paid them to drive us. Mentally, he was mechanically minded, and a good putterer, but at home when he tried to fix something and it did not work he would throw down his tools and say, 'To hell with it, call the plumber,' or whoever we needed to fix the job. After several flat tires, I began to become quite exhausted. We drove into some little town, and I said, 'John, I simply have to rest, that's all.'

When we began this trip, we were told that we could make the drive to Oaxaca in seventy-two hours. We arrived there after five days of far-from-comfortable travel. John and I rode in the back seat, and the two characters took turns at the wheel. Since there was no place to sleep you had to keep going, and, while Hans slept, Bill, who was like an exchange student – but today we would consider him a hippie-type – drove.

About halfway en route we came across a funny little hotel – filled with birds. 'I'm dying of thirst, John,' I said. Hans, the Russian, went into the hotel kitchen and came back with a can of stewed tomatoes and whisked them around in ice. In that part of the world, ice is practically unknown. Hans had to pay fifty cents for it. He whirled it like a bottle of wine to chill the tomatoes. That was lunch. As many travelers have found out, and I imagine always will find out, you cannot drink the water, and unless you arrived in a sizeable town, you were out of luck. In the small towns there were no restaurants, not even a cantina. It was possible to get tequila, or a tired, rolled-up taco, but that was about it. Even the gas stations had no restrooms. John took great pride in me in the manner in which I relieved myself, somewhere in Mexico, yet in a most ladylike fashion. I have always tried to be a lady, though on occasion have not quite entirely succeeded.

We finally reached Oaxaca, where there were two hotels, and we chose the best. By now, I felt quite ill because we had driven

day and night, and at night it was like the California desert –
between ninety and a hundred degrees during the day, but down
to forty-five at night. The car had no heater, but fortunately, I did
have that beaver coat.

We staggered into this hotel, and John, although quite tired,
insisted on showing me the ruins of Mitla. That was fine, but I
wasn't in any condition to go tramping around ruins. He also had
looked up a young newspaperman who was a descendant of
Cortez, according to Miguel Covarrubias.

The engineers who had built that hotel had made one little
mistake – the hot water did not come into the sink or the shower –
but into the toilet! We bathed as best we could, and I kept saying,
'John, I don't feel well,' and he would answer, 'Come on, you'll
come out of it.' John always would say there was nothing the
matter with me. I began to have terrible pains in my chest and
back, so I took a shower, a cold shower. John went back to look for
the descendant of Cortez because he wanted someone who could
speak perfect Spanish to take us to the ruins the next day. That
was alright with me. He departed, unbathed, and went down to the
bar and, still in a very rumpled suit, asked the man at the desk if he
could find his newspaperman. He said he would. In no time, John
returned to our room and found me lying down on the bed. I had
scrubbed myself off and taken a few aspirin. Aspirin always works
wonders.

'Can I stay in bed, please, John?' I asked.

'No. The newspaperman is coming, and we're going to have
dinner.'

We went downstairs and dined in the little dining room. We had *comida*, the big meal of the day that is followed later by *cena*, or supper. The opening chorus for *comida* was some tired-looking abalone, followed by garlic soup (John and I were both garlic lovers). The Mexicans take whatever leftovers there are to make a strong broth. Then they take five or six gallons of garlic juice, chop up the garlic, strain it and serve it. Well, after the abalone and then the garlic soup, I excused myself. I'm not a fragile woman by any manner of means, and will try anything once, but the abalone was warm, the soup cold, and I did not feel like chancing the beef. John had it all. I left the table while everyone else was downing tequila, and went upstairs. I began to feel absolutely horrible. I lay on the bed; time passed, and John did not appear. Anyone married to a newspaperman, a doctor, or any professional man knows you do not bother them when they're working. I understood this, and thought that John was making arrangements for our trip to the ruins. He finally arrived. 'How are you doing, dear?' I was lying in bed shaking with a malarial chill. It was well after midnight. John was feeling no pain, and I hated him for it because I would have loved a good drink myself.

'What's wrong, honey?'

'Don't know, but I feel awful.'

'Get up and have a good bath,' he said.

'How the hell can I, with the hot water running in the toilet?'

'I'll get in bed with you and keep you warm; you know I can do that.' He did. Then it turned icy cold. We got the beaver coat and cuddled – John was heated by tequila, but I was freezing to death. In between our body contact, John said, 'Gwyn, I met this American woman who's been living here, and you've got to meet her. She carries a big chain around her neck with a crystal ball. I looked at it and said, "What's that?" She said it's the clippings from her husband's beard! Believe me, darling, it looked like a wad of pubic hair.' We giggled, and then finally went to sleep in the twin bed in each other's arms. He kept me warm.

We awoke at eight the next morning and ordered coffee. Breakfast was delicious: fresh sweet orange juice, eggs from old-fashioned scratch hens, and home-cured bacon. John liked a hearty breakfast. When I had finished I was ready to take on anyone. In a suit and walking shoes, and my raincoat, I once more entered the clunk of a car. Its tires were now so covered with patches that they looked like a scotch-taped window. Then we were off to the ruins in the ruined car.

Halfway there it happened again. BANG! Another tire was gone. Fortunately, this time behind us was the young newspaperman, Senor Cortez.

'Get out, Don,' he said, 'we'll go the rest of the way in my car.' In Mexico, John is called 'Don.' We left Hans to sort out the damage and went on to Mitla, a beautiful and magnificent place. Everything John and I were doing we were doing together, for the first time, and everything but everything was in harmony. Such a beautiful word that. It was a happy time. We reached the ruins about nine that morning and stayed until sunset. We walked and walked; John wanted to see as much as he could. One thing about the man, he had this insatiable thirst for learning. The walking did not do me any harm, nor the baby. At one point I did ride a burro for a while. John rented it from a small boy. Yet, with all that walking, I finally became a little weary. We visited a museum and tourist shop next to it. They sold reproductions of the jewelry found in the tombs at the ruins.

'You've been a sweet, brave girl, honey,' John said, 'Just a minute.' He went into the shop and came out with a magnificent set of reproduction jewelry, all bells: toe bells, ankle bells. I was overjoyed, completely thrilled, in fact. It was a very jingly piece, and I like jingly things. Buying a present for me or any of his friends was one of John's better qualities.

It was a great day for both of us.

Back at the hotel, I said to John, 'I cannot go through that lukewarm abalone and garlic soup again, darling.' We both agreed, and also agreed that we needed a hot bath. We were feeling very uncomfortable and didn't feel like washing our hands, then going to dinner feeling sticky, grubby and with our clothes clinging to our dirty bodies.

'I want to go back to the ruins tomorrow,' John said.

'Well then, I must have a bath,' I declared.

John called downstairs and did get some hot water brought to the room, and I took a sponge bath. He had a cold shower. John liked cold showers. Afterwards, he said, 'I'm going to speak with the chef and order a good dinner tonight.' And he did.

That evening I met the lady who wore her husband's beard in a glass ball around her neck. She had come in to meet me and was reeling drunk. Hans, Bill, Senor Cortez, John and I had a few drinks, more than was good for us. I kept asking John to go to the drugstore and get me some Vicks as I still had the chest congestion. I finally left everyone drinking and went to our room. Again, I began to shiver. As I lay in bed, I could see the steam rising out of the toilet. I was freezing, so I got up, took a chair from the room, lifted up the toilet seat, sat on the chair and stuck both feet into the hot water. I was still there when John came in – at daylight.

'What are you doing?'

'Getting warm.' He was sweet and attentive, and he naturally laughed at seeing his wife sitting on a chair with her feet stuck in the toilet bowl!

That day we enjoyed the same breakfast and went to look at more ruins, about twenty-seven miles from Oaxaca. That evening a fiesta was going to be held, and I pulled myself together for it. After all, a fiesta is fun. The reason for the celebration was that the train from Mexico City was finally arriving. The reason local folks were going to celebrate so much was that they had heard a report, via the telephone, that the train, instead of eight days, was only going to be five days late! The local band was called in, and we all went down to meet the train, which also was carrying a lot of mail. It was a big party night; everyone was in high spirits. I became very ill and felt as if I were on a rollercoaster. 'John, I've got to get back to the hotel.'

'All right, I'll send one of the boys back with you.'

Hans took me back, and John stayed on. I climbed into bed and began coughing. John had said he would join me in a short while, but I did not see him for five hours. Some fiesta! At one in the morning I had no idea whatsoever where he was, and by then I had a temperature. I must say again that John could not tolerate sickness. He always wanted sympathy, but could not give it to others. He was very, very Spartan when it came to illness. By then I was ill. When he finally arrived back, I said; 'I think I have pneumonia.'

'Horseshit! You're always sick. So help me, Christ, you're always sick! Get up, and we'll put your feet in the toilet again,' he said, reeling in the doorway. I had just as much sympathy for him as I had for myself. There was I, ill and out, and there was he, feeling the effects of too much tequila and having trouble standing up.

'I don't know what I can do at this time of night; there's no doctor in this town,' he said.

'John, this baby is just tearing my insides out. It's just kicking like hell.'

'All right, I don't know what I can do, but I'll do something. Cortez must know someone, but even so, you wouldn't want a doctor from around here...' he said, then disappeared. When I think back on it I believe he was a little angry, but I did not quarrel with him. Two hours passed, and then he was back, loaded, and in his hands, he held a dirty old coke bottle, three quarters filled with paregoric. Then, reeling before me, he said, 'This is the best thing I could get. Here, drink some of it.'

'Guess how I got it? With my press card; we opened up the apothecary, and I got the newspaperman out of bed, so you better well goddamn drink it because I want to sleep!'

I drank half of it. It was like pouring half a pint of scotch, gin or vodka into an empty stomach. Naturally, I passed out. The next morning I could not breathe. All I did was chew on that dirty old coke bottle loaded with paregoric.

'John, I've got to get home; I don't want to lose this baby.' The baby was kicking beautifully.

'Do you want me to put you on a train?' Not 'us' but 'me.'

'Do that, and I'll be dead by the time I get to Mexico City if it takes nine days to five weeks to get down here.'

We went back to Mexico City the same way – riding in the back seat with John while the two boys were up front. The ride to Oaxaca seemed a pleasure boat trip compared to the ride back.

In Mexico City, we went straight to our hotel suite, and John called Dr. Ignacio Millán who, at that time, was holding the Chair of Cancer at the University of Mexico City. He came over and took my temperature, which was 106! How I ever kept that baby only God knows. I had pneumonia.

Natio turned to John. 'You stupid sonofabitch; how could you do this?'

'I'm tired, very tired of pregnancy,' John said. (*He* was tired!) 'Anything she can do, a police dog can do in ninety days and have nine more.' With that, he stomped out and went on a drunk, even with me in a semi-coma, and five months pregnant. I did not see him for two days. John was angry at the way Ignacio had criticized him. As I said, John hated criticism.

For a while, I was in a semi-coma state, and John came back. At night I would call him and reach out my hand, and he would help me.

But in the morning he would be gone.

The doctor wanted John to take me to the hospital, but in those days I was terrified of this idea. Today, I would not feel that way. I wanted the baby more than anything else in the world. I wanted John Steinbeck's baby.

After three days and nights in a semi-coma, I began to come

back to the real world. I had had sulfa and pills, and injections to make me sleep. I remember coming to, halfway through the night and calling downstairs for John. 'I feel much better,' I told him on the 'phone, 'will you come up?' I could tell he had had a few drinks. 'Yes, darling, I'll be right up,' he said.

'I'm hungry, and fancy some chicken broth.' I don't think there is anything better in this whole world than the way the Mexicans prepare chicken broth; not soup, but broth. The door to my room opened, and I started to focus my eyes on John. He had a cup in one hand, and behind him was a waiter with a soup tureen.

John said, 'There's somebody here, who wants to meet you.' I could hear a lot of giggling.

'Won't you stay with me, John? I'm so sorry I was ill, and we argued.'

'Jes a minute, babee,' he slurred. He stepped aside and then I saw two whores, women he had picked up in the bar and had known for years. I became mad. 'They're going to feed you soup, dear, and I'll sit on the edge of the bed...' I swore at him and threw the soup tureen at him. 'Fuck you, John,' I shouted. He left with his 'friends,' but came home later and behaved like a little-chastened boy.

I recovered my full strength, and all I wanted was Chinese fried rice! That was all I could think of, and the Hotel Nacionale had a Chinese chef. I had my Chinese rice and recovered from my pneumonia, thank God.

One night, after my rice hunger had been amply taken care of, John awoke, groaning. 'Oh no, oh no, don't bring her any more...' I woke him up and asked him what was wrong? 'I'm having a perfectly terrible nightmare, that you go into the Nacionale dining room and all they do is bring you bathtubs, yes, bathtubs full of fried rice, and that's all you eat!' he said. Dreams are such wonderfully strange things.

It was the fifth month of my pregnancy. I had some maternity clothes made for me in Mexico City, and John bought me a stunningly beautiful mantilla. I still had the clothes I wore when we were married. Why? Because, if you were married to John Steinbeck, you bought something that was serviceable and it lasted many years. He bought me more silk stockings, and had some lingerie made and some shoes. John loved my feet. He said I had beautiful legs and feet.

We spent the remainder of our time in Mexico City seeing friends, entertaining sometimes, but usually, I was in bed by nine or ten. Finally, I said to John, 'I'm in the fifth month, and it's about time I saw a doctor or an obstetrician.' I had not seen one before because John said Spartan women do not go to doctors. This time, however, he agreed. I was going to see a baby doctor.

12 – LASSIE SAVES THE DAY

En route to New York we stopped in Chicago, and I went to see Dr. Harry Ben Aaron. I was well into my fifth month. A fluoroscope was taken, and when developed I looked at the fetal picture of Thom, which included my spine and pelvis, and said to Dr. Harry: 'Isn't he cute?' The outer office heard that remark and asked me why I had made it. 'Because I just know it's going to be a boy.' Dr. Harry said to John, 'You know, if we study the bone structure in the picture, it's far too big to be a girl. Maybe Gwyn's right.' John said nothing but seemed to be pleased. I wanted Dr. Harry to come to New York and deliver the baby, but he did not because he had tuberculosis, and could not practice until he was well. The doctor had recently married a beautiful woman. That evening, we had dinner together and, thankfully, he told me everything was just fine and proceeding like any trouble-free pregnancy. He put me in touch with one of the New York obstetricians, a capable, qualified man. Anyone Dr. Harry recommended had to be the best.

We toddled back to New York, where Mother had held the fort with the two dogs, our Willie and her Lassie. Before we went 'traveling,' John had written several chapters of a new book, *Everyman*. Everyman was a young version of Ed Ricketts, who begins to travel on foot and arrives in a little Mexican town where he goes into a cantina. Tending bar is a cockroach. The young man begins to philosophize with the cockroach, and the insect introduces him to the remainder of his friends, all kinds of bugs. The young man tells that insects are going to take over the world. They start drinking, and the young man promises to help them.

John read what he had written to Pat Covici, his editor, who was a brilliant man. We had Pat over for dinner at our leased townhouse. During drinks, John revealed *Everyman* to him. We listened for two and a half hours, while he read five chapters and never said a word. Mother refilled our glasses several times, and, after John finished, there was what might be called a pregnant silence. John turned to Pat and said, 'Well, what do you think?'

Said Pat, 'That is a beautiful fire you have going there. Put the manuscript in it. Words were exchanged, and Pat told him, 'That's a piece of shit!' John did not destroy the manuscript, but he never continued with the story, and I never saw the script afterwar*d*. *Everyman* was never mentioned again.

Not long after that, John ordered a new set of Encyclopaedia Britannica. One day after they arrived, John, Mother and I decided to go out for dinner. It had been a cold New York day, and we had a fire going. Mother and I were dressed ready to leave when we saw John emptying out the fireplace and putting the ashes into the encyclopedia cartons. 'Good God, John, we've had a fire all day. I think you ought to put those ashes outside, not leave them here,' Mother said.

'I know what I'm doing, Bird Eyes, don't tell me,' he retorted.

'But John, perhaps there are still some hot coals left.'

'There are many ashes to smother them if there are,' he said. When John made a statement, that was final. He put the box of ashes beside the stairwell going up to our second floor, and then the three of us walked down to Manny Wolf's for dinner. As usual, the food was fine, but John's behavior made the dinner unpleasant. He was just plain nasty. If there was one thing he hated, it was a woman trying to tell him what to do. I had known that from the early days of our relationship, and never tried. By the time we finished eating it had started to snow, and when we left Manny's it was snowing hard. We walked home, and played a few records and had a drink before retiring.

Lassie refused to let Mother sleep. She was a watchdog, but John didn't like her because she 'barked too much.' She didn't bark, but kept scratching the side of Mother's bed. Mother finally left her bed and went to the door to let Lassie out. When she opened it she saw smoke billowing up the stairway. She rushed downstairs, turned on the lights, and found smoke pouring from the encyclopedia boxes.

'FIRE!' she yelled, and down came John in his pajama tops (that was all he ever slept in), and pulled a box aside only to discover the whole floor was burning!

We opened the front door and John dragged a box out, stomping in the snow in his bare feet. Mother and I grabbed anything we could find and poured water on the other carton until John took that one out. 'Don't call the fire department,' he said, 'they'll wreck the place!' Mother and I kept pouring water on the flames and managed to put them out. Minutes passed, and Mother and I completely forgot about John, we were so busy. Suddenly, there was an explosion outside. We looked out of the kitchen window to see flames shooting up from the boxes – and my husband with practically nothing on, fully illuminated on the streets of New

York, beating on the window and yelling, 'GODDAMN IT, LET ME IN! LET ME IN!'

At that, Mother and I broke into a laughing fit. People across the street were stopping and staring at this man in his pajama top pounding on the door as the snow fell in blizzard proportions. We let John in, looked at each other, and burst out laughing again. John did not share our sense of humor. He was furious. He stomped upstairs and spoke to no one for three days. On the fourth day, his first words to me were, 'When is your mother going home?'

Again, that was part of John's nature: he was right, and my mother had been wrong. Because he was proven wrong, he sulked, like a little boy. A great man indeed he was, but sometimes he acted like a little boy.

Mother left shortly after the fire incident. I still had the feeling that John was slightly upset with everyone, although of course, he would never show it, and I knew it would not be long before he would begin something else.

That something else was *Cannery Row*, a small, funny book that was to be another of his classics.

One day, after Mother had left, he suddenly said, 'I think I'll write about the Row. I want to tell the story of Ed.' Later he added, 'If we're going to produce – I think I will produce.' John wanted it to be a memory of things past, and he dedicated it his inspirational friend – *For Ed Ricketts who knows why or should.*

'Wonderful, darling,' I said, 'I think you should get back to work.' He had done the war journals, but nothing productive for eight months. Back in New York we had had a hundred and one conversations, and he told me such wonderful bedtime stories about Cannery Row; John's vignettes made me forget the unpleasantness.

It was late spring, but still very cold when he began to make notes for *Cannery Row*. Because of his relationship with Ed Ricketts, I think writing it gave him particular pleasure; in doing it, there were remembrances of his past and the association he had with Ed.

He began his same usual work schedule, the one he kept to whenever he wrote, no matter where we lived. He arose early and made his ranch coffee.

He wanted a good brand of coffee, and it was always ranch coffee. He began by measuring the grounds, enough for six to eight cups, and when the water came to a boil, he dropped an egg into it. Westerners make coffee that way; sometimes, if they have eggs for breakfast, they throw in the egg shells. The coffee pot was very messy to clean out. After the coffee, he poured in canned milk and quite a lot of sugar – brown, natural sugar. John was a heavy coffee drinker, and he drank innumerable cups of it.

After he made the coffee, he got me up, and we sat and talked, usually for an hour and a half, depending on the passage or an incident he was working on. A little past daylight he began his day, and after our coffee and talk sessions John, with his pajama tops and khakis, went into his nest, usually by seven or seven-thirty.

When he went to work, I sometimes went back to bed for another hour and then got up. By that time, he had finished his first pot of coffee and, with no other words or conversation, would yell, 'I need more coffee, honey!' On would go the coffeepot again, with the egg.

While John wrote, I cleaned the house, made the beds or took Willie for a walk. We did not have a maid. John did not like servants around because, he said, they made too much noise. He liked absolute quietness when he worked.

At lunchtime, he took a break, usually around noon. If going strong, he would only have more coffee.

He never talked, never said a word, and I would not speak to him. Usually, his average output in those days was anywhere from twenty-five hundred to five thousand words a day.

At the end of a working day, John was usually exhausted. He was like a long-distance runner who has used up all his energy. John burned up energy with frantic speed.

By three-thirty or four in the afternoon, he would leave his nest and, still with little or no conversation, go to the bathroom, strip off all his clothes, put the plug in the tub, get into it naked and turn on the hot water. He would step from the tub looking like a lobster, sweat pouring from him, and then he went and lay on the bed for a few minutes, or he might even sleep for half an hour.

In those New York days of 1944, we stayed home for dinner. Besides, John hated cooks. When he worked he never really knew what he wanted to eat. Sometimes, he might say, 'Honey, I've got something that's bothering me, I don't want to eat just yet.' Then he returned to his nest and worked for maybe another hour.

As each working day ended, he read to me what he had written. We would discuss the day's work, and he wanted my reaction more than my comments. I was always honest. If I told him that I did not feel something was right, he already knew it. 'Yes,' he said, 'that's the part that's bothering me. I must rewrite it.' My comments were purely a confirmation of what he already knew, yet sometimes he had to hear it from someone else. Never did I criticize him, I only commented.

Whenever he worked, John was not apt to be socially minded. Oh, people did drop by perhaps for dinner or drinks, but unless it was someone professional, maybe his editor and dear friend Pascal Covici, or his agents, he did not care to see anyone.

After dinner together, we usually listened to the radio, and John read every New York newspaper, and in those days there were quite a few: the *Tribune*, *Post*, *News*, and *Times*. His favorite was the *Tribune*.

John wrote Monday through Friday, and, come Friday afternoon, he stopped, took his usual end-of-the-day bath, and then we began to relax. He had his first drink of the week. I must say that John was a man who liked to drink, yet when working, he did not drink at all. John certainly made up for it on Friday nights.

His peculiarities did not affect our love relationship, yet there were times when I certainly had to work hard at the affectionate side of our marriage. Once, we were lying in bed on a Sunday morning watching the sunbeams through the window and listening to the birds singing. I reached over and touched him. 'You know, you haven't said "I love you" for about two and a half weeks.'

'Well, if I said it too often it would spoil you, and you would get used to it and want to hear it all the time,' he answered. Then he kissed my breasts. John could be very sentimental, even when he was creating. He would be generous and loved to surprise me with gifts, perhaps perfume or a fur coat, and he loved crazy presents, gag presents.

John worked in the front bedroom of our duplex on East 51st Street. I never left the house. John wanted me there to take care of everything. My pregnancy was proceeding well, and we were both very excited about our first child. John started to grow a beard that spring of 1944. I encouraged him. I even had a bet with him. I said with his beard, no one would notice I was pregnant. These were times when beards were not fashionable; men did not grow beards.

'If you win, and when the baby is born, boy or girl, I'll give you a thousand dollars cash and you can buy whatever you want.' I accepted the bet because I had a figure that made it hard to tell whether or not I was pregnant.

One of the many lovely incidents that happened during this time was with Burl Ives, the folk-singer-actor. When John was working on *Cannery Row* and making his first notes for *East of Eden*, John wanted Burl to 'meet his beautiful new bride.' So he invited him over for dinner.

'Mother Mouse, let's have some Mexican chili for him,' he said. Mother Mouse was one of his many pet names for me. Sometimes, he would call me Floppy, or Floppet, or Whoofenpoof, or Mrs. Whank, and he often referred to himself as Joseph Q. Whank, and he always signed his letters with a different name, because he thought it was humorous.

Now it takes an hour and a half to mince the onions for John's Mexican chili, and you either put it into Dos Equis beer or buttermilk with pepper. John loved chili, and he was famous for making it. He made his Mexican chili with 'diced' meat and Mexican pinto beans that are cooked a day before the actual chili making.

Burl came over for one of 'those evenings,' those great 'people' evenings, as I like to think of them, and we enjoyed Mexican chili. The next morning I came down to be greeted by a smell that was unbelievable. It was as if someone had tipped over a privy! And there, lying half-moaning in our circular couch was a large man named Burl Ives. He still had his shoes on, unlaced, his belt undone and his fly open. The rest of him was intact. 'You all right?' I asked. There was a low groan. 'Yes, I am, but I'd just like to know what the hell John put in that chili!'

It took a few hours, but we all rallied, and Burl finally left the house. I went back upstairs for a little rest with my beloved who was not smelling much better than dear Burl.

Cannery Row was taking shape, and I was getting larger. We still had no full-time help, but we did have a big, elderly colored woman, Emma – six feet, three inches tall, a half-Cherokee Indian and half-Negro who came in once a week to dust and sweep floors. In my seventh month I had to buy a maternity dress, and even with that, I kept myself chic. A woman should, whenever she can, and pregnant women, too, should try always to be well groomed and feminine. John liked me to be smart, which I was, and very proud of it. The doctor had told me to keep exercising, so I did the cleaning. However, I was cleaning the upstairs bathroom, which was uncarpeted, when I had an accident that almost made me lose Thom. I used to get on my hands and knees to scrub the floors, then wax them. I believed there's no better position for a woman four or five weeks away from having a baby than being on her hands and knees. This particular time I came downstairs with a pail of water, and slipped. John was away that day. I slid all the way down the flight of stairs, and when I landed at the bottom, I was scared. I began to have terrible pains in my legs. I called John at Viking Press, and he rushed home, called the obstetrician, who came and gave me a shot and ordered me to take a dose of castor oil! I did. Nothing happened. I was dying of the heat, in fact, I thought I was going to die. John called up an office agency, and two big office fans arrived at the house, one for the living room and one for our bedroom. Those fans almost blew us away – out of bed, out of the living room – they were so big – and so was I, but still no baby. From that time on, after that fall down the stairs, I was in a state of labor off and on.

That summer of 1944 in New York had been long and hot, the hottest since 1929. I suddenly found out that John could not take the heat, either. Remember, he was a Salinas boy, and Salinas has a temperate climate. If too hot back then, he could always escape to the seashore. In New York, we could not, and John became impatient, very impatient. A few days before I went to the hospital, Bob Capa called. 'John, I want you to meet Hemingway,' he said.

'I don't want to meet him as long as I live,' replied John. He automatically hated Ernest Hemingway, because Hemingway had won the Nobel Prize before he did. I must say that I think *The Grapes of Wrath* was a much better book than the one for which Hemingway won his prize.

'I want you to come to Tim Costello's,' Bob said.

John said he did not know if he would, but after putting the telephone receiver down said to me, 'Capa wants me to do it, so we'll do it.' Before the evening, we took a ride into the country to Burgess Meredith's home. We went in 'Baby,' the last Lincoln Continental that was made before the war.

'Let's stop in New Jersey and get some corn,' John said. He adored corn. Unfortunately, his teeth would not permit him to eat it all the time. We took that ride in the country, five days before our first son was born. It was another happy memory. In those days, it always seemed much cooler on the other side of the Hudson River. We stopped at a farmer's stand and bought two mesh baskets full of corn on the cob, and some fresh eggs. When one talks about 'the good old days,' I think they were. We bought two huge bags of corn, some four dozen ears – for fifty cents!

'Let's take it down to Tim's,' John said. He was in a good mood. Burgess wasn't at his ranch, so we started back, and, as we crossed the George Washington Bridge, it began to rain. We went home and changed clothes. I put on a new maternity dress and one of the last four pairs of silk stockings, plus lots of jewelry, and then we went to Tim's.

That evening at Tim Costello's is a famous part of Carlos Baker's book, where he described John Hersey, Bob Capa, John Steinbeck and Mrs. Steinbeck. But he does not say which Mrs. Steinbeck. That was the night, too, when Hemingway broke the blackthorn over his head and ordered John O'Hara out. The way Baker put it is not quite the real story. The blackthorn happened to have belonged to John's great-grandfather, and John had given it to Tim who was hanging it over the bar. Also contrary to what Baker said, O'Hara did not leave the place in a huff. He stood outside looking through the window, whimpering like a child. That is the truth, and when John and I left, there was O'Hara, weaving back and forth in the middle of Third Avenue.

'Let's do something,' I said to John.

'Oh, that poor sonofabitch, that poor sonofabitch,' he said, 'he'll get into a fight, don't let's get near him because he'll want to start a fight.'

We left another merry writer and tottered home. John had yanked me by the arm and said, 'Leave O'Hara alone,' and we moved off for home on 51st Street after what had been an eventful dinner at Costello's. John and Hemingway were quite cordial (the drinks helped). It had been a fun evening, enhanced not only by the company of great men of words but by our fresh corn on the cob.

Two days later, I began to start having pains. 'It's on the way,' the doctor told me in his office. I was more than happy at the news and went home. On the doctor's orders, I drank castor oil again. I went into labor, and John was like a boy. He was so excited.

After twenty-four hours the pains left, and still, there was no baby. I was told to drink another pint of castor oil. What with that and the New York heat, life was pretty unbearable. John was now upset, too, that the baby had not appeared. We went to a couple of dinner parties, and at each there was a pot of boiling water on, ready. I went to those moaning and groaning and praying for the birth. Nothing was happening. After one party, I saw the doctor again, and he said, 'You have got to go into hospital.' John sighed with relief. The waiting was coming to an end.

13 – INTRODUCING THOM STEINBECK

I was quite frightened about having a baby. I think any woman is, the first time; if not visibly, then deep down. I was ushered into the Harkness Pavilion on a Sunday night; no waiting in line as the wife of a famous man. Doctors looked at me, and nurses measured me and took my weight: 140 pounds. When I married John I was 143 pounds. The nurses did all the things they do to expectant mothers. Settling down to await the moment – every birth is a great moment – I continued to work on the needlepoint rug that I was making for John's dressing room. I was wheeled back and forth to the labor room, but each time it was a false alarm. The pains would come, then go, and I returned to my stitching. It began to become a comedy act, one that went on for three days. The whole time I was pumped full of drugs and more castor oil. After what seemed years, a doctor came in and said, 'It's your first, and you have a tough water sac. We'll have to break it.' I was terrified. When you have had a child you realize you are not much better than a cow: that is after the obstetrician gets through with you, poking around in your body and lower organs.

I was in an operating room, and the doctor took something that looked like an auger bit and stuck it into me. Never in my life had I felt such pain; I had no anesthetic, not even half a grain of phenobarbital. I screamed and cried, and then it was over, and I was back in my room.

John was there. 'I've brought you two of Macy's last bottles of pink champagne,' he said, proudly. 'Thanks very much,' I muttered back. I was feeling pale and stayed that way. It seemed like fourteen doctors came into the room and each one had his hand in me. Every time they pulled the baby down, the baby's heartbeat would stop. I thought I was going crazy. I was also frightened out of my mind. The doctors finished their plowing, and I was in agony. All I wanted was to have a baby!

John left and came back with a rhododendron plant. 'Our rhododendron has finally bloomed, darling,' he said, handing me a bloom. I sneezed. Everyone was happy. They thought that if I sneezed hard enough, I would have the baby. I did not. The doctor came back. 'Mrs. Steinbeck, I'm worried. We did everything we could this morning. I thought you had a tough membrane, but this is not your first child, and you've told me that you had abortions before. Every time I try to bring that baby down, the baby resists. It is transverse.' He turned to John. 'Mr. Steinbeck, your wife will have to have a Caesarean.'

Hearing those words, John went into a state of hysterics. He tore up and down corridors. 'DON'T TELL HER! DON'T TELL HER!' he yelled, adding, 'I CAN'T STAND IT!'

The head nurse came in and calmly remarked, 'My God, he's worse than Oscar Levant.' (Oscar was the great jazz and concert pianist.) She took John away and gave him some coffee. I lay in bed, still stitching.

John was finally allowed to return to the room where I was all covered and ready for surgery. 'I don't want you to worry,' he said.

'I'm terribly disappointed.'

'I'm disappointed in myself,' I said.

Then John said, 'I chose you as the woman to bear my children without problems, and here I am, working on a book, working with my editors, and you have complicated my life.' I fell apart. I felt crushed because I was so in love with him. Now I had complicated his life. I was sure he loved me, but I did not know what to think. I do not believe he even knew what he was saying. I was wheeled away to have our baby.

I came to in intensive care. I was in shock, and the first thing I saw was my husband's face with hospital cap and gown covering it.

'DAMN, I'm so proud of you! They've given you scopolamine. You didn't say one dirty word or talk about sex or anything like that,' he said, sitting beside me.

'My baby, is he dead or alive?' I said.

'That doesn't matter; you're uninhibited, you have a soul so great,' he said. Later, John was to say I had a soul too big for its britches. I kept asking about the baby. John kept talking. 'In just a few days we'll be back in bed together and it won't matter. There'll always be other babies...'

'My baby....my baby...'

'You're such a clean woman, Gwyn, you gave me a son.'

With that, he got up and walked out. I did not see him again for four days, and then he brought me two more bottles of pink champagne – and a praying mantis he had found on our other rhododendron!

I had given John Steinbeck the son he wanted to keep his name alive. And so Thom Steinbeck, weighing six pounds ten ounces, was born in New York City at seven-thirty in the evening of 2 August 1944.

I remained in the hospital for two weeks because I had suffered shock. One day, John came to visit, and he said he had been talking to 'the girls' at McIntosh & Otis, his agents (he always referred to them as 'the girls'), and said, 'You are going to have a nurse.' Not long after, a nurse arrived. Her name was Miss Diehl, a very, very large woman with dark curly hair, black eyes, and in her nursing cap and gown. She was a graduate in baby nursing from Albany State Hospital. She turned out to be quite a woman, and very efficient. Then Miss Diehl and I, and my new and beautiful son, went home.

14 – TWO MORE MOVES OR THREE?

John continued to work on *Cannery Row*, but I knew that he was becoming his old restless self once more. As for me, I had the post-natal blues and was still ill and very thin. Fortunately, we now had Miss Diehl, who took over in her most efficient German way. She was so organized that John began to hate her, and even wanted to get rid of her. I did not, and she stayed. John returned to his daily work on *Cannery Row*, to his routine with his ranch coffee breakfasts and hot baths at the end of the day. He was never much of a domestic man. 'I'll always take pride in the fact that I will never learn to pin a diaper,' he remarked. But John loved his new son very much and liked to play with him from eleven to noon in the morning. If company came (friends dropped in every day at first with presents) he took pride in showing him off, even if it meant breaking his work schedule. He was every bit the doting, loving father as I was the doting, loving mother.

Slowly, very slowly, I regained my strength, but John began to get annoyed with me. Once he said, 'Get up and get on your feet, Goddamn it! I want somebody to love. I want somebody to talk to! I cannot speak to this nurse!'

I did try hard to rally, but could not. I just did not have the strength. I began to hate Miss Diehl and John. Hate is a strong word, but I guess that's what it was. I was still in a depressed state, although happy and proud that I had given him a son.

One night, John said, 'Get your glad rags on, old dear, we're going to Café Society and watch Jimmy Savo. We're going with the Fraziers.' I did. That night I had four vodkas and felt terrible. It was the first time I had tasted vodka; I had been a gin martini fan, I admit. I arrived home in a semi-coma with what seemed like the aftertaste of ether in my mouth. Miss Diehl marched in as John helped me through the door.

'How dare you take this woman out. Don't you know she is very ill?' She threw a tirade of admonishing words at John, who said to me afterward, in almost a mumble, 'She has got to go tomorrow.' Miss Diehl stayed with us for a good many years before she went.

A few weeks following that incident, in September 1944, John said to me over a cup of late afternoon coffee, 'I can't stand New York, I must go back to Monterey. I must get back to my roots. I'll take Willie, and we'll drive to California and find a home.' After discussing it for several hours, he decided he would leave within two weeks while I stayed and took care of the packing. He left me and drove to California with Willie. I loved my home in New York and our friends, but John even more. Within two weeks he called me from the West Coast and said he had found a 'beautiful home' in Monterey, and to come. I called in the movers, sold some of our furniture, packed, said goodbye to our friends, and Thom, Miss Diehl and I headed West by plane. Between Miss Diehl and myself, I think we cleared everything up in New York within two weeks. I was becoming quite proficient at packing! Whenever John made a decision, that was final. No one could ever change his mind. He had that strength and sheer confidence. Of course, that shone through in his writings.

We would never have made it to California if it had not been for some old contacts of mine, the Neiman Marcus family. We flew out but were being dumped off plane after plane, and poor little Thom had broken out in a rash and began to vomit. When we reached Dallas, Texas, I called Henry Marcus.

'Henry, I can't get out of here. I've called Leonard Lyons in New York to see if he can help us, and I told him John's waiting for us in California. Thom's sick and vomiting, and he has prickly heat. His formula's gone sour. Could you possibly help?'

'Send your nurse over, we have a dietary kitchen in the restaurant,' he said.

Miss Diehl went and took over the restaurant kitchen in her native German way, and returned with food and a new formula for Thom. He recovered from his prickly heat, and was able to go to the bathroom again. Henry Marcus helped us get out of Dallas and on to California through his influence with the airline officials. 'Who you know' can help first.

I was happy to see John again, but somehow I had the feeling that he was not particularly glad to see me, nor his son. I know he did not care about Miss Diehl. His whole manner that autumn – it was October – was one of remoteness.

This time John had rented a terrible house. I called it the 'White Cliffs of Dover,' because it perched on a cliff, fourteen miles out of Monterey. John spent most of his time in Monterey. His old friends were there. I was at the house that faced the sea with Miss Diehl, our 'Virgin Queen,' my son and Willie. In those days the greatest enjoyment for me turned out to be climbing down steps to the beach with my baby and Willie. John bought me a Ford convertible, and I learned to drive, and later took trips to see my old friends from my singing days in San Francisco.

Every day John drove into Monterey with our allotment of two gallons of gasoline, all we could get then since the war was still on. He said he had to see Ed Ricketts, usually about *Cannery Row*. He saw Ed, and others, like the poet Robinson Jeffers, and Ritch and Tal Lovejoy. Ed and John took walks on the beach and, he told me, they talked about the Row, the sea, the war, and the meaning of life. I honestly feel that he was so bored with his domestic life at this point. To him, it was a kind of game. It was difficult for him to accept responsibility and fatherhood; he thought it trapped him, although we still enjoyed sex.

The house was practically all glass and looked out over the ocean. But when the wind blew, hell, it howled as on the moors of *Wuthering Heights*. When John came back at night, perhaps he would take Willie for a walk along the beach and watch him play with the seals. Willie even rubbed noses with them, and John liked that. Anything dear Willie the sheepdog did, John loved. John did not talk much to me about *Cannery Row*, but of all of his writing, this was his great fascination. He did not have to research – he had lived there for so long.

At the 'glass house,' one of my most prized possessions disappeared – the beautiful ring I had bought with the thousand dollars John had given me for having Thom. It was a rose-cut diamond ring, made like those rings you keep poison in, with an opening on the inside. When John gave me the thousand dollars after Thom was born, I went to the Hammer Galleries in New York and bought that ring. I adored it.

We had a big party at Ricketts's lab. Guests asked me where I had got the ring, and I told them, 'John gave it to me for having Thom.' Later, when I helped clean up the dishes, I took the ring off and put it on a shelf above the sink. I never saw that ring again. It had to have been stolen by one of John's friends. I think that what happened was that I made the mistake of saying that John had given it to me for having Thom – and that it had cost a thousand dollars.

However, on 25 October 1944, John came home with a tied, antique string of amber beads. It was a beautiful birthday gift, and he gave them to me because, he said, I was a woman who 'belonged to the sun and the earth.' Those were his exact words. How about that? He never gave me anything that was not blue, green or gold. That birthday, too, John brought home a fresh tuna, which I stuffed, and John, myself and Miss Diehl sat down to my birthday dinner of a beautifully baked tuna. John resented Miss Diehl dining with us, but she did. 'I hate sitting down with the servants,' he once told me. I could not understand his thinking then, as there were only three of us.

By the time Thanksgiving came around, I had begun to shriek a little, to complain about my life which, after all, was rather dull. It was a routine, day-to-day existence at this 'glass house' by the beautiful sea, and the only bright aspect was that it had a library. Yet John was gone practically all the time. I never knew where he went, although I believe, as I have said, he was escaping from his life of domesticity. After all, what man would leave a young wife all day long with a new baby, and a nurse who did practically nothing but knit? Then one day he came home and said to me, 'You hate it here, don't you?'

'Yes, yes I do. How long can a person talk to the seagulls, sea lions and Miss Diehl?'

'Well, I've bought us a house,' he said, smiling.

I was delighted, although by now nothing John did ever surprised me. I threw my arms around him and hugged him. It was a happy moment.

'Yup,' he said, smiling again like a little boy with a new toy, 'ever since I was young, I've always wanted to live in this house. I've bought it because I've just heard from the girls at McIntosh & Otis, that I've got a few dollars. I've bought an old adobe house in the heart of Monterey.'

That night was a warm one in his arms.

And so again we moved. Our new home was an old adobe and needed work. It was a landmark in Monterey, dating back to 1830. The plumbing did not work correctly, and the only heating was from a little ceramic stove that we had, a wedding present from Henry Varnum Poor. The kitchen was a lean-to, and John could not stand up in it. Now it was November, quite cold, but nothing compared to New York. We set to work on the house, whitewashed it inside and out, and John wired it. An old friend, Lloyd Shebley, whom he had known when he had lived in Lake Tahoe, helped; so did Ed Ricketts. Suddenly, I felt alive again. That little adobe with its walled-in garden, also only a few blocks from the sea, became a happy traditional home, while the world in Europe and the Far East continued to go mad.

Christmas came. We had so looked forward to it in our new home, but it turned out to be miserable. Thom had come down with pneumonia, and then Miss Diehl had it, and then, last but not least, I did. Christmas morning John came into our bedroom and said, 'I'll see you later, I'm going to spend Christmas Day with my sisters,' (he had three, Mary, Beth, and Esther) in Watsonville. Before I could say anything, he had left. I never even received a present from him that Christmas. I don't know why; I shall never know.

Old Dr. Hoyt, who had removed John's tonsils, made a house call. Each of us had a temperature of 104, and I ended up taking care of Miss Diehl. Doc Hoyt could not understand why John was not there, but he wasn't.

New Year's Day, 1945, was an entirely different story. It was like old times. We had lots of friends over. I cooked beef tongue in wine, and we all sang and danced. John invited old Lady Gregg and all of his friends to the house. Old Lady Gregg became slightly drunk, and she talked about the days when she first lived in Monterey and she used to watch the fishermen bring in the whales, and bull and bear fights were held for entertainment. John and I danced the varsovienne, a lovely dance at which John excelled. That was a Happy New Year, for all of us.

In Monterey I did find it difficult to get along with John's family. I liked them but met with little success in my efforts to establish a relationship. Except for his sister Mary, they were all much older than John, and they all adored their baby brother. To them, I was an outsider. Even when they came over to see the baby and I brought Thom out, they would make some excuse and leave. It was an uneasy situation. They plainly did not want me there.

It turned out that we were not in Monterey long, and in January of 1945 John said to me, 'I think I'm going back to Mexico. I'm going to write *The Pearl of La Paz*. I can't stand it here anymore.' John was his usual restless self again. To me, it seemed a great shame as we had cleaned up that little adobe and he had made the garden beautiful, too. He had repaired the fence with the help of nails and hammers he had 'borrowed' from the Holmans, our neighbors. John stole all the time from them. He never went out the back door without grabbing a handful of nails, a fistful of screws, and a few hammers. He had quite a habit of 'borrowing' things.

John packed and left for Mexico City with Willie, and Miss Diehl and I closed up the house, and then we went and stayed with my beloved sister-in-law, Beth Ainsworth. We stayed with her in Oakland for a few weeks until we boarded a plane for Mexico.

15 – NO MORE KIDS

Before we went to Mexico, John, Thom and I went to San Francisco to see Ernie Pyle, the beloved-by-the-troops war correspondent. We stayed at the Palace Hotel and were with Ernie the night before he took off to get killed. We went because Ernie wanted to see Thom before he left. Ernie was Thom's godfather by proxy. We checked in and went to Ernie's suite.

'Beloved mother, give me my godchild,' Ernie said. I gave him Thom, and he put the chubby baby into a playpen that had dozens of cellophane sheets in it. Thom had a ball. John got mad because he had not thought of that. We went downstairs for dinner and to listen to Eddie Oliver play his famous piano (Oliver later moved to Palm Springs, California, and played for many great parties). Eddie played *Warsaw Concerto* at Ernie's request. Back in Ernie's suite, we found Thom asleep amidst the sheets of cellophane. We had a long talk that night, a night I shall never forget. We talked about the war, good times, how we longed for peace, and about the foot soldiers, who Ernie cared for so much, and who cared for him. We talked into the daylight hours, and that was the night Ernie said, 'I won't ever come home again.' At that, John remarked, 'Horseshit.'

Somehow, Ernie knew. Before he left on an unscheduled briefing flight, he said, 'My number's up, I feel it.' He put his arms around me and said, 'I love you, little mother.' I replied 'I love you, too, Ernie.' That was the last time we saw him.

We received the news of his death while we were in Mexico that summer. John shrank into a shell, just as he did when President Franklin Roosevelt died. John went to bed for seventy-two hours straight. He had lost a great friend. John had ideals about his friends. I think that is why I loved him.

At the end of the seventy-two hours, he went back to his work on the script of *The Pearl,* but it took a long time for him to get over Ernie Pyle's death.

My Great-Aunt Lila and my Great-Uncle Frank lived in Cuernavaca, and it was through them that we found our next home. They lived in the Zapata house there, and John stayed with them while we looked for our new base. He had a hard time finding somewhere, because nobody wanted John Steinbeck. He was disliked there for some unknown reason. During his home-hunting time, he and my great-aunt and uncle also found time for recreation.

They all got drunk together.

My Great-Aunt Lila was quite a woman. She was a former professional swimmer, and every morning thought nothing of diving into her pool regardless of the temperature – and at forty-eight hundred feet above sea level, that can be pretty cold!

Thanks to Great-Aunt Lila and Great-Uncle Frank we did find an adobe, with a spacious living and dining room and three bedrooms, plus an enormous swimming pool – seventy feet long. The water went down a barranca, which looped off down into a refreshing pool.

John was glad to see me when we arrived that summer of 1945

in Cuernavaca, and I was overjoyed to be reunited with him. He began his usual work routine with the ranch coffee and eggs, and writing Monday through Friday. While *The Pearl* took shape, I endeavored to learn Spanish from a woman in the nearby village and helped John on research for a new work about Zapata, the great Mexican revolutionary. John had told me to learn Spanish. I think he resented me a little for my Spanish because, and I'm not boasting, I was told I had what is known as an accent *'perfecto.'*

In the mornings, while John worked, I usually read for an hour or more, and then Victor, our Mexican servant, and I went to the market. Cuernavaca is a small city, smaller than Palm Springs where I live now, and the people are friendly. Our evenings during the week were spent quietly together, drinking on the portal. We drank good aged tequila. John could drink tequila by the quart. Saturday nights, John and I would get ecstatic listening to the local town band *à la* John Philip Sousa, and watching the weekly parade. They were really happy times in my life with John. Those Saturday nights, Jack Wagner, Max's brother, would join us. John and Bolton Mallory had made him assistant director for *The Pearl*.

Despite the good times, life began to get boring for me; sharing the days with Miss Diehl was very tedious, yet I did have my dear son Thom, for which I was thankful. John was then working on *The Pearl* with Emilio Fernandez, Pedro Armendáriz, Jack Wagner and Óscar Dancigers, the producers. Jack, who lived in our guest house, complained that he was sick and tired of having the *Indios* (Indians) urinate against his wall every morning on their way to work. He told the story to Pedro Armendáriz, who encouraged him to do nothing about it. Pedro had had the same problem and had his hacienda illuminated, but the *Indios* came by in the morning, squatted down, went to the bathroom and read the paper!

I left John in Mexico at work on *The Pearl* and took my son to Florida, to see my father. While there, my birthday came, and John sent me some earrings and jewelry. One was a piece that Armello Fernandez had bought for Olivia de Havilland, because he was 'mad for' her, but which she would not accept.

During that Florida trip, I discovered I was pregnant again. When I returned to Mexico, I met John in Acapulco and told him I was going to have another baby. He said, 'I don't want it, I don't want any more kids.'

'You can't bring up one child alone; you're the one who wanted to have a big family,' was my answer.

'I'm too sick, I'm too sick,' he said. 'I don't want any more children. Go to the hospital in Mexico City and have an abortion.'

'I will not, I've had too many already,' I replied, firmly.

'I don't want any,' he repeated. He was content, he said, with the fact that he had already fathered a son. Then I told him that the doctor said I could not have sex after the third month, because of the effects of amoebic dysentery (we both suffered from dysentery that summer in Mexico), and I was going into my third month. With that, he snapped, 'If I can't have you to myself, then I'm sorry that we had children at all!' I was lost for words, but I was very determined to have the baby. I could not understand the thinking of a man whose letters had expressed love and desire to have children.

Along with my return to Mexico, I also had found a very sick husband. He was suffering from beriberi and scurvy. He bled, he had hemorrhoids, and he was covered with sores. He was in absolute agony, and I thought that his condition had made him say what he did about wanting no more children. Fortunately, I had left Thom with Miss Diehl, so I was able to devote my full time to helping John back to health. John told me that he had been faithful to me while I had been away; his illnesses told me quite plainly that he had not. Once, he had written to me from a cave in Salerno, Italy, during the war, and had told me: 'I was horny and slept with a woman, and I stole her perfume bottle, and I'm sending it to you.' He did. John was like that. He recovered and went back to work. I stayed on and helped with the rushes of the film, *The Pearl.* I stayed on for three months, and then, in my sixth month of pregnancy, decided to return to America. John stayed to complete *The Pearl.* He wrote me that he was returning by car, in 'Baby' with Willie and Victor, and he asked me to look for a furnished apartment.

16 – A LOVE DIES

We did not move into a new apartment, but into a new home, at 175 East 78th Street, a side street not far from Central Park and Manhattan. John bought two brownstone homes next to each other, so we could decide who would rent it and be our neighbors, and also because buying property then was a good investment. He was a shrewd investor. It was in our house that I almost lost John Junior before I had given birth to him. John had returned from Mexico, and I had been in the house all day with the architects. Both houses needed practically total repair and remodeling. Late that particular day John showed up with some of his agents. I showed them the living room, and then John said, 'Take them through the rest of the house.' It had been an exhausting day. It seemed as if I had climbed the five flights of stairs up and down a dozen times. I was completely tired out and just did not have any more energy left.

'I cannot climb another flight of stairs today,' I said, smiling. John looked at me as though he would kill me. We were standing on a landing. He swore at me and tried to kick me down the stairs. I fell about five steps. I grabbed the rail as the agents stood with their mouths open.

'Come on,' he said, 'I'll show you the place.' They followed him meekly, and I sat on the stairs until they came back down. I was so angry with him but knew that my refusal caused his anger.

After we moved in, John had to make a quick trip back to Mexico to continue *The Pearl*, and I stayed on in New York to finish the house. To stay active, I helped out at the Presbyterian hospital with the English war brides. When they arrived in the United States, these brides from 'over there' were kept aboard ships outside Hudson Bay and the Statue of Liberty. As a volunteer aide, I helped them establish themselves, and worked in the clinic.

During this, I caught their dysentery. My doctor ordered me to stop working, and then gave me the news: 'I have to take your baby sooner because you are getting too dehydrated.' Another Caesarean. The doctor promised me he would not tell John until the last minute.

John Steinbeck Junior was born 12 June 1946, under the sign of Gemini, and two weeks premature. John and Lynn Loesser took me to the hospital, where the nurses fed me intravenously, and then John and Lynn took off. John was born early in the morning, and when John Senior showed up late that afternoon, I introduced him to our funny-looking red-headed son.

'I would like to call him John,' I said.

'I won't have it,' he answered.

'Why not? I love you, and this is our son.'

'I don't want any son named after me,' he said. I insisted on the name, and he finally gave in, one of the rare times in our life together that he did.

We went home, and life began again on East 78th Street. Miss Diehl, in her efficient German manner, took care of John as she had taken care of Thom. When John was about six weeks old, he started to vomit after each feeding. John Senior and I both knew that Miss Diehl was a damn good nurse, and was doing everything she could, but one night she came to our room, knocked on the door, and said, 'Mrs. Steinbeck, I think John is dying. I can't get a pulse.' I jumped out of bed and went to him. John was a deep blue. We naturally called the doctor, who came and gave him an injection, which helped. The next morning we took him to the top pediatrician in New York. John and I were in his office watching. John wanted to be there. What he was doing was analyzing his sperm, not me. John looked at the doctor and said, 'Why don't you open *it* and do an exploratory?'

'You don't do an exploratory on a baby six weeks old! You want him to die?' the doctor snapped back. 'I can't guarantee anything, Mr. Steinbeck.'

With that, John said, 'Well then, I've just been wasting my fucking time!' And he stalked out. Miss Diehl and I just stood there, completely shocked, as was the doctor.

The doctor said he would try a formula change, which he felt might be the answer. Miss Diehl and I took the baby and left the office. John had already gone. We went home, and all young John would do was scream, scream all the time. I called the doctor back. 'Take him to the hospital, and we'll transfuse him to keep him alive,' he said.

For several days I went to the Presbyterian hospital and watched my son dying in front of my eyes, with blood pumped into him through his feet. Any mother knows there is such a sick, helpless feeling inside watching a sick child and being unable to do anything.

John continued working on *The Pearl*. Then came the moment I dreaded, but felt would happen. 'Mrs. Steinbeck,' the doctors informed me, 'there's nothing more we can do for your baby.'

'Is he going to die?'

'Yes, we're very sorry, but he is, unless we can find a formula that will agree with him.'

'Then I'll take him home,' I said.

The second night he was home, he screamed all night long. I was with him when John came down from our bedroom, burst through the door and said, 'I wish to Christ he'd die, he's taking up too much of your fucking time.'

That was the moment when love died.

John walked out, yelling, 'I can't work and listen to this goddamn brat of yours scream!' It was my brat, not his, not ours.

I am a believer in many things, and I prayed that my son would live. He did, thanks to a doctor named John Dorsey Craig. I remembered what an able man and doctor he was, so I called him and told him my son was dying. He came over immediately, put his finger into Johnny's stomach and said, 'My God, he's got pyloric stenosis, take him off milk and give him mashed potatoes and beans on the end of a butter knife, and lots of butter.'

I did. Today John is a healthy young man with a wife and daughter.

While our son recovered, John discovered from his agents that he had a lot of money from royalties in Europe. He also was scheduled to go to Norway to receive the Liberty Cross from King Haakon for *The Moon Is Down*. The award, usually given to World War II resistance fighters, John received for his inspirational book,

The Moon Is Down.

By now, Johnny Junior had fully recovered, so I went on that trip with John. We left the boys at home, and off we went, by ship. Like every trip I took with John it was an experience never to be forgotten. One never knew what was going to happen next.

We left for Europe in October 1946, and stayed for five weeks in the beautiful city of Copenhagen, Denmark, before going on to Stockholm in Sweden.

In Denmark, there were, naturally, parties, and the artist Bo Beskow painted us, and then painted John in Sweden. While we were in Sweden, I caught pneumonia! Sweden is such a beautiful country, but not when you have pneumonia (or, for that matter, any illness) and I was only able to see a little of it. The hotels had no heat then, and it was COLD! Being ill in a foreign country, where you don't know about doctors or hospitals, is not exactly the best thing for one's morale. Besides, I missed my sons, and by now it was nearing Christmas. I told John I wanted to go home and spend Christmas with our children. He did not want me to. Because he was *my* child, that is why.

While I recuperated, John went on to Norway to receive the award from King Haakon. I was disappointed that I could not be with him. John told me that the old king stabbed him as he pinned the medal. Apparently, the king's hand was shaking, and it went right through the skin. John winced a little, he said, and commented that it was the only wound for which he received a medal.

Most of the time we were in Sweden, John left me alone. We made a few shopping trips together to buy gifts for McIntosh &

Otis, and Pat Covici, and some of our other friends. But I wanted to go home. I was determined to, no matter what happened. In fact, we had a battle of words over returning home, and since John had had several drinks, I did not take his 'words' seriously.

'I don't want to go home. I want to buy a farm in Upsala. Send for the children, and we'll have them here in the spring,' he said.

'NO!' I insisted. 'I want to spend Christmas with my family in my own home.'

'Then you go home without me. I've got to go on writing.'

'Well then, I'm going alone.'

Twenty minutes after I arrived at the airport John showed up with two newspaper friends. We had several drinks, and by the time we boarded the plane all was peaceful. We were the best of friends, filled with the spirits of Christmas and we went home, back to a wintry and snowy New York. John and I had a wonderful Christmas that year, 1946.

17 – A LAST HAPPY CHRISTMAS

That Christmas, 1946, was one of the happiest times of my life with John. Of course, there were many other times when we had great fun, but 1946 was very special. John was not in any of his restless moods, and his attitude towards the children was one of devoted fatherhood – although he paid more attention to Thom, his firstborn.

He wasn't working on anything that Christmas, and he could fling himself into those family moments with the same energies he used when he worked. That year, I gave him a painting by Luigi Corbellini, of a little red-haired girl, and also lots of other gadgets, and shirts and bow ties. He loved bow ties. He looked very well in them. He gave me an antique diamond and ruby ring to replace the one I had bought for myself after Thom was born.

We threw a party. John invited a hundred and sixty people, but it seemed three hundred showed. That was typical in those days; anyone who gave a party knew they would expect many more than their guest list. The afternoon of our party, John and Nat Benchley had the time of their life getting very toodled making John's famous punch. That's where you begin with fresh peaches and brandy, and when the peaches are black, you add lemon peel and then begin with white wine and more brandy, then champagne and end up with a big ice float. John and Nat made sure we had enough punch. They made it in the bathtub in the cellar! By the time they had finished, about five o'clock, they were lovingly crocked. Somehow I managed to get John into his clothes for the evening, which, like every party we gave, was one great big happy blast.

We celebrated Christmas night at the 21 Club. We went with the Benchleys and, by the time we left, the snow was several feet deep. It was snowing so hard, and there we were, after a memorable evening, about to march home in the snow. John loved it. He loved to walk in the snow. I wore a beautiful black velvet evening dress which, after we had walked blocks from 52nd Street to our apartment on 78th, was in a sorry state. But we didn't care. John was so excited by the snow that when we reached home, every one of us was sopping wet.

'Isn't this wonderful and exhilarating?' he said. 'Let's change our clothes and shovel snow.' We did. All night long. The next morning, after Bloody Marys, John and Nat decided to buy some sleds. They did, and the snow kept falling. That was one of the few times I saw John in a boyish mood. He had a great time. We built a snow fort in the backyard and had snowball fights, the girls against the boys. By the second day of the snowfall, the city ran out of milk, and John thought that was wonderful, too. 'This is how you rough it in the frontiers,' he said, loving every minute of it. He was that kind of an outdoor man, had been all of his life. The world discovered more of Steinbeck, the outdoor man, in his *Travels with Charley*.

As usual, when New Year's Eve came it was time for another party. Doesn't everyone on New Year's Eve? John did not like to go out on New Year's Eve and fight crowds, but he enjoyed having people in and staying up, and drinking all night, which he did. John never made any resolutions. He thought that kind of thing was silly. But he made private resolves and always kept them to himself.

The winter of 1946 was a time when it was becoming increasingly evident to me that John was slightly jealous of his two sons, and of the time I would spend with them. He would do peculiar things. Sometimes, John would come into their room, where I would be sitting in an old-fashioned Boston rocker with the children, singing to them, and he would stand at the door like a little lonesome child standing in front of a candy store window. When I invited him in, he refused and said he was just watching. He usually stayed a few minutes; then perhaps he would play with Thom for a few minutes, then stand in the doorway for a while longer; then go back downstairs to the living room, always asking when I would be coming down. When I did join him, he started to read his newspapers. He never wanted to be disturbed while he read the news, and he did digest it thoroughly. It was just his idea that I should be in the room with him. I would just sit there with my drink. He might look up from his newspaper and say, 'Are we ready for another one?' 'Yes, I've finished mine,' I would answer, then add, 'What do you want for dinner, dear?' His answer usually was, 'I don't know yet.'

And so I sat and waited until he made up his mind and finished reading. Every New York newspaper was stacked by his green leather chair in the corner. In those days we did not have a cook. John did not like them, anyway. He hated to sit down for meals at certain times. His hours were always flexible. Besides, he claimed that he enjoyed my cooking. If he were in the mood, he would say to me, 'Call up the Benchleys and see if they'd like to come over for the evening.' Perhaps it would be the Benchleys, who lived next door and were great friends and neighbors, or some of his writer friends like Stuart Clooney, Ivan Anderson, or maybe Bob Capa. Sometimes, evenings with his friends might end early, or they might go on until three or four in the morning. It all depended on John's mood. I suppose I was what one might call a very patient wife, but you had to be if you lived with John.

We stayed home most of the time in those early months of 1947. We had company, if John was not working, playing records, singing or reading poetry or having literary discussions. We never entertained more than eight people at one time as John liked to hold court. John was a man, too, who always was interested in the favorite singer of the time. In one of his letters, when he was covering the war, he asked me to keep him informed of Frank Sinatra's progress. 'Every generation needs a Jesus Christ,' he once said, 'and, apparently Frank Sinatra is the new one.'

Occasionally, we might go to a nightclub, the Colony or 21, or perhaps go to the Café Society Uptown or Downtown for an evening of dining and dancing. John liked to dance, and he was a good dancer. But mostly we made our entertainment at home, and that can be the very best kind.

During that winter, John had written a play for Fred Allen, Johnny's godfather, but nothing could be done about it because Fred was very ill, so he had put it aside. As he later described in *A Russian Journal*, he was helping his blues in the bar of the Bedford

Hotel when Bob Capa came in. The two of them got to talking over drinks, and the idea of going to Russia was born. He came home that night and told me he and Capa were going to Russia to write a book on the Russian people, to find out how they were. He would write; Capa, the photographer, would capture life and people on camera. He asked me how I felt. I thought it was a great idea. Another phase of our life was about to begin.

18 – A RUSSIAN JOURNAL

We still 'loved' the Russians in 1947. Although many were not happy with Stalin, John's whole feeling about going to Russia, which is evident from *A Russian Journal*, was that he felt we should know something about the Russian people; we should know about *them*, not their leaders and their policies. Saying, as many people do, that all Russians are bad is like saying all Germans are, or all Irishmen are, and that, of course, is baloney. John felt he could bridge that gap that then existed, between two peoples.

Somehow, John and Capa wangled an invitation to a reception at the Russian Embassy on Park Avenue. We went, and it was a memorable occasion. Our Russian hosts were charming, but John and Bob were quiet and withdrawn. The outcome of that little affair was that the Russians had to 'think about it' before they decided whether or not to give John and Capa visas. That embassy reception also led to Steinbeck and Capa throwing a little party for the high officials of the Russian Embassy. The idea was for John and Bob to talk about visas away from the embassy. Capa and John were like two war brides who had never given a party before. It was to be a very modest affair.

'There's no sense in having caviar as their caviar is far superior to ours,' John said. I suggested we have hors d'oeuvres catered, but this idea was shot down quickly. 'You don't put on a fancy affair for the Russians,' said John, 'you make the hors-d'oeuvres,' and I did.

The Russians were to arrive at five-thirty, and all day John and Capa fussed around, nervous and excited. I was, too, but I refused to let the Russians upset me. I was still feeling weak and had never really recovered my full strength after Johnny was born. I took my time and stayed calm, and decided for this special occasion, which meant so much to John, to wear one of my pretty chiffon afternoon dresses.

When John saw me, he almost fell over. 'MY GOD! You can't wear that!' he exclaimed. 'You're too dressed up. Go back upstairs and put on a cotton housedress, and take off all that jewelry'. I did as John asked, and when the black limousine arrived, the scene was something like a Whistler painting. There was I, in my simple housedress, my wedding ring my only jewelry, sitting in a chair doing embroidery with our two sons at my feet. I was, in every aspect, the good, simple 'American' housewife.

The limousines lining up, John and Capa began to sweat a little. They had had a few drinks, but as the Russians arrived, they became serious. Whether or not they would get their visas depended upon the gentlemen who were coming to our house. We exchanged polite greetings and shook hands. Then the Russians looked at Thom and John and chucked them under the chin. They made small talk about how sturdy the children were, how healthy looking. After a polite interval, I took the babies upstairs and returned and resumed my embroidery. I said little but smiled a lot. John had ordered that only he or I were to serve, not our butler. Everything was to be quite simple and homey.

John served first-class vodka (he served first-class drinks), and also some aquavit that we had brought back from Europe. He always kept that in the deep freeze in a block of ice. The Russians liked that. Then there were the hors-d'oeuvres I had whipped up, including some three dozen deviled eggs that I had made. John seemed as if he were eating them all by himself; he was so nervous. I must say that our Russian guests were absolute gentlemen; to me, they all seemed to look like Khrushchev. I passed hors-d'oeuvres and served more drinks. When everyone was on their second or third vodka, I discreetly left the room. By now, John and Bob had entered into a serious discussion, between mouthfuls of deviled eggs, aquavit, and the vodka. John explained, and repeated to me later, the reasons why he wanted to go to Russia, and our guests had listened. I believe they may have liked the idea, but they were still suspect at the end of two hours. Then John buzzed me on the intercom, and I went down to say goodbye. The Russians kissed my hand in the manner of the elegant European, and left. John and Bob collapsed in chairs. For them, it had been like an opening night, but they still had to wait for the reviews.

They had no idea what impression they had made, and they sat there, each with a bottle and a glass, and both emptied their bottle. It was not long before numbness prevailed.

As well as trying to get a visa for himself, John also was trying to get one for me. He had discussed it with Mrs. Ogden Reid of the *Tribune*, and she had devised the idea that possibly I could accompany John and Bob and write a cooking column of Russian recipes for the *Tribune*. This column, she said, would make me a member of the 'working class.' I loved the idea. But fate decided otherwise.

I knew how much the trip meant to John, and he had a 'good neighbor' policy within him. He wanted desperately to go to Russia. It was not all because of his desire to find out about the Russian people, but he was like any good reporter; he was a great reporter, somewhat of a snoop. During the war, he told me, he had met Russians and found them to be just like himself.

'We'll never get along with these people – or any people – unless we know something about them. I must go and see for myself. They just can't be all that bad as we hear they are; after all, they were our allies.'

It was spring in New York, 1947, and John was as nervous as an expectant father. He could not concentrate on his work; he was working on The *Wayward Bus* then, and we saw very little of him. The strain began to show in him, his attitudes, and his daily life. I could not do anything about it, but I worried about him. Then word came: John and Bob were to be granted visas. Mine had been refused. John was excited about his but disappointed for me. While I was disappointed, I was happy for John and Bob. I knew they would be gone several months and would be traveling all the time. Besides, I was not very strong and had been working on nervous endurance.

John was so excited about going to Russia. He decided that he and Bob would go to Europe ahead of me, and I would join them in Paris. John said he wanted to see what royalties in pounds he had in London, and how many francs in Paris. He also had more than three million rubles piled up in Russia and was full of plans. 'When I get to Russia I'm going to buy you a full-length sable coat.' He still had the idea that he could get me a visa. My attitude was that if I got one to do the stupid cookbook, then I got one. If I didn't, that was life.

John and Bob were to leave early in May, and I was to join them in Paris in June. John decided instead of bringing the money he had in Europe back to America, he was going to spend it all over there. 'There's no sense in bringing it back, let's spend it and enjoy it like king and queen.'

So that was what we did.

Before he left, he fell out of a window and hurt a leg, as he fell about twelve feet. I had to have a tooth extracted, and did, and John was in one of his 'moods.' He wanted to go out, and I did not. It was a wisdom tooth, and that can be painful, as anyone knows who's had one pulled. The dentist told me to go home and hold scotch on it. I was feeling a little pale, but John expected me to be a Spartan woman. He was too keyed up about Russia, but was sympathetic.

'Do you think you'll be well enough to go out to dinner?'

'Hell, no!' I answered.

'What did the dentist say to do?'

'Hold whiskey on it.'

He thought that was a great idea, and got a bottle of scotch and two glasses. He was a scotch drinker. We drank and discussed dentistry, but I knew he was restless with all of the things going on in his mind. I had three drinks in my jaw.

The Benchleys lived next door, and I heard a cab draw up. It was a fairly pleasant spring day, and the front windows were open. They were French windows, with iron railings across the lower part.

'Look,' I said, 'that's Bench coming home from work.' He was writing for *Newsweek*, and doing book reviews there. 'They may want us to go out to dinner.' I was lying stretched out on the couch, a fourteen-foot-long couch. On one side there were two chairs. John had been sitting in one. 'John, for God's sake, isn't that Bench?' I said, impatiently. No answer. The curtains fluttered in a light breeze. I called out to John again. Still, no answer.

He had leaned on the window railing and it had given way, dropping him down onto the entrance way. He just missed being impaled on the pointed railing. I screamed. All I could see was a pool of blood. John had on a pair of leather sandals, and his usual khaki, his writing clothes. He had cut a thin artery in the big toe of his right foot, and also damaged his kneecap.

Bench came in. We rushed down and brought John into the house, to the living room, and put him on the sofa. He was white with pain. He was too frightened to curse. The doctor arrived and patched him up. We wanted to put him in hospital, but John, stubborn as always, refused. John was terrified of hospitals.

'My wife will take care of me,' he said. 'Look what a great job she did on my toe!'

The doctor, Bench, and our butler took John upstairs and put him to bed. The doctor gave him something for the pain, but was worried about any possible internal injuries. The painkillers were strong; I gave John one pill every four hours.

'Can I have a drink, doc?' asked John.

'Yes, you can.'

John gulped down half a pint of scotch!

The doctor turned to me and said, 'I would like a urine

specimen.'

'Why?' John asked.

'To see if there's any blood in your urine.' There was. John still refused to go to the hospital, and for three days he suffered. Then he went to the hospital.

John was six feet tall and weighed two hundred pounds; he tipped the scale usually at two hundred and eighteen pounds. But his bowels had not moved. They did in the hospital.

John recovered and, patched up, he and Capa went off to London and Paris as scheduled. John was angry at his misfortune, but he limped and bore it. He was not going to miss his latest adventure.

Life would not be life without its twists and turns, and while I was taking care of a few last-minute details relating to the running of our house – I injured my foot! Willie, our beloved dog, who had not been right since we had been in Mexico, had turned and growled at Johnny, and I lifted my foot to him. Willie ducked, and my left foot went smack into the wall.

When I arrived in Paris, I left the plane with a cane, limping as badly as John!

I arrived in Paris early morning. John met me, and Capa was waiting for us at our suite at the Hôtel Lancaster – with plenty of Bloody Marys, cold champagne, good French wine, and salads. It was a very, very happy reunion. Of course, I did not get any sleep, but I did manage to get a hot bath, unpacked, and from then on we never stopped. It was a great Steinbeck merry-go-round in Paris. We went to every show, the museums, which John enjoyed immensely, and we shared some lovely evenings and dinners with John's publisher, Harold Guinzburg and his wife, Alice. John liked the French country people, but not the city French. He once told me, 'I think the French hate us because they owe us so much. They don't like us, but they love our money.' I think John was right in his feelings about the French. He used to say, too, that the French will make fun of you, if you mispronounce a word, yet if you make the same mistake in Spanish, your host or hostess will lean over and politely tell you, not laugh at your mistake. Still, John did love the beautiful French countryside, French wines and, God knows, loved the food. He was, however, slightly unhappy that I had hurt my foot. Still, my foot kept swelling. Knowing John's mind, I did not say anything, but it pained all the time as if someone were dropping a sack full of bricks on it every minute.

I had been in Paris a few days when John went for an interview with *Le Figaro* daily newspaper. I stayed in our suite at the Lancaster. Capa came over for coffee and to take some pictures of me. When he walked into the room, he noticed that I was limping badly. 'I think John's a little put out with me for having this foot; you'd think I did it on purpose, Bob, but I can't even get a shoe on!'

'Hasn't he suggested you see a doctor?'

'No.'

'To hell with this, what's with him? Even if you've got a damn headache, he gets mad at you.'

'I don't know,' I said, 'but I do know my foot hurts like hell, and I don't know what to do.'

Capa made up my mind for me. He took me to an American

hospital that afternoon. An X-ray showed I had broken every toe in my left foot. I went back to the Lancaster with a cast. John did not particularly think much of that, either. It's no fun to be in the wonderful City of Light with a leg in a cast!

That evening, John and I were to attend one of Elsa Maxwell's famous parties, a costume affair. John hated costume parties. He thought they were phony, but his curiosity demanded that he went.

'I'm a sonofabitch. I'm not going to get a goddam costume!'

He didn't get one, and because of my respect for him, I didn't, either. We went as ourselves. John wore a suit, and I wore a chic black dress with a delicate slipper on one foot, and a shiny white cast on the other.

Burgess Meredith and his wife, Paulette Goddard, were living at the Lancaster, and they were going to the party, too. John and I were in the lobby when down came the elevator and out stepped Burgess and Paulette. Burgess wasn't in costume, but Paulette, a beautiful woman, was dressed like a French shepherdess of the Marie Antoinette period, complete with a large hooped skirt and shepherd's crook. I thought John was going to explode, but he didn't, not outwardly anyway.

The four of us were quite a sight, one limping couple, one French shepherdess and her summer-coated escort getting into a taxi for the trip to Elsa's party. Our entrance quickly became a conversation piece. Everyone wanted to know what had happened to the limpers.

'It just so happened that we fell out of the same bed,' I told them. Everyone laughed. Apart from our entrance, it was somewhat a dull evening, and that was most unusual for the great, legendary party-giver. Her parties usually were all glitz and glitter showpieces with a blast.

People like Elsa Maxwell fascinated John. Whenever he met people like her or people he was especially interested in, then his cold blue eyes explored them on the spot, and mentally he made notes. They were undressed. Elsa had the treatment. Before we managed to tear ourselves away, Elsa tapped John with what he said was the 'Louella Parson's hook,' the kind of hold it is so hard to escape. John was polite; we had a few drinks and then left for the Lancaster, where we met some friends. John had us all laughing over dinner with a rather lengthy description of his impression of dear Elsa.

The four days that followed, John and Capa were kept busy setting up for their trip. There were more visits to the museums, and John spent his royalty francs the way he wanted to (the way he always spent them), and I bought some beautiful clothes at Jacques Fath.

John enjoyed those days and nights in Paris in 1947, again, like a little boy, just having a wonderful time. He had me all to himself; no children, no housework, no paying bills, just one continuous time for playing – eating, drinking, making love, spending money.

During one of our 'playing' times, on Bastille Day, July 14, John almost got himself killed. He tried to steal a sailor's cap for me. Everybody loves everyone else on Bastille Day, but that sailor did not love John. We were in the streets sharing in the general celebration and the dancing and the drinking. John did his share of drinking, as he always did, and I did mine. We found ourselves at a table with some French sailors, and one of them asked me to dance. He apologized when he saw my cast. Then he asked another lady, and left his pom-pom hat on the seat, at the back of his chair. Now John Steinbeck could be quite light-fingered if he wanted to be, and he wanted to be at that moment. He tried to put the pom-pom under his jacket. Capa told him to put it back, but he persisted in keeping it. By then, he was feeling no pain. The sailor, a rather burly specimen, returned and found no pom-pom. He looked around and saw the bulge under John's jacket. He came over and began to berate him. John could read French, but could not speak it fluently. However, he did manage to tell the sailor it had all been a joke and the incident blew over – but not before the sailor had politely but firmly given John a 'Go to hell' message.

Not long after that, John and Capa began their journey to Russia. My clearance had not arrived, and I was going home. I wasn't particularly happy to go back alone, but I would be glad to see my boys again. Capa took me to the airport. John said goodbye in the hotel. As I have said, he hated goodbyes. I flew back to New York, and John and Capa left Paris for Stockholm, and then they went on to Helsinki, where they began the travels in *A Russian Journal*.

19 – A VERY JEALOUS MAN

While John and Bob were roaming around Russia, I tried to keep myself busy in New York. Of course, everyone leaves the city in the summertime, but I stayed with Miss Diehl and our excellent colored butler, Neal. Sometimes we made a picnic lunch, and the five of us would pile in the car and go up the Hudson River for a picnic, or maybe visit Burgess Meredith at his farm in Spring Valley. That summer, too, I saw an awful lot of theater, and I would entertain a few friends in the evening now and then. Everything I did was usually on the spur of the moment. 'Let's go to the country,' I would say to Miss Diehl, and off we went and bought fresh fruit and vegetables, sometimes barrels of apples. Then we would come home and make gallons of applesauce for the babies, and freeze the rest in the navy reject deep freeze that John had bought. It held something like seven hundred and fifty pounds.

There was little mail from Russia, and for the first time in any of our separations there were few letters from John, but many from Capa. I knew they were busy, of course, and traveling most of the time. Besides, they were subject to censorship so when I did receive a letter I was happy and contented, but I did not get upset if for days I received no mail. So when I wrote to John and Robert, I would begin a letter Monday and finish it Friday, filling it in with a journal of events and happenings of the week.

I would write of lunch with Elizabeth Otis, his agent, or about a visit to Rye Country Club with the Benchleys, where Thom and

Johnny would have fun playing in the sand on the beach, or about visiting Lynn and Frank Loesser. John and I and the Loessers were very close. I had known Lynn since I was a teenager, and knew of the times of struggle for Frank before his shows made him a success. Great men, and women, of achievement usually have their time in their life of striving and loneliness. Frank Loesser was a quiet man with a wild sense of humor. Without any hesitation, I say he was one of the most talented people who ever lived.

That long, hot summer of 1947 I kept myself busy, and I missed John very much, despite what some people might have thought. Why not? I was still very much in love with him, and when you're in love and apart from your love, you miss that love.

Time has a strange, awful habit of passing so quickly, too quickly, and before I knew it the summer was over, and I had received a wire – 'Be home tomorrow. John.'

John came back from Russia shattered. Once more he had put everything into his work and, as always, it had taken every ounce of his strength. Despite his exhaustion, he went straight to work on *A Russian Journal*. For John, that experience in Russia had been, as he told me, 'simply fantastic.' He admired the Russian people and their country, but then, John said he loved all peoples. Which in his way, he did.

He told me of the vast Russian landscapes, the Orthodox churches, the sad hotels, and the peasants, the farm people, all vividly described in *Journal*. One thing that especially impressed him was that there were mostly old men and old women or very young boys and very young girls. Russian manhood had been decimated by the war, and this upset him.

I remember him telling me, 'You know, I don't think I'll ever be able to bridge the gap and be an active Communist, because I believe in the individual creation. I don't think five men can write a book, or ten men can paint a painting, or twenty men can make one piece of sculpture.'

He did not bring me back the sable coat he had promised. He was able to collect his rubles, but he did bring me back an exquisite beryl from the Russian state of Georgia, and a hatful of antique garnets, a necklace, a huge cross, bracelets, earrings and all kinds of other things. Naturally, he also came home with some excellent Russian vodka.

He was glad to be home, and he was happy to be with me again, and with Thom, the son whom he adored, and yet by then Johnny was such a handsome and cute child. Within me, I held a deep hurt that John showed so little affection for his second son. I always asked myself why, but there was never an answer.

The first few weeks he was home he spent days with his publishers and agents. We usually spent the evenings together, relaxing at home, talking about his trip, or sometimes having the Benchleys or other friends over for dinner and drinks. John was even beginning to enjoy our sons, and life for me began to be full again. We were a complete family. Summer had gone; it was autumn, and it was my birthday.

As in each of our lives, there are good birthdays and bad ones. That year, 1947, was one the best. Friends took me to lunch, which I thought was rather long, but when I returned home, I learned the reason. Surprise! John was a like a child when I arrived, and then took me into the living room and stood, very proudly, before my birthday present – a full Hammond organ, the kind used in recording studios. I was ecstatic. John knew I liked to play, and I had already set some poems to music. From that day on I began to write more songs. I wrote twenty-four of them, and twelve were recorded. I received that Hammond organ and spent some delightful moments with Thom and John sitting on my lap as I played for them.

In our lives at that time was a man called Mark Hanna, a close friend of Alice and Harold Guinzburg. Mark was a theatrical agent, and the only one the beautiful and talented star actress Helen Hayes ever had in her later life. He also was Nat Benchley's agent. One night, John asked him to dinner and to hear some of my songs. He heard them and said they were – this is the exact word he used – 'magnificent.' Anyone who creates anything likes to hear praise like that. 'Something should be done with them,' Hanna said.

'What the hell for?' was John's response.

'There's so much love in these songs,' Hanna said. I've always been a loving kind of woman.

John became irritated. 'She doesn't need to make a living.' That seemed odd coming from a man who had encouraged Nat Benchley and me to adapt a book he had always adored called *The Circus of Dr. Lao*. (It later became a motion picture – *7 Faces of Dr. Lao* – starring Tony Randall).

Despite John's comments, Mark encouraged me to get an arranger. I found a talented man called Charles Hale, and together we made a demonstration record. I paid for it out of my own money. I took it home, and we had some friends in to celebrate the occasion. Everyone said it was a beautiful record, and that made me, naturally, proud.

As the evening progressed, John became very cranky. I began to suspect it was because somebody else was stealing the spotlight, which he adored. Yes, John Steinbeck loved the spotlight. He always had to be center stage. Of course, he earned it and deserved that bright light, that brilliant light that glowed.

Late that night, John leapt out of bed and went downstairs. Time passed, and he had not returned. He finally buzzed me on the intercom. 'Come down here, I want to talk to you,' came the command. I went down, and there he was, pacing the floor and in a terrible mood. He had been drinking scotch. Finally, he turned to me, pointed a finger like a lawyer in court, and said, 'I don't know why the fuck you feel you have got to get in competition with me!'

Naturally, I was shocked. 'What do you mean, competition?' I was managing to remain calm.

'Well, you are trying to publish that goddam music!'

'If you feel that way, then that is the best compliment you ever could have paid me.' I turned, and went back to bed, his yelling and screaming following me. To keep peace in our family, I reluctantly gave up my efforts as a songwriter. Sometimes now I wish I had continued writing songs, but then I just had to stop.

Peace did come, as did Christmas. That Christmas 1947 came and, like our other years, it was party after party. I was, I admit, a 'party girl,' but no more than John was a 'party man.' We had our usual tree-trimming party and open house. As usual, we followed the same partying pattern through to New Year's Eve; everyone around us seemed to be lovers with liquor and feeling no pain.

John began to become his old restless self. He became unsettled to the extent that suddenly he decided he did not want to live in New York any more. 'I think I want to farm in upstate New York,' he suddenly said one day. Here we go again. And the search was on for a farm.

We finally found one through a real estate friend of Burgess's, a dairy farm. When we went and looked at it I knew, for once in my life, I was going to say a firm 'NO!' to John. I could imagine myself stuck out there for the rest of my life if he bought it. John was always trying to push me away to some corner where there would not be another soul around. He never realized it, but he was a very jealous man.

I love the country (as John did), but then I was not prepared to be put away in it. When I climbed back into the real estate man's car, I tersely said to John, 'I will not live there,' and I did not speak to him again until we arrived home. It was one of the very few times I ever really went against John. It all boiled down to the simple fact that I had had it. I was tired of being torn up or dismantled, mentally or physically, and as we entered into 1948, I began to turn away from John.

It seemed as if a climax had been building up for years, and suddenly I had realized it. We had had our arguments, like other married couples, but that day on the farm trip, and as I sat and looked out of the car on the way home, I changed.

I discovered at that time that John was taking aphrodisiacs. He would get drunk and swallow those pills and then want to plunge into his conjugal rights and have heavy sex. It is common knowledge that a man who has had a little too much to drink will not be at his best when it comes to making love. John usually tried when he was in that condition, though there were times when he was half in that way, and even when he was just a little merry.

Our relationship as husband and wife continued, but I knew that unless there were some drastic changes in John's attitude toward me, our marriage could not last. He was now hardly ever home, and when he was, he worked long hours in his 'nest' or would say little to me. Always, always there was no reason for his behavior. Only John knew why. I never did.

But I still loved him. I always will.

I got up in the middle of the night at Easter and blew out several eggs, and painted them for the children – and for John. He was thrilled to death when I gave them to him the next morning.

But moments like that were now rare.

John's attitude, generally, towards me was cold. Like any good father, he spent moments playing with his children, but rarely Johnny. It was always with Thom, the firstborn.

That summer of 1948 his restlessness grew. He was now working on *Viva Zapata!* and had several things running through his mind. He hardly had time for his sons. He was always preoccupied with something, was going somewhere, and I never knew where. John was drinking more than was good for him. I became so miserable as a woman, as I lived what had become a daily routine with my children. But at least I had two sons whom I loved very much.

So many things happened that summer. Johnny had chicken pox, which John did not care about and, as usual, left it to me to take care of the matter. Then there was the day of the Shriners' parade in New York. John's father had been a Mason, and he hated Masons. When he found out about the parade, he took his shotguns and went up onto the roof. Strange, but it is true; he had decided that if the Masons hit our house, then he would react – with bullets.

Sometimes during that summer, too, we would be out socially, and he would erupt into screams and yells at me, and I would break down and cry, and go home alone. When he returned, he had a habit of saying, as if nothing had happened, 'Why did you leave the party?'

When he decided he could not stand Miss Diehl, or 'Platterfoot' as he called her, nor stand the children, nor stand anyone else, he left our house at 175 East 78th Street and took a suite at the old Hotel Bedford. He had found another 'nest.' He took all his notes on *Viva Zapata!* with him, and said to me, 'I think I'm going to write a history of my family.' That, of course, eventually became his classic novel, *East of Eden*.

John's hatred for Miss Diehl could only have one ending. Miss Diehl went. In fact, it was a mutual parting, and when she left, she came to me and laid the key to the house across my hand and said, in soft tones, 'I hope no one ever treats me again in my life as John has.' He refused to write her letters of recommendation, but I did.

Through the Benchleys, we acquired a new nurse, Kathy Gunther. She was a sweet, efficient girl and came at a time when life for me had become unbearable.

As much as I loved John – and I did very much – I knew I could not live with him anymore. It was just impossible. And then one night in 1948, as we danced together, I quietly told him, 'I want a divorce.'

He thought I was joking, but found that I was not. He did try hard to stop me, but it was no use. With Kathy Gunther and my two sons, I went to Reno, Nevada, in September 1948, and divorced John on the grounds of incompatibility.

John went off to Mexico. A world for me had ended, and an unknown one had begun.

20 – BAD DAY IN COURT

It seemed a violent storm had passed on, and now my land was a gentle, refreshing wind. Of course, in any divorce – and ours was quite nasty – adjusting to a new life is not easy. God knows there are many sleepless nights. Thom and Johnny couldn't understand what had happened to their mother and father. I felt for them. No way could they understand. It's always the children who get hurt the most.

John often visited us at our house on East 78th Street. He would come and say, almost demand in fact, 'I want the children for the weekend.' But he would add that he could not take them because he was so poor. Poor! John Steinbeck, poor! That was hard to believe, but that was what he told me.

He was not poor. I believe he was either trying to get back at me for divorcing him or he simply just did not want to be bothered by his sons. But what kind of father would be like this?

Then there were times when he would call me in the middle of the night, even come to the house and throw stones at the window! He did not want to talk to me; he just wanted to find out if I was with a man.

There were times when he would visit, and we sat and talked about the past; trace our life, from when we met in that hole of a hotel room.

In the years between 1948 and 1954 John often told me he was not working very well, but then he turned around and said he was doing 'good things now.' He did write another beautiful story, another classic, *The Red Pony,* in 1949, which became a memorable family movie, and he did the script for the film, *Viva Zapata!*, which starred Marlon Brando. And, there was *East of Eden*.

He married Elaine Scott in 1950, but before, when he lived with her, he still used to come to the house. He wanted to see me and to talk, and even after they were married, his visits continued. Perhaps she knew about it, maybe not. I don't know. I believed he still loved me as I had loved him.

Any woman who has experienced a divorce knows the pain and anguish involved. It is there, no matter how coldly one looks at it.

I was the one who made the break, make no mistake about that. I was the one who said, 'It's over.' There was still the hurt of knowing how much I loved him, but knowing the end was inevitable. You could not change John, and I never tried. He was such a giant of a man.

There were moments I experienced before and after the divorce when I burst with anguish inside, watching him pour his affections onto Thom, and leave nothing for Johnny. Finally, he did recognize his second son, but it took a long, long time. There was a story repeated to me, and I had no way of checking it, that it was Elaine who said to John that if he did not recognize Johnny, she would not marry him.

Trying to analyze anything is not easy, even though so often we try. I feel now that John could not stand my rejection of him, and thus decided to show it to me by rejecting his youngest son.

One night, after the divorce, he yelled at me, 'It's all your fault!' John stood outside the house and had awoken me by throwing stones up at the window. It was about the time he wrote *East of Eden*. I shall never forget seeing John standing there, saying, 'My editors say that I have to rework this whole book, and I have never rewritten anything in my life.'

He calmed down, and I invited him in. I told him, 'John, dear, you are one of the greatest writers in the world, and maybe you have two books in one?'

'Harold Guinzburg has never turned me down before, and they'll never buy this book as it is.'

'What did you come to me for then?' I was irritated.

'It's your fault!' he snapped back.

It was as if I was taking all his money away from him. God, he had such a phobia about his money. He always thought everybody was after his money.

Our relationship continued on a talking basis until 1960, when Johnny and Thom came to me and said they wanted to be with me. They even wanted to sue John. In the meantime, they had lived overseas with him, and I am sure it had not been a happy time. They had everything in the world going for them. They were now grown-up boys when they came to me, and while we did not have John's money, we shared a one-bedroom apartment. John had cut off my support money for them during their stay in Europe. I guess I was wrong for not doing anything about that, but I didn't. I was so upset I could no longer control my sons at that point. They were adolescents, and reaching out and doing all kinds of things, behaving as young, growing people often do, and their behavior got them into trouble.

They defied me continuously, and I was tired of it. The respect I wanted and deserved (like any mother), was gone. I just could not play the dual role of mother and father.

I must say that unbeknown to me, in 1958 and 1959, they were being brainwashed by their father. He kept telling them how awful I was, how I wasted money that I did not have. I know this for a fact.

It was John's jealousy again. What was wrong with having a beau or two? After all, I was divorced from him, and by now he was happily married to Elaine. Was I supposed to become a nun?

John thought so. He did not feel I should have any friends. He wanted me to be the maid and wet nurse to his sons, and his sons in those years were being pulled apart by their parents. They finally reached the point where they did not know what to do or who to believe. They were flunking in prep school, so John pulled them out and sent them overseas to a private tutor. I am sure they learned much from that experience. They were growing up, and their intelligence and awareness were, naturally, increasing too.

Thom and Johnny loved their father, very much, but they were never close to him as sons should be. They were never allowed to become close, to share the father-son relationship that can be so precious. Their association with him did increase in the last years of his life, but until then he had always been 'too busy' to be bothered by them; he was constantly moving around, traveling, doing something that kept them apart.

Finally, my sons said that if they could not get any money from their father other than my alimony – which, incidentally, was all spent, all of it, on them – then they would sue him. And they did.

I called my attorney and said I did not want any part of the court action since it would look as if I had urged them to file it, had collaborated with them. 'If the boys want something like this, then it's going to be horrendous, and they should appoint their separate lawyer,' I told mine.

At this point in their life, my sons were floundering. They found an attorney and told him what they wanted to do, but they did not really know what they wanted.

The boys' attorney felt they had a case against their father, and one day I was notified to appear in family court. I went, and I did ask for support money, as by then Thom and Johnny were back living with me.

Unfortunately, at that time Thom had a girlfriend, and he spent a great deal of time with her. Sometimes he never came home at night. Being a mother, that naturally upset me, but there was nothing I could do about it. Growing teenage boys have a determined mind, often the mind of a man.

The three of us shared a little apartment in Sutton Place, a cooperative I had bought from a friend. I was proud of it and had created an attractive home, although it was still far too small for three people.

Before we reached family court, there were several interviews with psychiatrists who, naturally, asked me all kinds of questions. On the day of the hearing came a blow. I marched proudly into court to be told that my sons could not be there, although they had brought the action.

Elaine was sitting with John that day, a day I shall never forget.

I turned to my attorney and said, 'If my sons cannot be here, I don't know why she should be here. It's none of her damned business.'

The excuse made for Elaine was that John was not at all well, and she had to be present in case anything happened to him. It was a feeble excuse.

That experience in court was one I wish to forget, but never can. It was a traumatic day for me as I was pummeled with questions. John's attorney had gone to the trouble of finding Christmas bills from the liquor store, the implication being that I could drink a lot of scotch or gin, but not John. From the accounts that bore my signature, his lawyers claimed I was somewhat of a drunk. I admitted I signed for the liquor – but it had been consumed by me, John and our many friends.

Then came accusations that I was living with a man, which I was not. Besides, whatever I was doing with my private life, I felt was my own damned business, and I was at an age when I hardly thought I had to account for every moment of each day and night. No adult woman, or man, should have to; personal life is personal life, isn't it?

John's attorneys questioned me for four hours, and, at the end of it, I was completely physically and emotionally exhausted. At the end of it, my sons were allowed into court.

'Do you want to stay with your mother or go back with your father?' asked the judge.

They both said they wanted to stay with me. I was deeply moved, and there was a lump in my throat as the boys said that.

All they asked for was twenty-five dollars a week. The judge ruled that they were to receive twenty-two dollars and fifty cents a week. I would get three hundred and twenty dollars a month for both of them.

When I had divorced John, I received three hundred and forty dollars a month which, at the time, was perfectly adequate for two small boys, three and four years old. Later this was not enough for growing boys who needed new clothes every year and shoes every three or four months.

The judge ruled that John still had to pay for his sons' education until they were twenty-one, and he also was ordered to pay a clothing allowance twice a year, although this was not to exceed three hundred dollars.

That day in family court was a day of nitpicking by John's attorneys. I shall always maintain that it was wrong that my sons were not allowed to say anything, and that everything was directed to make me appear 'The Wicked Lady.'

In a way, it must have been most difficult for Thom and Johnny. Perhaps they wanted some recognition from their father, or were trying to force him into a corner to say, 'Sons, I love you.'

I believe the problem was that emotionally, John could not stand the fact that his sons loved him – and me at the same time. I just feel he did not know how to express his love for his sons, but that he had no difficulties expressing his hatred for me, a hatred that began to build and one I have never, ever been able to understand. Why?

So often in our life together, he had expressed so great a love for me.

The winter that followed our 'day in court' was an unpleasant one. I began to have terrible attacks of asthma, and my sons and I would argue over many things. Each time would be a greater torture for me because I loved them so much, and I went through torment in those moments of very ugly word exchanges.

Easter came, and Thom became restless, showing the same kind of restlessness that his father always had. He could draw well and began to show an interest in movie animation. In fact, Thom could do anything with his hands.

It so happened that a friend of mine saw a piece of his work and said Thom ought to be in the Chouinard Art Institute in California. I discussed the idea with Thom, and he liked it. I made arrangements with my old friends the Davises, and Thom was going to stay with them in California. They would get him into the art school and, out of my money, I paid my friends a hundred dollars a month for Thom's keep.

So young Thom Steinbeck went off to California, and Johnny stayed with me. Johnny was a boy who kept to himself; he was hard to control, stubborn as hell, just like John, but then, when boys begin to enter manhood they usually are that way. With Thom in California, life in New York went on somewhat routinely from day to day. Then a disastrous occurrence happened to Johnny that landed him in hospital.

He had been associating with a group of wildish young people, and I imagine he was smoking pot. One night, there was an escapade. In the building where we lived, there was a man who had a brand-new motor scooter, a Lambretta. Taking one of my hairpins, and his bicycle key, Johnny managed to start the motor. It was late at night, very late, and he went with his girlfriend for a ride on this Lambretta. He was a little high, I imagine, and the two of them ended up hitting a stone wall. John broke an elbow, smashed his face in, and injured his spleen. Fortunately, his girlfriend was not too badly hurt.

That particular night I was out visiting with Lynn Loesser. I had been led to believe that Johnny and his girl were going to a movie, and so I decided to go visit Lynn. She persuaded me to spend the night, which I did, but at eight the next morning I received the news of Johnny's accident. A friend called and told me he was in the hospital. I threw on my clothes and returned to our apartment. There was blood everywhere. The Lambretta was a total wreck. My dear friend had paid off the police, for which I was grateful.

I dashed to the hospital to find my son looking pretty terrible. His father came in, limping, with his cane, the top of which was a mace, ball, and chain. I ran to him, but he took his cane and brushed me aside. 'This is all your fault,' he said in a soft, but angry, voice.

'I don't think it is, but let's not argue about it, John; our son is badly hurt.' I was in no mood to battle with my ex-husband then.

John went to his battered son, the son for whom he had shown so little love, so little affection. He became very stern and wanted to know what happened. By that time, John had already suffered a heart attack in Capri, and anyone associated with him had to be careful because of his health. I decided the less said about Johnny's Lambretta ride, the better, and I omitted any mention of the young lady passenger. He would find out but then was not the time.

He found out sooner than I had hoped, and when he did, he turned to me, anger in his voice and showing on his face, and said,

'Why have you lied to me? All your life you have done nothing but lie to me, lie to me...'

Again, he had attacked me for no reason; attacked me viciously. His words were all untrue. How can you lie to a man you still love? If you do, you cannot.

'I have not lied to you!' I fought back, 'I merely did not say anything about it, because the girl was terrified of you. She has been examined, and is alright.'

He threw a volume of words at me, none of which I care to repeat, and walked away.

I felt crushed, and alone.

That night will forever remain with me, not only for the anguish it caused me as a mother, but because when John walked away from that quiet hospital room, it was the last time I ever spoke to him or saw him.

That night in New York, a life that had given me so much, that had begun years before in a dingy hotel room in California, had taken me to so many people and lands, that had been so beautiful in so many ways and yet so terrible in so many other ways – ended. And a light went out.

Johnny recovered, and spent the summer with my mother in California. They had a happy time, and while they did, I began to suffer one asthma attack after another. I have a great sympathy for all people who suffer from this illness. However, I am sure that the attacks were aroused by the stress I had experienced.

The summer passed quickly, and in the fall I was able to rent our New York apartment and move to a little house in Palm

Springs. I had spent some pleasant winters in that resort city while Thom and Johnny were in prep school, and I had taken a liking to that small, then quiet, and later world-famous, community in the corner of Southern California.

John went back to Elaine and back to his work. I think – I am sure – that he was miserable, but because of his complete stubbornness would never tell anyone.

I began my new life in Palm Springs while my sons began to grow into men. I stayed on the edge of the desert's many-sided 'social life.' After all, I had experienced so much that was real, and with so many famous and great people, and had enjoyed so many pleasurable times that I would never again have, that any attempts to emulate the happiness of the past could only result in failure and depression.

Life in Palm Springs for my two sons and me was quiet, and I found many hours to reflect on my time with John.

And then one day came the news that John Steinbeck had died at his New York home on Friday, 20 December 1968.

I felt terrible. I went all to pieces. I had been so upset at the news that he had been ill. I had heard from radio and television that John had gone back into the hospital, but I had not dared to call anymore. My mother had called the hospital and was told that he was better and had gone home. My mother was never allowed to speak to John, but had spoken to Elaine. I had no conception of how ill John was, although I knew he had not been well in recent years, and yet he pushed himself to all kinds of superhuman limits.

But when I heard he had died I went into a state of absolute shock. I hated myself, and always will, for not trying to talk with him again. I heard of his feelings about me through his letters to our sons, and from his conversations with other people. I know he wanted his thoughts to get back to me, even if he did not admit it.

I am convinced he was driven by hatred for me that bordered on love. He wanted me dead, and he wanted me to suffer. Believe me, I did, yet when I heard that he had died I was so very sorry, and I felt sad for Elaine. I cried and had several vodkas. With his death, the world had indeed lost a literary giant, but one who would live forever.

21 – A GREAT MAN IS DEAD

So John died, and took so much with him, but left more, an immortal legacy. At home in Palm Springs, I thought so much about our life together. I cried, God knows how I cried for him. I drank more than was good for me. Love is not gone because there is death. No, love as mine was for John is always there, every moment. When he died, there were no thoughts of the bad times, the ugly times, the tragedies in our life – just long remembering of all the moments two people shared together. Everywhere I turned, he was there. Everything I looked at; it was always John Steinbeck.

When I heard of his death, I thought back to his diaries where he wrote of his preoccupation with dying, even when he was in his thirties. Once, he said that he would commit suicide – except that he should wait. He would die, but did not have the courage. While alive, he had the courage for many things, and the greatest of these was his urge to write. The relentless drive of the man was unique. Here was a man who sacrificed everything for the sake of his work. To him, the writing was a miracle drug.

Although I had not communicated with John for a long time, it seemed in my daily life that he was always there in a strange, spirited form. When he died, I became surrounded by a void, something completely unexplainable.

I sat at home and thought of, and wished for, many things; I could see John at his desk, in his 'nest,' writing furiously, and with incredible speed with his right hand. He had his way of holding his pen. If his fingers grew tired, John moved his pen to the next digit.

John loved to keep his writings neat. Almost all of his works were in old folios or books, or on legal pads. Only late in his life did he resort to the typewriter.

John also was a man who needed constant attention. He needed care every moment: would say one thing, and I would act according to his wishes. Then, he would turn right around and say something else. John was the only man I ever knew who changed his mind so often and thought nothing of it.

And always he sacrificed everything for his work.

When he worked, he became a superhuman machine. When a book was complete, he sank into states of depression and turned to a new location for his life: a new city, a new town, new people, a trip to anywhere that took his fancy.

He always wanted to do everything, to do so much, to burn his life with each moment. Once, when he was young, he decided to be a fighter, but his uncle told him he would end up like an animal and be bought and sold. He gave up that idea, although he did enjoy boxing.

Later in life, he became interested in baseball, while he abhorred golf. 'Any man who spends his time chasing after a little ball is wasting his life; he might just as well sit and play solitaire,' he said. John did not believe in 'killing time.' To him, as I learned so well, all time was very precious, especially the many hours I spent with him.

Until his legs became painful, he used to ride horses and liked to swim. But whatever he did, he was clannish about it. I think scholars should note that in some of his letters, in the flyleaf of *Journal of a Novel*, he said he was writing *East of Eden* so that his sons will know who he was and the background to their lives. *East of Eden* is all about him. That was his ego – it was always John.

Often I am asked about my years with John, how I considered them. The simple answer – it was a tragedy.

Yes, a tragedy, but a beautiful one.

From the beginning, I think we were star-crossed, and that I was not the woman for him. I was too soft, too feminine; he needed a mate built of brick.

There were many beautiful moments of happiness, but I do not believe people are meant to be happy all the time. It is like Harold Rose said to me one night when I told him something was wrong with my relationship – that I was unhappy – and Harold said, 'How is that relative? Who is happy?'

Our marriage ended, but I do not believe it was anyone's fault that it failed. We both tried, but something got in the way. Sometimes I feel it would have been better if we had just lived together, but social attitudes in those days did not approve of such behavior, as today. If we had lived together, we would have both felt freedom within our love of each other.

We did have a trial run for years – maybe all couples should have one – and we were not married sooner because I felt John's subconscious was at work. He had fears about being 'trapped' in marriage, enclosed in too many obligations.

My mother once described our relationship, as a 'Trilby and Svengali set-up.' Perhaps it was because I walked about in complete awe of this man. Only as I began to mature during my life with him did I then want things for myself as an individual.

I was so proud of John, my husband. Who could not be? I was proud, too, in knowing that it was me whom he relied upon to protect him from people, to make sure his 'image' was always there whenever he circulated in public. Like so many writers, he had several lives, and in each, he was spoiled, and in each, he felt he was king. Perhaps he was.

I know I made a mistake. From the time John awoke to the time he went to bed, I had to be his slave. Whatever he wanted to do, I did.

Being married to any famous man is one rocky hard row to hoe. It takes every single waking and sleeping moment of your life; your life is his. You have to sacrifice anything that would break the pattern, that might interrupt the way of life of the man you love.

But that is the way of when you truly love.

I suppose the story of Gwendoline and John was a love story that was not a love story, but still a love story. In my five years and eight months of marriage, and my three years of living with him before that, I saw and knew his struggles, his agonies, his fears of criticism. He hated critics. It destroyed him to think that someone attacked his work. Yes, John was a man terrified of public reaction, although he had no reason to feel that way. He could not understand it if someone said to him, 'I don't like you.'

Fortunately, I could take it, and did while he could not. When criticized, he wanted to strike back with venom. He went into fits of rage, and anyone associated with him was well aware of them. No, John Steinbeck was not a man to cross – ever.

Not all times were like that. There is the story about John in Cuernavaca, Mexico. We were living there during the shooting of *The Pearl of La Paz*. Every morning we would breakfast under a large tree that resembled an English oak. The bakery men, with their baskets on their head, would pass by, and our servants would buy their sweet rolls from them: 'pan dulce,' as they are known. Then Jack Wagner, the producer, would appear, and then John. Usually, I was the first to arise.

One morning I was sitting with our son, Thom, and Willie the dog, when a little bird flew down and hovered over me as if it knew me. I threw some crumbs to it. It ate them and flew off. Next day, the bird returned, became brave and came back with some of its friends. More crumbs. Soon, one bird was brave enough to sit on the edge of my cup and share my morning coffee. It became quite a pastoral scene with the hummingbirds hovering around me, this little bird drinking from my cup, with our child in my arms and our dog at my feet.

Jack and John began to make remarks about how amazing it was that I had such a way with animals and birds. Well, one particular morning we were enjoying our usual breakfast, and this one little bird was taking the sweet roll from my mouth. Jack and John sat there, watching, John with a slight hangover. I looked down at our swimming pool and saw something coming towards us. 'What's that?' I asked a very bleary-eyed husband.

'What's what?' he muttered.

'That, coming towards us.'

'I don't see anything.'

I persisted. 'Of course, you do, it's a little thing, some animal.'

The 'little thing' kept crawling until it came to my feet, where it collapsed. It was a baby possum.

At the moment it collapsed at my feet, John looked at me, then at the possum, and said, 'Jesus Christ, St. Francis, don't you think you've gone far enough?'

Such was the wit of John Steinbeck.

As I have always had a great love for animals, I got a shoebox and an electric light bulb, tore some sanitary napkins apart and lined the shoebox with them, put the light in and kept the possum alive. Sadly, it died after a week, too young to be alone. Our houseboy found the mother and four other baby possums dead outside our garden gate, killed by a vehicle. So sad; no one knew why. John was upset, too, and buried them.

22 – I WAS HIS FRIEND; HE NEVER MINE

All the real love any woman could ever give a man, I had spilled out in my life with John. I could never love that way again after my divorce. John maintained his drive, and it seemed as if it was revenge, as if everything he did was to punish me for divorcing him. He often told mutual friends that there were too many women around.

Too many women? Strange that, considering his whole life he was surrounded by women. His top agent, Elizabeth Otis, was his confidant, and there were Mavis McIntosh, Annie Laurie Williams, Mildred Lyman, who worked in the office, and Mary Abbott – it was almost like a flock of mothers! John wanted the adoration of women; he liked to be with them, yet he felt that our sons lacked male companionship. He could not wait to send Thom away to prep school. Thom was then nine, and miserable at having to go. He was a homesick child, and his grades suffered because of it.

With Johnny, there was a time when Dr. Juan Negrin, head of brain surgery at Lenox Hill Hospital, believed there was something wrong with the way he acted. Johnny was lonesome because his brother was away, and he was sent to the psychiatric department. After an encephalogram, they decided to keep him under observation. There had been occasions, I told them, when I had returned home from a luncheon appointment and found Johnny huddled in a corner. I suppose I made the mistake of discussing that episode with John.

So young Johnny had psychiatric tests, the peg-into-the-round-hole kind of thing, general association tests, and I sat beside him as he went through them. Suddenly, he looked up at me and said, 'Mother, am I insane?' I became covered with gooseflesh.

'No, you are not. Not at all,' I said.

'Then why is all this being done to me?'

I paused then answered, 'Your father feels you're unhappy.'

The next day, John called and told me the test reports showed that Johnny Steinbeck was an ordinary child who was living in an abnormal world.

I could not accept that. If Johnny's world was high-key all the time, I had only tried to be a good mother. Our sons were clean, well fed, they were taught manners, how to read and write, and heard only the best of music and met only the best of people.

Shortly after John's call with the test results, the hospital called. Johnny had disappeared.

A search began, and this six-year-old child was found in the men's ward – hiding under a bed in sheer terror.

I made up my mind. I went to the hospital and took my second son home.

Predictably, John called and wanted to know the meaning of my action. I told him, and that was that.

The following summer, John took Johnny away to a camp in Maine, New England. That year they enjoyed, for a brief while, a happy father-son relationship. I hoped that perhaps a bond would grow between them.

When Thom was thirteen, John decided he also needed psychiatric treatment. He said Thom's behavior warranted it. Thom was ducking out of school; why, I don't know. Looking back now, I can understand why our two sons might have been disturbed, because all the time they were being pulled one way or another.

John seldom looked back. I believe his whole attitude toward me after the divorce concerned revenge. I have mentioned that John Steinbeck was gentle, but when he found an enemy, he roared!

I shall never forget the many times he would tell me how he hated critics. Edmund Wilson was the principal target for years. Wilson always gave him bad reviews, and it was a long time before he met the man.

'If ever I see him, I'll kill him!', was a frequent remark.

One day, on First Avenue in New York, John met him. John was out walking with George Frazier, and Wilson was out walking his sheepdog. 'There's Edmund Wilson,' said George. 'Why don't you meet him.'

And John did.

John came home and told me of the meeting at a hotdog stand. 'I feel sorry for him,' he said, and he did not kill him.

Yes, John was in a position where he did not have to care about anyone. Success can and does do that to people. He worried a great deal. Once when we were on 78th Street, and he was talking about a bad review, he said, 'For two cents I'll show them and never write again in my life. Then what would they do?'

I laughed. 'That's the silliest thing in the world because that's what you do, will always do. Besides, everyone gets criticized.'

'I am sick and tired of critics,' he said.

His distaste for them may relate back to an unknown episode in his life. In the beginning, as his diary shows, he had many rejections and struggles, and never forgot any of them. Perhaps he blamed his later frustrations on this. He believed in himself (as everyone must), yet many times in our life together, it was easy to see he was insecure. But then, aren't we all at some time?

To the world, John was a hard, determined and rugged man. Underneath, as I know so well, there was a very soft, warm man; a man John was afraid to show the world. There was a funny person, a man who could love so strongly yet turn and hate in the same way.

There was, too, a man who had moments of cowardice and who, to protect himself, turned rude and mean, or walked away.

John Steinbeck was a man whom I felt, in the end, was taking away my right to live, for some unknown reason; a man for whom I could do nothing right. God knows I tried because I loved him so; how I loved him. I could be an Amazon, but my makeup was too feminine for him.

John, the super-sensitive genius, was always worried about time, and he lived with the frustration of not being able to accomplish in life all he wanted.

A prime example of this was the time he and Elaine went to England. He wanted our sons with him, and was going to research a piece about Ireland and the early times of the monks. John loved history, and the mysticisms of the past held a permanent fascination for him. He never did write about Ireland and the early monks, despite that research. Time did not permit him.

Being married to John was hard work. When I married him, I suppose I was looking for my father and wanted someone to lean on, while he was looking for a mother image. I leaned on him – yes, that I admit – but not when there were crises, or if he became ill during his own 'down' periods (and there were many) and his 'white nights.' Those were times when he just could not sleep, and often I would find him wandering about the house, or in the kitchen drinking coffee. Morning would come, and he would go back to his work, exhausted, always forcing his mind and body onwards.

During those 'white night' periods, I withdrew, and John had his way, no matter what it was.

Any marriage has its arguments, and that's only natural. We, of course, had our exchanges of emotional words – but never a fight, and such times happened when he felt like roaming off on a tangent or decided he wanted to change his life.

It has been said and written that John was a self-effacing person, who did not like to be recognized. I know he wanted everyone, the whole world, to love him, and he would get a tremendous feeling of enjoyment whenever anyone recognized him, anywhere. If you asked him, he would deny it, but if someone did not notice him, he felt slighted.

Life with John Steinbeck never lacked for excitement. He lived on the edge of excitement, with everyone around him aware how he was going to be.

Sometimes, he invited our friends over for an evening, and just after they arrived, he would change his mind and let forth with phrases like, 'You can sit around all night if you want and drink everything, but I've got to get up in the morning and make a living.' Naturally, this would hurt his friends, but his action was definite.

John had to be selfish with himself when he worked. He was only a man, but I do believe he wanted to be a saint and never made it. Why do I say that? Once, I flew from New York to California to let Carl Sandburg hear the records of my music, and, hopefully, win his approval of them. From Carl, I learned something that told me John would never attain saintly status. Carl was in Hollywood doing *The Life of Christ*. When I arrived, he was about to be interviewed by a young man from Israel. He allowed me to stay and, during the interview, the young man said, 'You know, Mr. Sandburg, we think of you as a saint.'

Carl laughed as only he could, and said, 'Well, you better get that out of your mind. I am no saint. Any man who has killed or contemplated murder is no saint.'

Like Sandburg, John was a gutsy human being, although he shied away from many things. He backed away from people he was in awe of, people like Carl and Ed Ricketts. Many people were afraid of him, too, because they knew John could explode within minutes.

Yet John had the habit of being gentle with people he did not love. John could solve the problem of a friend or a stranger with ease, yet when it came to anything near or dear to him, he was helpless.

Yes, that was John. I believe John wanted to make our world a better world. He may not have gone about it in the right way, but then, most of us never do.

If he suffered because of mistakes, I am sure it was never more than I did, or anyone else did or does.

We each have to suffer for our mistakes, and, in the final analysis, we pay for them one way or another. My debt is over, too. I gave what I had, and I am only sorry it was not enough. I believe I was the wrong person for John despite our many moments of happiness. I was his friend, while he was never mine.

You have to be friends as well as lovers, you know.

As I sit alone now, thinking, I know that our life could have been better, had we just lived together without the locks of marriage.

John liked to live outside of society, yet he still wanted to conform to it. He lived the way he wanted to live – doing everything he wanted to do.

He loved the way he wanted to.

And somewhere our love for each other was turned off, for a moment. That moment was enough to change two lives.

But I know that the love we shared with each other never really ended, and never will.

END

NOTES AND SOURCES

Chapter 1

1. Carol Steinbeck – see Dramatis Personae.

2. Little Bit of Sweden on Sunset Boulevard – the restaurant where Gwyn and John went on their first date.

3. 'Black Marigolds' – a thousand-year-old love poem (in translation) written by Kashmiri poet Kavi Bilhana.

4. Robert Louis Stevenson – Scottish novelist, most famous for *Treasure Island, Kidnapped* and *Strange Case of Dr. Jekyll and Mr. Hyde*. Stevenson met with one of the Wagner family on his travels. He died aged 44 in Samoa.

5. Synge – probably the Irish poet and playwright John Millington Synge.

6. Matt Dennis – bandleader, pianist and musical arranger, who wrote the music for 'Let's Get Away from It All,' recorded by Frank Sinatra, and others.

7. Dr. Paul de Kruif – an American microbiologist and author who helped American writer Sinclair Lewis with the novel *Arrowsmith*, which won a Pulitzer Prize.

8. Ed Ricketts – see Dramatis Personae.

9. The San Francisco State Fair – this was the Golden Gate International Exposition of 1939 and 1940, held to celebrate the city's two newly built bridges – the San Francisco-Oakland Bay Bridge and the Golden Gate Bridge. It ran from February to

195

October 1939, and part of 1940. At the State Fair, early experiments were made with radio; Steinbeck heard Gwyn singing and called her, some months after their initial meeting.

Chapter 2

1. *The Forgotten Village* – a screenplay written by John Steinbeck and released in 1941. Narrated by Burgess Meredith – see Dramatis Personae. The New York authorities banned it, due to the portrayal of childbirth and breastfeeding. The film was restored and rereleased in 2011.

2. *Sea of Cortez* – a joint effort by Steinbeck and Ed Ricketts – a mixture of travelogue and data – which was not well received due to wartime conditions and its style being so different to anything Steinbeck had produced before. It was based on an expedition made in early 1940, on which Carol accompanied them. She is never mentioned once in the text, although all other crew members are. The first separate printing was published by Viking in the USA in 1951. A reworked narrative only reappeared in 1959 under Steinbeck's sole name. This interested Steinbeck's enormous following because of its description of his relationship with Ed Ricketts, and how he contributed to Steinbeck's thoughts and writing. The Sea of Cortez is the Gulf of California.

3. Helen Morgan – an American singer of sentimental ballads who died in 1941. Gwyn took some of her singing style from her.

4. Pacific Grove – the Steinbeck family had a holiday home for many years at Pacific Grove. John and Carol bought a house at 425 Eardley Street – which he kept after they split.

5. Boris Karloff – the stage name of English actor William Henry

Pratt. Karloff specialized in roles in horror films, notably his portrayal of *Frankenstein* in three major films in the 1930s, based on the novel by Mary Shelley. He chose his stage name to avoid embarrassment to several of his family, who held high-ranking posts in the British diplomatic service.

6. Carol was presumably referring to the decisions she had made about having children, saying she would 'rather have rabies than babies.' She had told one friend that she wanted children, but John did not – insisting his books were his children.

7. *The Wayward Bus* – published in 1947, describes an eventful bus journey in the Californian mountains with an assorted bunch of disparate passengers. Dedicated to Gwyn, it later became a film in 1957, starring English actress Joan Collins and blonde bombshell American, Jayne Mansfield.

Chapter 3

1. Lewis Milestone – a Moldavian-born American filmmaker who directed *All Quiet on the Western Front*, Steinbeck's own *Of Mice and Men* (1959), and later *Mutiny on the Bounty*, starring Marlon Brando.

2. *The Red Pony* – this was written in 1933. Early chapters were published in magazines and the full book in 1937. It was later filmed – directed by Lewis Milestone and starring Robert Mitchum and Myrna Loy, with music by American composer Aaron Copeland.

3. Ellwood Graham – painter/artist who knew Steinbeck, and who sponsored some of his early work.

4. Burgess Meredith – see Dramatis Personae.

5. Elia Kazan – a Greek/American writer, actor and director, best known for directing Steinbeck's *East of Eden*, starring James Dean, Burl Ives and Raymond Massey. The film won two Oscars. He also made *A Streetcar Named Desire*, starring Marlon Brando and Vivien Leigh, and *On the Waterfront*, again starring Brando, together with Rod Steiger.

6. Ed Ricketts – see Dramatis Personae.

7. *The Moon Is Down* – for this film Steinbeck received, from the King of Norway, the country's Freedom Cross. The story told of the occupation of an unnamed state by unnamed invaders. It was never implied that they were German, but the book inspired Resistance fighters in Occupied Europe. It became the best-known book of U.S. literature in the Soviet Union during the war. The title comes from Macbeth. Banquo's son, when asked the time, replies, 'The moon is down: I have not heard the clock.'

8. Mickey Finn – knock-out drops used to incapacitate drunken customers before robbing them. The name probably originated in a Chicago bar, owned by one Mickey Finn, which closed in December 1903. Incapacitated patrons would be carried into a back room, robbed and then dumped in an alley, waking up the next day with no memory of what had happened.

9. Snedens Landing – sometimes known as 'Hollywood on the Hudson.' It has been home at various times to Bill Murray, Uma Thurman, and Angelina Jolie.

10. Maxwell Anderson – an American playwright, author, journalist and lyricist who wrote the words to 'September Song.' A prolific writer, one of his plays was named and may have coined the phrase *Candle in the Wind*.

11. Paulette Goddard – an American actress and Ziegfeld girl. One-time girlfriend of Charlie Chaplin, and, if they were ever married, she was granted a divorce from him in 1942, and married Burgess Meredith. Later, she had a brief relationship with Steinbeck.

12. Kurt Weill – a German composer who moved to the United States and wrote *The Threepenny Opera*, which included the classic standard 'Mack the Knife.'

13. Henry Varnum Poor – an American architect, painter, sculptor, and muralist. As an architect, he did house renovations for Burgess Meredith and Maxwell Anderson. He painted a portrait of Gwyn together with John and son Thom.

14. Pare Lorentz – an American filmmaker who made documentaries. His film *The Plow That Broke the Plains* (1936), about the creation of a dust bowl which leads to Okies moving to California, influenced Steinbeck. Lorentz made state-funded films about aviation, and one of the Nuremberg Trials.

15. Helen Hayes – American actress nicknamed 'The First Lady of American Theatre.' Winner of an Emmy, a Grammy and an Oscar, she was a lifelong philanthropist.

Chapter 4

1. Cannery Row – the first cannery opened in 1908, and by 1918 'The Row' became a boomtown of corrugated canneries producing 1.4 million cases of sardines. After World War II, the sardines disappeared from Monterey Bay, and the fishing industry collapsed, as predicted by Ed Ricketts.

2. Jacques Cousteau – a French undersea explorer and

filmmaker, who co-invented the Aqua-Lung – the breathing device for scuba diving. He became a world-famous advocate of environmental protection.

3. The proposed trip to the remote, hostile Queen Charlotte and Aleutian Islands was abandoned after Steinbeck's fall of twelve feet, from an upstairs window, in New York, when a balcony gave way. He heeded the medical advice that such a trip on the lines of the Sea of Cortez mission would be very unwise. He was told that with the varicosities in his legs, a slip while gathering specimens could cause a troublesome embolism. So instead, he hobbled to Russia with Robert Capa.

Chapter 5

1. Paul de Kruif – an American microbiologist and author famous for his 1926 book on that subject. As a young man, de Kruif fought in Mexico during the Revolution.

2. Kit Carson – Kentucky-born frontiersman, Indian agent, and U.S. Army officer. Carson in the American Civil War led a regiment of Hispanic volunteers from New Mexico on the Union side. He later led forces to suppress Navajo, Apache, Comanche and other Indian tribes. He was a western comic-book hero to a generation, married three times and had ten children, dying at age fifty-eight. Carson was involved in the Bear Flag revolt by American settlers in 1846 against Mexican authority, and Steinbeck's *Sweet Thursday* was first entitled *Bear Flag*.

3. Route 66 – a road of some 2,400 miles opened in 1926, it ran from Chicago through Missouri, Kansas, Texas, New Mexico and Arizona, before ending in California; a historic migration route for

those leaving the Dust Bowl in the 1930s.

4. Barney Oldfield – an American pioneer racing driver, Barney was christened Berna, but changed his 'sissy' name to Barney as a teenager. Graduating from cycles to motorbikes and then cars, he became a household name, setting a world land speed record at Daytona Beach, Florida in 1910 of 131 miles an hour. He became the first 100-miles-an-hour racer at the Indianapolis Raceway and later he raced a Fiat car against bi-planes at county fairs – earning a fortune and surviving long enough to spend it, dying peacefully in 1946, age 68.

5. Las Vegas (New Mexico) – the county seat of San Miguel County, New Mexico, 65 miles east of Santa Fe and some way from Las Vegas, Nevada!

6. Romanoff's – a restaurant in Beverly Hills whose proprietor was once described as 'the most wonderful liar in 20th-century U.S.A.' Mike Romanoff claimed to be a Russian aristocrat, but was born in Lithuania; real name Hershel Geguzin. At lunchtime, the second booth to the left was sometimes occupied by Humphrey Bogart, while the proprietor often dined with his large dogs at his table. Patrons who could not get the best tables said they were sometimes forced to sit 'in Siberia.'

Chapter 6

1. Elizabeth Otis – see Dramatis Personae.

2. Sir Alfred Hitchcock – an English director known as the Master of Suspense. Son of an English greengrocer, Hitchcock was intensely disliked by Steinbeck, despite his being one of the most renowned English filmmakers of the time. Films like *The Lady*

Vanishes, Jamaica Inn, Rebecca, and *Psycho* made Hitchcock world-famous. He often had a quick cameo appearance in his pictures, usually near the start, because he knew filmgoers were waiting to spot him, and he did not want to divert their attention away from the story.

3. John Hodiak – starred in the film *Lifeboat,* opposite Tallulah Bankhead.

4. Tallulah Bankhead – a striking American actress from a prominent political family. Her grandfather and uncle were U.S. senators. She struggled with alcoholism and drug addiction and was famous for her uninhibited sex life – her husky voice made her far more famous than her film appearances.

5. Lon Chaney Jr. – American actor who played Lennie Small in the film *Of Mice and Men.* He made dozens of films, playing monstrous characters such as Frankenstein. He appeared in the film *High Noon,* and later as Chingachgook in *Hawkeye and the Last of the Mohicans.*

6. *Tortilla Flat* – Steinbeck's first major success, in 1935. One of three Cannery novels, the others being *Cannery Row* and *Sweet Thursday.* The film in 1942 featured Spencer Tracy, Hedy Lamarr, and John Garfield.

7. Henry Fonda – Henry Jaynes Fonda played Tom Joad in the adaptation of Steinbeck's *The Grapes of Wrath.* Part of a famous acting dynasty, his family included Jane Fonda (Hanoi Jane) and Peter Fonda, star of *Easy Rider.* Fonda finally won an Academy Award in 1981 for his last film, *On Golden Pond.* In 1973 he starred in *The Red Pony,* based on the Steinbeck novella. When he died, the New York Times reported that by his family's wishes, his body was

to be disposed of, 'without ceremony of any kind.'

Chapter 7

1. Higgins the boat builder – Andrew Higgins was described by President Eisenhower as 'the man who won World War II for us.' He designed landing craft which were so flexible, reliable and fast, that the Americans could reach many parts of the coastline, not just the established ports, giving the Allies an option of landing spots in North Africa, Italy, and France. Higgins (like the Wright Brothers) had a problem in convincing the American military of his achievements; that a small boat builder from Nebraska could have the necessary answers.

Chapter 8

1. The Hotel Monteleone – founded in 1886 and still exists in New Orleans.

2. Ramos fizz – a New Orleans gin fizz.

3. Dr. Paul de Kruif – see Chapter 1, note 7.

4. *Lohengrin* – coincidentally the character is a Knight of the Holy Grail – a theme which intrigued Steinbeck throughout his life.

5. Lyle Saxon – a writer, journalist, and historian on New Orleans.

6. Antoine's – a renowned French-Creole cuisine restaurant, founded around 1840. During the Prohibition era, one of the back rooms (such as used for the Steinbeck wedding) was the 'Mystery Room.' It acquired its name because patrons would go through a door in the ladies' restroom to a secret room, and exit with a coffee cup full of booze. The protocol phrase at table, when asked from

whence it came, was 'It's a mystery to me.'

7. It seems likely that Gwyn knew the identity of Lady 'M' but felt it best not to identify her, in as much as she worked at McIntosh & Otis.

Chapter 9

1. George Frazier – travel and entertainment writer and jazz critic.

2. Sam Spewack – a Ukrainian-born writer who, with his wife Bella, wrote the libretto for the musical *Kiss Me Kate*, with music by Cole Porter.

3. Quentin Reynolds – war correspondent, and journalist and associate editor for *Collier's.*

4. Fernet-Branca – a bitter Italian herbal liqueur.

5. Red Norvo – a jazz musician who recorded with Billie Holiday, Frank Sinatra and Dinah Shore.

6. Virginia Mayo – star of some fifty films. Best known for her comedies with Danny Kaye, but also played opposite James Cagney, Bob Hope, and Paul Newman.

7. Burl Ives – a rotund folk singer and actor who was born Burl Icle Ivanhoe Ives. He sang with Woody Guthrie and recorded songs like *A Little Bitty Tear* and *The Blue Tail Fly*. Later he became a character actor, appearing with Paul Newman and Elizabeth Taylor in *Cat on a Hot Tin Roof*, and in 1955 played Sam the Sheriff in Elia Kazan's film production of Steinbeck's *East of Eden*. He won an Oscar for his portrayal of Rufus in the epic western *The Big Country*.

8. Robert Ruark – a columnist and big game hunter.

9. Hazel Scott – Trinidadian jazz pianist and singer.

10. Adam Clayton Powell – congressman for Harlem and one of the first black Americans to be elected to the U.S. House of Representatives.

Chapter 10

1. Mitla – a renowned archaeological site near Oaxaca in Mexico, where buildings up to 1,500 years old are to be seen, well preserved by the extremely arid climate.

2. 21 Club – opened in Greenwich Village in 1922, but moved to its current location at 21 West 52nd Street, New York, in 1930. The old site later housed the Rockefeller Center. When raided during prohibition, the shelves on the bars would automatically tip all liquor through a chute and into oblivion. The cellar was next door to the club, so staff could truthfully say there was no booze on the premises. After prohibition, it housed private wine cellars for such names as Sophia Loren, John F. Kennedy, Ernest Hemingway and Frank Sinatra. Even today, the club, owned by Belmond Ltd (formerly Orient-Express Hotels), does not allow jeans, and all patrons must wear a jacket. If they forget, they can hire a 'loaner' jacket, by designers such as Hugo Boss or Ralph Lauren. The club has played host to almost every famous American from the world of sport, politics, and entertainment, many of whom are associated with specific tables in the club.

Chapter 11

1. Everett Hoagland – a West Coast big band leader.

2. Avenida Cinco de Mayo – a place of celebration which commemorates, annually on 5 May, a Mexican Army victory over

the French in 1862.

3. Ilya Ehrenburg – Russian writer and journalist who wrote a book, *The Thaw*, which outlined a change in Russian foreign policy after the death of Stalin, and the growth of Russian liberalism.

4. Diego Rivera – a painter and muralist of working-class people and natives in Mexico.

5. Oaxaca – a state in Mexico, whose city of the same name is noted for its creative atmosphere and museums, fascinating markets and cuisine.

6. Iganacio Millán – was a leading figure in Mexican medical and political circles; one-time student of Albert Schweitzer, and a close friend of Diego Rivera.

Chapter 12

1. Manny Wolf's – a chophouse located on 3rd Avenue and 49th Street. Founded in 1897, the noisy, crowded atmosphere soon became very popular, with dancing after ten o'clock. Marilyn Monroe frequented the restaurant, which closed in the mid-1970s but reopened in 1977, a project of Alan Stillman, who founded T.G.I. Fridays. He picked the name of the restaurant, which is now *Smith & Wollensky*, simply taking at random two names out of the New York phone book.

2. *East of Eden* – Gwyn asserted that Steinbeck was planning *East of Eden* as early as 1944.

3. Dos Equis – a Mexican beer brewed for over a century; the brewery is now owned by Heineken.

4. John Hersey – a Pulitzer Prize-winning journalist and writer, author of a piece for the *New Yorker* about how survivors

experienced the bombing of Hiroshima.

5. Carlos Baker – a Princeton professor who wrote the 1969 authorized biography of Ernest Hemingway, entitled *Ernest Hemingway: A Life Story*. His book describes in detail how John O'Hara had a walking stick, blackthorn, which Steinbeck had given him. Hemingway bet O'Hara fifty dollars that he could break it over his own head, and did so, much to Steinbeck's disgust.

6. John O'Hara – a prolific Irish-American writer of novels and short stories. Originally a journalist, his best-known works are *Butterfield 8* and *Appointment in Samarra*.

Chapter 13

1. Macy's – a store in Herald Square, Manhattan, New York, which was the flagship department store in a group founded in 1843. It was justifiably famous for its Christmas window displays.

2. Gwyn had told the doctors supervising Thom's birth that this was not her first child, and that she had had abortions before. She said she had the first shortly after meeting Steinbeck, and a second at an early stage on a road trip with him to California in 1942.

3. Miss Diehl became known as 'Platterfoot' because of her size, and her shoe size being greater than Steinbeck's.

Chapter 14

1. Jimmy Savo – a Broadway, vaudeville and nightclub comedian and entertainer, juggler and mime artist, famous for the comic rendition of songs such as *That Old Black Magic*.

2. Neiman Marcus – a department store founded in Texas in 1907, famous for its Christmas catalogs. The store on one occasion

exhibited twenty rare Gauguin paintings, to enhance its artistic reputation.

3. White Cliffs of Dover – this house was miles out of Monterey, and Steinbeck used the two gallons of wartime fuel the couple were allowed to visit Ed Ricketts and other friends in Monterey, even though Gwyn had her own Ford car.

4. Robinson Jeffers – an American poet and environmentalist, known for his descriptions of the central Californian coast. Jeffers built a granite house in Carmel called Tor House and Hawk Tower. The tower was named after a hawk, which appeared during its construction and disappeared on the day of its completion. Jeffers was much admired and discussed by Carol and John Steinbeck, Ed Ricketts and Joseph Campbell.

5. *Wuthering Heights* – the only novel of English lady novelist Emily Bronte, published in 1847, the year before her death, aged thirty.

6. Hammer Galleries – founded in 1928 by industrialist, Occidental Petroleum oil tycoon and philanthropist, Armand Hammer. Hammer met Lenin in 1921 and began collecting Czarist art, such as Fabergé eggs, for which the gallery became famous, together with its later exhibitions of Impressionist paintings.

7. Soto House, Pierce Street, Monterey – this was the adobe house acquired after the rented property Gwyn recalled as the 'White Cliffs of Dover.'

8. Lloyd Shebley – friend of John Steinbeck, who found him a job at the Lake Tahoe fishery, where John first met Carol Henning.

9. Varsovienne – Polish dance, a combination of waltz and polka, the most poignant version of which appears in a scene from

the film *A Streetcar Named Desire* by Tennessee Williams. The sequence featured Karl Malden as Mitch and Vivien Leigh as Blanche.

Chapter 15

1. Ernie Pyle – Pulitzer Prize-winning journalist, who would have had much in common with John Steinbeck, writing about rural towns in America in the Depression. He then became a well-known aviation and war correspondent of almost legendary status, lauded by President Harry Truman. Having survived the D-Day landings, Pyle was killed on a Japanese battlefield at the end of the war at the age of forty-four. He was awarded the Purple Heart, had a plane named after him, and his life featured in the film *The Story of G.I. Joe,* with Burgess Meredith in the title role of Ernie Pyle.

2. Emiliano Zapata Salazar – a leading Mexican revolutionary, who headed a peasants' revolt in 1910 and was assassinated in 1919.

3. *The Pearl* (*La perla*) – the 1947 film based on John Steinbeck's short story *The Pearl.*

4. Dame Olivia de Havilland – at the time of publication Dame Olivia, who played Melanie Hamilton in *Gone with the Wind,* is the oldest Dame of the British Empire ever, at age 101. Born in Tokyo to British parents, she won two Oscars and received the National Medal of Arts from President George W. Bush. She is the sister of actress Joan Fontaine, with whom she had a bitter sibling rivalry for some 40 years, until Joan died aged ninety-six.

Chapter 16

1. Lynn Loesser – wife of Frank Loesser, Broadway composer of musicals, of which *Guys and Dolls* is the best known. As a lyricist, his songs included 'On a Slow Boat to China,' 'Two Sleepy People,' and 'Baby, It's Cold Outside,' the last of which won him an Academy Award.

Chapter 17

1. Luigi Corbellini – an Italian artist specializing in painting portraits of children, who exhibited his works at New York's Hammer Galleries.

2. Nat Benchley – Steinbeck's New York neighbor, Benchley was a writer, humorous critic and actor who worked at one time for *Newsweek*. He wrote a biography of his friend Humphrey Bogart, and his son Peter Benchley wrote the horrific tale that would become the smash-hit film *Jaws*.

3. *Travels with Charley: In Search of America* – the book, published in 1962, describes a road trip Steinbeck made with his dog Charley in 1960. Feeling his mortality, Steinbeck chose to travel without human company, to rediscover parts of America and to reflect how the country had, in his view, deteriorated.

4. Robert Capa – see Dramatis Personae.

5. Fred Allen – godfather to John Steinbeck Jr., Allen was a comedian whose topical radio program ran for many years. Among other things, it featured a mock feud with comedian Jack Benny. Apart from Steinbeck, fans included President Franklin D. Roosevelt, and writers William Faulkner and Herman Wouk.

Chapter 18

1. Mrs. Ogden Reid – part of the Reid family that owned the *New York Tribune* newspaper up until 1958, which was known as the 'writers' newspaper.' She had previously helped Steinbeck get a passport when he went to Europe as a war correspondent in 1943, and she stepped in again to help him with his visa for his Russian trip with Robert Capa.

2. Elsa Maxwell – A gossip columnist, songwriter and famed party-giver, she claimed to have introduced Rita Hayworth to Aly Khan, and Maria Callas to Aristotle Onassis. She devised treasure hunts and organized themed parties for the celebrities of her day. She knew and met everyone – Marilyn Monroe, Mussolini, Gary Cooper, Jackie Kennedy, the Duke of Windsor and Mrs. Simpson amongst them.

Chapter 19

1. *East of Eden* – a book published in 1952, although Steinbeck had been planning the major work for some years. He wrote to Gwyn herself about it in February 1948. It then became a 1955 film directed by Elia Kazan, starring James Dean, Raymond Massey, and Julie Harris.

Chapter 20

1. Sutton Place, New York – an affluent neighborhood on the East Side of Manhattan.

2. The family court hearing lasted three days. Gwyn says she was on the stand for four hours one day, during which time the well-paid attorney for John Steinbeck was more interested in

damning her character, rather than assessing whether the boys' claim for increased maintenance was justified. It was the last time, but one, she ever saw her ex-husband.

3. *The Wicked Lady* – presumably a reference to the 1945 film starring British actress Margaret Lockwood, in the title role as a nobleman's wife, who secretly becomes a masked highwayman for the excitement it brought her.

4. Chouinard Art Institute – a Los Angeles art school, founded in California in 1921, which developed strong connections with the Walt Disney studios. Disney used Chouinard as a breeding ground for animators for his timeless *Snow White and the Seven Dwarfs*. Disney took over the school financially, which in 1961 became part of the California Institute of the Arts.

5. Lambretta – a name synonymous with motor scooters, initially manufactured in Milan, Italy.

Chapter 22

1. Walter Mitty – James Thurber's character, from *The Secret Life of Walter Mitty*. Mitty is a mild man, with a vivid fantasy life.

2. George Frazier – an American journalist, his 1942 column in the *Boston Herald* was the first regular jazz column in an American big city daily. Known as 'Acidmouth', he had an acerbic wit and wrote the song 'Harvard Blues' for Count Basie. His favorite word was 'duende' – roughly meaning 'grace, wit, and class.'

3. Edmund Wilson – a writer and critic who influenced many American authors, including Scott Fitzgerald, whose unfinished works he edited for publication. He was very critical of many authors: for example, he described Tolkien's *The Lord of the Rings*

as 'juvenile trash.' He was reputedly a very difficult man to please, but influential nevertheless, reviewing books for *The New Yorker* and others.

4. Carl Sandburg – an American poet, folk singer, writer, and editor, who won three Pulitzer Prizes, two for his poetry and the third for his biography of Abraham Lincoln. He was awarded his second Pulitzer in 1940, the same year that Steinbeck received his, for *The Grapes of Wrath*.

5. During the time of the relationship between John Steinbeck and Gwyn, the following books were published or developed: *The Forgotten Village, Sea of Cortez, The Moon Is Down, Cannery Row, Bombs Away, The Wayward Bus, The Pearl, A Russian Journal* and *East of Eden*. Also completed were *The Moon Is Down* as a play, the screenplay for *Lifeboat*, and the wartime articles which became, in book form, *Once There Was a War*.

DRAMATIS PERSONAE

Olive Hamilton Steinbeck (1867-1934)

Steinbeck's mother, Olive Hamilton Steinbeck, was born one of nine children and had four sisters. She left the family farm – her father was a model for some of the Sam Hamilton character in *East of Eden* – and worked hard to qualify as a teacher. She was ambitious, wishing to escape the uncertainty of farm life and was teaching in a small school by age eighteen. She traveled by horseback to school each day.

Well organized, determined and strong-willed, she wanted to live in a town and so was attracted to a handsome accountant and manager John Ernst Steinbeck. They married in King City, California but moved to Salinas, where he ran the flour mill until its closure. Their Central Avenue house was in the most fashionable street in the town, radiating its inhabitants' class aspirations.

Olive craved and worked hard for status. She was outgoing, firm and 'proper,' and her forte was taking charge in both local and family life – getting things done. Steinbeck was thus born into a house full of sisters, books, poems recited, an unassuming father and a dominant mother. As a child, and as the only son, he was undoubtedly spoiled. 'He was spoiled,' his sister said flatly. 'Everyone took care of him. We were close to him, all of us...' (Parini 25)

Steinbeck, ever the magpie, had no trouble in painting a picture of Molly Morgan, who was based on his mother, in *The Pastures of Heaven*. She knew she had a talented child, even when he took advantage and was not prepared to be told.

Her husband took his only son to see the damage caused in Salinas by the 1906 San Francisco earthquake – this was Steinbeck's earliest memory and it's surprising that 'the magpie' never used this in his writings. Meanwhile, Olive, the ex-teacher, read extensively to him, prodding him to understand. When Steinbeck could read unaided, there were periodicals such as *National Geographic* and *Collier's* to feed a voracious, growing mind, and he soon graduated to books like *Robin Hood* and *Treasure Island* hence, perhaps, his first novel about pirates!

As Olive's son had no brothers to play with or taunt him about his bookishness, his bedroom at the top of the substantial house – dark and secluded – became the first Steinbeck 'nest,' where he read widely. This hunger for books led him to high school a year early, which delighted Olive. She would have been pleased when he became yearbook editor at Salinas High School, and ecstatic when in 1919 he was accepted for Stanford. With her belief in education, she foresaw her son as a professional; a step up from his father.

She was to be sorely tried and disappointed.

Olive took charge when financial disaster hit the family – first, her husband's redundancy, and then his ill-fated foray into business. She must have ridiculed John Sr., and Steinbeck hated her for it. Through her social connections she helped her husband get a bookkeeping job, as a stopgap, and then the county treasurership of Monterey, which enabled them to live quietly but well enough to maintain sufficient social status.

Her youngest daughter, Mary, had married a wealthy businessman, Bill Decker, later killed, missing in action in World War II, but Olive cherished hopes of Steinbeck becoming a doctor or lawyer. From the time he went to Stanford, up until her stroke in March 1933, she must have chafed at what she saw as Steinbeck's non-success and moral decline.

She railed against John's belligerence from college onwards, and his embrace of 'roaring twenties' behavior. Her pet name for him had been 'my little squirrel' (Parini 25), surely something that would have made Steinbeck cringe as a 'cool' Stanford student.

As years passed, the relationship between mother and son deteriorated. She felt let down by John's apprenticeship adventures in the fifteen years before her death – his menial jobs at Lake Tahoe, and in New York, and his antics in Panama and the fleshpots of San Francisco. These had not yet borne literary fruit. By the time of her death, despite the publication of three of his books, he had not yet broken through as a successful writer. What effect did Steinbeck's conduct have on the relationship between Olive and her taciturn husband, who had financed their son from meager resources for several years? Was this against her will, or was she unaware of it?

Posthumously, she would have been very proud of her son's success, if not of some of the earthiness and morals depicted in his writings, although when she was alive, her hostility undermined his self-esteem. She wrote him many letters while at college, bewailing his progress, which greatly angered him.

It was ironic that after her stroke he was the one to be recalled to the family home, with Carol, to care for her, as his sisters had other responsibilities. John and Carol's duties, as companions and nurse, created a problem as Steinbeck felt he could not write while under duress; but he did. It was eleven months from the time of her stroke in March – a month she hated – until her final death in 1934. Steinbeck was anxious that his mother should live to see his success and not remember him as a failure and a leech. John Sr., too, wondered if he could look after himself if he became a widower. If ever there was a time when Steinbeck looked likely to falter in his ambitions, this was it. However, as happened twice more, the crisis up to and including his father's death was to see the preparation and publication of significant works, *The Pastures of Heaven, To a God Unknown, Tortilla Flat* and *In Dubious Battle.*

This time might be considered the first of a trio of crises – the second when he crafted *The Grapes of Wrath* and the third when *East of Eden*, so long in gestation, became the writer's second 'big book.'

Olive's death gave Carol and John respite, although their domestic troubles were just beginning. The cost of Olive's care ended, and although her husband's health was fading too, other problems were manageable.

Assuredly, it was Olive Steinbeck who fired her son's imagination. Perhaps her doubts drove him to succeed, so that her actions and attitude, her belief in education, together with the support of her husband, were vital ingredients in Steinbeck's ultimate success.

John Ernst Steinbeck Sr. (1863-1935)

John Steinbeck's father, his namesake John Sr., was born on his father's farm but became a disillusioned man. Even his death was sad in its timing. It came after years of his support for his only son, just five days after the publication of *Tortilla Flat* – his son's breakthrough novel.

John Sr. ran a flour mill in Kings City, California, married wife Olive there, and then moved to Salinas to run a larger one when his son John was eight. That mill too closed leaving him redundant. He used his life savings to start an ill-fated feed store – not a good idea given the impact of tractors and cars on the agricultural landscape at that time, with the demise of natural horsepower and the feed that powered it.

A bookkeeper by profession, he was fortunate to have influential friends in Masonic circles. He and his wife were respectable and well regarded, and a fellow Mason found him temporary work at the Spreckels sugar plant – a major Salinas employer. Then the county treasurer died in office, and John secured the post at a modest salary, but acquired assured employment and status in a time of deepening depression. The treasurership was political, which enabled John to delegate duties from time to time to both John, his son, and John's wife Carol, when he was ill or depressed.

He was a respected man in the community – tidy, neat, punctual and fastidiously dressed, but his wife Olive, the matriarch of the family, undoubtedly wore the trousers.

The couple had four children – Esther (born in 1892), Beth (1894), John (1902) and Mary (1905). Despite the feed store misadventure, they prospered enough to have a substantial house in the best street in Salinas, Central Avenue, and later buy a small holiday home at Pacific Grove, a few miles away. Steinbeck used the latter at various times between 1930 and 1948 as one of his many writing 'nests.'

Belying his status, and probably to escape Olive, John Sr. gardened and raised chickens, and had at one time a cow and a pig, which he butchered himself. He kept a horse and would ride alone, perhaps to escape a house full of women. He had a horse-drawn buggy, in which he would take some of the smaller children on outings to the Pacific Grove cottage.

Although he was quiet and withdrawn, he gave his writer son financial support for several years – first at $25 a month and then $50 a month from the date of John's marriage to Carol in 1930, equivalent to over $700 a month today. He tinkered with John's old car, paid $100 for a steam ticket for John to Panama, and smuggled meat to the young marrieds as they struggled – probably not telling Olive. On two occasions, apart from treasury assistance, he was able through his connections to set up temporary jobs for John. He was genuinely concerned for his son's welfare, once promising him a gold watch at twenty-one if he abstained from smoking. Steinbeck smoked in secret and probably deceived his father.

His son, too, was never satisfied with just financial support. He wanted his father to face up to his dominant mother. She might have succeeded in dominating his father, but not her son, in whom she often despaired. Even when John was twenty-six and returned from Lake Tahoe, John Sr. left the house rather than mediate in a bitter argument between mother and son, when she was losing patience with Steinbeck's progress, prospects and general behavior.

Steinbeck himself was hard to please – and perhaps took his father for granted – despising him for his timidity and deference to his wife. John Sr. had his family responsibilities, which he could not escape: John Jr. could, and did. Although his father could not, his fortitude after his redundancy and business failure, his saving to purchase Pacific Grove, and raising four children, was something son John would never replicate.

When Steinbeck was finally published, his father reputedly carried round a copy of his son's book and walked into a local bookstore, albeit one that had refused to stock the novel. In August 1933, worried by his wife's poor health, John Sr. collapsed with heart trouble and was unwell after that – the problem made worse by shattered nerves and failing eyesight. He was also shortly to lose the treasurership of the county. He had to stand for election, which was an anathema to his natural shyness.

With both parents now ill, even with the unstinting work of Carol, his sisters living elsewhere, John the writer, now thirty and his career at a critical stage, struggled to move forward. Fortunately, he could spend time at Pacific Grove, but his mother's condition worsened. When she came out of the hospital in December 1933, she went back to the Central Avenue home, where she died the following February. John and Carol had followed to nurse her and look after John's father.

John then took his father back to Pacific Grove for a while, although later John Sr. arranged for old friends to stay and look after him at his house in Salinas in exchange for rent. John Sr. died in May 1935, but days later the tide turned as *Tortilla Flat* was published, confirming his son's early promise. Steinbeck relented a little regarding his opinion of his father, as he wrote to his godmother, Elizabeth Bailey: 'I can think of nothing of him so eloquent as silence. Poor silent man all his life. I feel very badly, not about his death, but about his life, for he told me only a few months ago that he had never done anything he wanted to do.' (LIL 110)

Thus, Steinbeck the writer, profligate and awkward in many ways, paid tribute to a father without whose financial support he would not have survived until recognition beckoned. In the deprived thirties, John Sr., Carol, and Ed Ricketts provided the financial, emotional and intellectual stimuli to Steinbeck, whose alchemy and cussed determination then produced so much rich, varied and memorable prose.

Carlton 'Dook' Sheffield

Carlton Sheffield was a Stanford classmate of John Steinbeck and instructor and assistant professor at the Occidental College in Los Angeles, California. Steinbeck never graduated; Sheffield did, and the two corresponded for forty years, right up to the time of Steinbeck's death.

Gwen may have met Dook only a few times, as she and Steinbeck lived mainly in New York, but Sheffield was the center of a commune of would-be writers and poets in the Eagle Rock area of California. He helped support Carol and John Steinbeck, as

Steinbeck sought to find space and time to find his voice before his writing would support him.

The relationship between the two men had highs and lows, but Dook was privy to the thoughts – good or otherwise – of a great writer.

Sheffield was a year older than Steinbeck – his first marriage to a lady called Ruth lasted only a short time before a divorce and her early death. She must have been shocked to receive a letter from Steinbeck after their wedding which read, at one point, 'I love this person (Sheffield) so much that I would cut your charming throat, should you interfere with his happiness or his manifest future.' In the same letter, Steinbeck wrote, 'We are constantly together. Do you (Ruth) wish to interfere in this, so that you may have him more surely to yourself: I do not know you. Undoubtedly, each of us supplies a great need for him, take care that you do not overstep your need and your usefulness.' (LIL 12)

Hardly a letter a bride would expect, and doubtless explains why Steinbeck was not at their wedding.

Steinbeck and Sheffield had boxed at Stanford – Steinbeck invariably won, and perhaps Dook was in awe of his college mate – and they shared early adventures together. Before departing for an ill-starred stay in New York, Steinbeck stayed with him at Eagle Rock, picking up old times. Once, Sheffield invited Steinbeck to speak to his journalism class, but the latter lasted a few minutes before fleeing the ordeal, for which he was manifestly unsuited.

Sheffield had married his second wife, Maryon, by the time John had met Carol when they met again in late 1929. Dook and Maryon invited the writer and his girlfriend to share their home. John wanted to escape his parents in Salinas, so they were happy to agree. Maryon thought John should marry Carol and, history has it, she arranged a time for the judge to marry them without their knowing in advance. The Sheffields then took the two of them hostage and hauled them into the judge's office, where they married in January 1930.

The foursome acquired further friends for the house party, a Richard Lovejoy and his Alaskan wife Tal and her sister. The house was inevitably lively with uninhibited outdoor sunbathing, perhaps fueled by the eighteen gallons of homemade beer that Dook would make every five days.

Soon after, John and Carol found a shack close by, which they were allowed to occupy for a nominal rent if they did it up. The fun times continued, subject to the group's meager funds, which were subsidized by Carlton Sheffield from his salary of $2,000 per year.

The group wasted valuable resources on a Heath-Robinson venture dubbed The Faster Master Plaster Casters whose aim was to make accurate plaster casts for Hollywood celebrities. Others became involved, drank some of the beer, but the venture fizzled out. John and Carol then vacated their shack; the owner wanted it back, now it was habitable. The Steinbecks moved temporarily in again with the Sheffields but then out, this time to the Steinbeck family summer cottage at Pacific Grove.

Thus they survived through part-time jobs, Carol's work and frugality, and Dook's support. Carol and John returned once more to Eagle Rock a year later, and there was an incident between John and Maryon Sheffield, who, aided and abetted by Carol, dyed

Steinbeck's hair pink, a result so outrageous that sister Mary refused to meet him and Carol for a local beach outing.

Following this, the Steinbecks returned to the Steinbeck family home in Salinas, forced by the need to take care of Olive Steinbeck, who had suffered a massive stroke.

Steinbeck wrote letters, almost as a warm-up exercise before starting writing work. The recipients, other than his agents, film rights people and lawyer, were varied: among them Carl Wilhelmson, Sheffield, Edward Albee, Steinbeck's various early girlfriends, the artist Bo Beskow and several others. As Steinbeck's fame grew, he would write to many well-known people, including President Franklin D. Roosevelt and his wife, who was sympathetic to the plight of the Okies, presidential candidate Adlai Stevenson, both John and Jackie Kennedy, and star of *Casablanca*, Ingrid Bergman. He fell out, unsurprisingly, with many friends, but with Carlton Sheffield the links lasted – in spite of his being very upset when Steinbeck proffered a loan to Sheffield to enable him to seek a master's degree at Oxford or Cambridge. (LIL 710)

He revealed to Sheffield very private thoughts, saying in an early letter (when aged thirty), 'I should love you to have this book and my reasons are all sentimental and therefore of course unmentionable. I love you very much. I have never been able to give you a present that cost any money. It occurs to me that you might like a present, that cost me a hell of a lot of work.' (LIL 64)

In another very long letter, while he was married to Carol, Steinbeck wrote: 'I just want to talk, and there is no one to talk to.' (LIL 74)

Of his firstborn son, just seven weeks old, Steinbeck wrote to Sheffield, 'If I can, I am going to build a cell for him, because that's where they belong for several years. They are mean little animals. That is that.' (LIL 272)

In 1952, Steinbeck indicated his fragile, ever-wavering mindset to his old roommate. Aged fifty he wrote, 'I think I am changed in some ways, calmer, maybe more adult, perhaps more tolerant, but still restless. But I will never get over that, I guess – still nervous, just short of a manic depressive, I guess. I have more confidence in myself now, which makes me less arrogant. And Elaine has taught me not to be afraid of people (strangers) so that I am kinder and better mannered I think.' He continued to Sheffield, 'You drift toward peace and contemplation, and I drift toward restlessness and violence.' (LIL 459)

Of his abandonment of California, the writer told Dook, 'I didn't belong there…I discovered what I should have known long before, that I don't belong anywhere.' (LIL 763) In lighter vein, he wrote of his Nobel Prize, 'The prize is more negotiable than the Americas Cup, although both are the product of wind.' (LIL 744)

Steinbeck was not always gentle in his remarks about his friend Sheffield. To another correspondent, Carl Wilhelmson, he wrote, 'I haven't heard from Dook in a long time as he seemed so touchy that I gave up.' (LIL 288) A little later, to Pascal Covici, his editor, Steinbeck wrote, 'His is a very little mind. In many ways, he has the qualities of a medieval school man. I don't like him. Perhaps I never did.'

The remarks were somewhat unkind to a good friend from harder times, and Dook eventually found out about these remarks after Steinbeck died. However, Sheffield generously expressed his appreciation of such a talented writer – which he probably would have wished to be – by forgiving such comments.

By the time of his death, Carlton Sheffield had indeed amassed not only many letters to and from his former college roommate, but also many press clippings and articles about John Steinbeck, which are now in the Stanford archives.

Webster (Toby) Street

Webster (Toby) Street was a Stanford classmate of John Steinbeck. He became a Monterey lawyer, in whom Steinbeck confided during turbulent and other times throughout his life. Toby and John were both members of the College Running Club, and also members of the English Club.

Street abandoned hopes of being a writer but contributed to the pantheon of Steinbeck's work in as much as he turned over an early project of his, *The Green Lady*, to John to do with what he liked. This, after rewriting, became *To a God Unknown*.

As a young man, Steinbeck was interviewed by the mother of Frances Price as to the suitability of Toby as a husband for her daughter. Apparently, John gave the right answers – even if the couple were later divorced. Toby might just have found John a maintenance job at Lake Tahoe – where John met Carol, his first wife – as a favor in return. Street also remarked that when Steinbeck escaped his mother Olive's grumblings, he had been relieved to do so.

Steinbeck later claimed he never wanted to be married, that he would not make a good husband, since his work was his passion.

Toby then relayed to Carol, 'You are not as important as his work.' (POM 49)

Letters from Steinbeck to Street often revealed insights. In a letter from Steinbeck, in 1934, about his writing, he said, 'Comfortable and comforting. What an extension of life this pen is. Once it is in my hand, like a wand – I stop being a confused, turgid, ugly and gross person.' (Parini 189)

The young Steinbeck had a quaint attitude to money. Street, who handled both his divorces and his dealings with Ricketts's Lab, asserted that his client, Steinbeck, needed to think he was poor. Later, Paramount Pictures paid $75,000, plus a share of the profits, for the film rights to *The Grapes of Wrath* in 1939 – equivalent to $1.3 million in 2018 – which perplexed him.

On leaving Carol and after their divorce, Steinbeck told his lawyer friend that he was 'a wife deserter and cad.' (LIL 234) 'I guess,' he said, 'Carol hates me very much, and I don't like being hated,' (LIL 239) and also, 'I was cruel to her physically and mentally.' (LIL 242)

Soon after they met, according to Gwyn, she became pregnant with Steinbeck's child; in the absence of any firm course of action from him, she confided in her mother, who then arranged for Gwyn to miscarry.

So it was hardly surprising that at the height of the love triangle between Carol, Gwyn and John, Gwyn's mother, known as Bird Eyes, went and challenged Toby Street. 'What was John going to do?' After a pause for consideration, Street said: 'Well, I'll tell you, Bird Eyes, once upon a time Carol was a sweet girl.' Toby may have had a fondness for Carol. 'John made her into a monster, and if he gets Gwyn, he will make her into a monster too.'

A prescient remark that came true – as eight years later Steinbeck, on Gwyn leaving him, was to tell Street that Gwyn, as she was now known, wanted a divorce. 'I am inhibiting her and she can't stand me,' (LIL320) he told Street. She was prepared to divorce him on the grounds of incompatibility – the only grounds that he would accept without demur. Steinbeck then added, wistfully, 'As usual my wife gets about everything I have.' (LIL 324) He also said that, 'I'm pretty banged up,' (LIL 321) from the combined blows of the divorce and Ricketts's horrific death. After a year the divorce was finalized.

Steinbeck and Toby Street remained friends, despite the distance between New York and California, one of the few friendships from college days as Steinbeck moved in new circles. Toby visited the famous storyteller as late as August 1968, four months before Steinbeck died.

Carol Henning Steinbeck (1906-1983)

Carol met John Steinbeck in California in June 1928, when she wandered with her sister Idell into the Lake Tahoe fishery in search of a friend, Lloyd Shebley. Lloyd was John's work colleague and housemate, who had got him a job there. Though Lloyd was away, John eagerly showed the girls around the hatchery. Her banter and his confession of being a 'midwife to Lady Trout' (Parini 97) ignited a spark between them. John quickly seized his chance and set up a double date for that evening.

Steinbeck's 1994 biographer, Jay Parini, described Carol as 'tall and slender, she had rich brown hair that she wore long.' Steinbeck, himself, depicted her as red-haired in eleven of the twenty-five poems he wrote to her in the early days of their relationship. He was hooked, and for three weeks until she left, the couple were inseparable, drinking, dining, dancing in the mountain resort, becoming lovers within days. One adventure in the rowdy railroad town of Truckee involved the bar owner lending John – who loved weaponry – a revolver to protect the girls on a wild night out. This included an infamous bar, The Bucket of Blood. John had had a girlfriend before, showgirl Mary Adarth, who finished with him for having no prospects. After two years (including harsh winters alone) John was as hungry as a bear – for an all-consuming, exciting relationship.

He asked Carol to stay, but she wished to remain loyal to her elderly employer who had funded her holiday, and returned home. John was devastated, lovesick when she left, taking to his bed for a week. Weeks later he narrowly escaped retribution after a drunken assault on a pretty young friend after she rebuffed his advances, albeit that she may have led him on. He held her upside down from an upstairs window, but his pal Lloyd rescued her and conveyed Steinbeck's abject apology next day, which the young lady, fortunately for John, accepted.

Another wild night out in Truckee, where John produced his revolver and Lloyd again intervened, ended any further contact between Steinbeck and pretty Polly Smith. John then pursued Carol to San Francisco at the end of the tourist season. He was fired after wrecking the hatchery boss's new pickup truck. He got a job in a warehouse, Carol worked for the *San Francisco Chronicle*, and they spent all their spare time together. John had modest rooms, until his quiet but generous father suggested he use the family holiday home at Pacific Grove for his writing. There Carol would visit (and often stay), and use her secretarial skills to type, and tidy various drafts, and the couple would discuss their content.

The lovers were almost caught out one Sunday as Mother – the church-going Olive Steinbeck, with husband in tow – turned up unannounced. Carol exited partly clothed – the rest in hand – out of the back door. By autumn, the couple were inching towards marriage. They even bought a license, but postponed its use more than once.

Carol had involved herself in left-wing politics and had a social conscience. She tried to interest John, but he was wrapped up in his writing and less concerned. Across America, recession was edging towards depression, businesses closing, lives wrecked – it was the time of the 1929 Wall Street Crash. As they argued about the depression, this may have planted the seeds in Steinbeck's mind which would later germinate into *In Dubious Battle* and *The Grapes of Wrath*. A strong partnership was forming, and this a year before John met Ed Ricketts.

The couple intended to marry in Los Angeles, but their car expired, so they ended up with Carol's parents in San Jose for ten days. 'They didn't really like me,' Steinbeck said. (Parini 118) When mobile again, they moved on, staying with Carlton 'Dook' Sheffield – a former Stanford classmate, then teaching, and his second wife, Maryon.

It was Maryon and Dook who drove them to Glendale in the San Fernando Valley for a civil wedding to which they were the only witnesses. Understandably, John's parents were particularly upset, and one wonders if Olive knew of the couple's doubled allowance to $50 monthly, from her husband, as Carol became the first Mrs. John Steinbeck in January 1930.

The couple had little money, and from time to time took handouts from Carol's father, a moderately successful realtor. Like Steinbeck's father, Carol's too had a dominant wife from whom he would escape to the golf course.

The couple moved afterwards to Pacific Grove, where Carol got a job with the Monterey Chamber of Commerce. John worked on. Carol found Pacific Grove quiet and stuffy, and sometimes wildly funny. Imagine the reaction of their Eagle Rock set, The Faster Master Plaster Casters, to the following 1932 swimsuit ordnance of Pacific Grove:

'It shall be unlawful for any person wearing a bathing suit or part thereof, except children under the age of ten years to appear in or upon any beach or in any place open to the public, unless attired in a bathing suit or other clothing or opaque material. This clothing or material shall be worn in such a manner as to preclude form, from above the nipples of the breast to below the crotch formed by the legs of the body. All such bathing suits are to be provided with double crotches or with skirts of ample size to cover the buttocks.' (POM 62)

Pacific Grove was quite a buttoned-up town and must have seemed in sharp contrast to Monterey, where John, with his fund of stories, and Carol with her sharp wit and wild antics, were part of a contemporary group who gravitated to Ricketts's Lab. Ed Ricketts's Lab became established there, both as a business, and a social meeting place. For the first time, Carol had to share John with others.

When Steinbeck was down, Carol would liven up the house with her jokes, energetic conversation and gregariousness. She would give Steinbeck little presents to cheer him up, such as chocolate and flowers. She would also tidy up his writing. Steinbeck misspelled and was no master of punctuation. She was his technical editor. Carol then started an advertising business with a friend, Beth Ingels, who proved a rich fund of local stories, many of which John wove into his writing. With Carol's unflagging energy, the couple coped with the deepening depression. They lived on fish they caught, cheap wine, rolled their cigarettes, played chess, listened to the radio and got on with it, content in their lifestyle and youthful independence.

It was about this time that Carol's sister, Idell, introduced Joseph Campbell to the group. She had met him on a steamer trip, some years before, when her mother had treated her, alone, to a Hawaiian holiday, which was a bone of contention between Carol and Idell. He was an unemployed classics scholar, who had spent time in Paris and who shared with Steinbeck a fascination for Arthurian legend. Campbell joined the tight-knit group of John, Ed, Carol, Ritchie and Tal Lovejoy. The six bubbled with conversation and adventure. (POM 105)

So absorbed was Steinbeck in his writing that Carol felt starved of affection, and perhaps a little bored. The handsome Campbell, who like most of America was out of work, had the time and inclination to woo Carol. She too liked to think of herself as a free thinker, and he loved her directness, humor and antics – 'she was a tree climber,' according to Ed Ricketts Jr. 'She just liked to climb pine trees,' at least once clad in nothing but black gloves. (POM 109) Campbell, who later became a well-known writer, said, 'Before, when I visited John and Carol, I had felt myself to be the visitor…now it is John who seems the outsider. He is like someone who captured the girl that I was meant to have married.' (Parini 155)

They had a strong affection for each other that they were incapable of hiding, although it seems Campbell and Carol were never lovers. Carol was unlikely to have left with Campbell – an Easterner – as she loyally wanted and indeed craved success for her husband.

Both men were aware of the situation, and Steinbeck discussed it with Ed Ricketts. Campbell approached Steinbeck; they argued the matter earnestly, but Steinbeck prevailed, advising Campbell to leave town, at the point of a gun. Campbell agreed to withdraw and left California in mid-1932.

As the 'loser' in the triangle, Campbell was not well disposed to Steinbeck, particularly concerning the couple's childlessness. John, he said, had refused Carol, 'an old fashion honor-virtue marriage, with children, as well as denied her a modern marriage with mutual freedom.' Campbell went on, 'he has split the thing, giving her an honor-virtue, 50-50 responsibility, childless, husband-dominating monster of marriage which looks very cozy at first glance, but pretty sad on a little inspection. Carol has been jipped.' (POM 114)

Carol may have seen this lost chance as increasing her sacrifice in not having children, which she and John had agreed upon to sustain his writing drive. She may later have recalled, with regret, her quip, 'Rather have rabies than babies.' Susan Shillinglaw's excellent and very readable biography of Carol, *Portrait of a Marriage* (POM), tells of one or possibly two abortions for Carol around 1934, albeit in mitigating circumstances, given both the Steinbecks' financial woes and their nursing commitment to Olive and John Sr. (POM 145) 1934 was confirmed as the date by her third husband, Bill Brown. There is also a reference (Parini 277) to Carol having an abortion after Christmas 1939, at John's insistence, which led to a complete hysterectomy, but there is some doubt concerning this; it was probably earlier. If she had had a hysterectomy years before she would not have been pregnant around 1940; this was perhaps her desperate strategy to try and persuade John to stay with her.

The overall effect was to undermine the Steinbecks' relationship.

John, despite his acquired social freedom, had been brought up in a strongly religious family and that his wife should even have admired another man – let alone take that admiration to its foreseeable climax – was, in his mind, a betrayal. Carol was probably never forgiven; Steinbeck rarely forgave. Months later, the couple returned to Salinas to nurse Olive Steinbeck, who had become ill after a stroke. Carol worked tirelessly, nursing both her husband's fragility of mind over the supposed 'affair' and Olive's physical and mental deterioration.

Despite this, the time could be thought of as the first crisis; when the circumstances bore Steinbeck 'fruit,' in as much as Steinbeck produced both *The Red Pony* stories and the novella *Tortilla Flat*. Given that 1933 was the nadir of the recession and both his parents were faltering, and John and Carol had the responsibility for their care, his continued drive to write and succeed was remarkable. He even wrote while at his mother's bedside. His two divorces, in turn, coincided with periods that saw both *The Grapes of Wrath* and *East of Eden* materialize.

Before the breakthrough and in the aftermath of the 'Campbell affair,' and Olive Steinbeck's death, the couple were struggling. Steinbeck himself said, 'I think Carol is the same way. There is a haunted quality in her eyes. I am not good company to her. I cannot help her loneliness, and she can't help mine.' (POM 139) Indeed, it seemed to Carol that they had begun to live separate lives. (Parini 188) Olive died in early 1934 and John Sr. in May 1935. The family then sold the parental home but retained the Pacific Grove cottage. *Tortilla Flat* was a success and, at last, there was an end to poverty.

These welcome funds brought lighter moments, as when Steinbeck and Carol drove to Mexico City; some undertaking in 1935. Carol had fun buying sculptures and knickknacks and caused a hilarious uproar in a Mexican market when she loudly declared, '*Quiero un toro*' (which means 'I want a bull or stud'), causing much Mexican mirth. John didn't work, and the interlude enabled the couple to relax together for the first time in years. (Parini 201)

Not surprisingly after eight years together, Carol wanted a home of her own and she found a Los Gatos property in April 1936. She was eager to get away from Ed Ricketts, now sixty miles distant, but who had seemed to monopolize her husband and ignore her. (Parini 212) She worked on the house, which included a cot for Steinbeck in his writing room. He may have wanted solitude, but this did not reflect well on the couple's marriage. Steinbeck liked the property because it was remote and had no electricity or telephone. Carol had a garden, and for a time, she had John to herself, away from 'the boys at the Lab.' That summer, she wrote poems and doodled; together they gardened, did the house up and their relationship improved.

However, on a trip to New York, she went crazy at a party and disappeared into the night, causing frantic inquiries at police stations and hospitals, before turning up disheveled the following day. His sister said of Carol, 'That wild side was too much for John. I think she frightened him. He never knew what she might do next.' (Parini 233) The dust settled, however, and they both enjoyed a trip to Sweden and then a somewhat mysterious trip to Russia shortly after, during which Carol, to be contrary, joined the Communist party. The couple began to argue about money. Carol wanted John to help some of the people who had written to him with begging letters, but he was vehemently against this. Poverty had bound the couple: wealth unbound them. Carol saved each royalty check, 'squirreling it away for lean times that would surely come,' whereas John had moved from the need to be poor, to considering money 'bright stuff and I wanted to spread it around.' (POM 205)

She began to resent her husband's success and reflect that, in her terms, she had achieved nothing – no career, no Campbell, no kids. She needed to make her own mark. Although committed to John's career, she didn't want to disappear into his words. (POM 191) Typically, her husband ignored the problem and buried himself in his work. (Parini 244) Despite their improved finances; they bought a car each and cashmere coats, but still Steinbeck fretted about money and intrusions, even after further success with *Of Mice and Men* in 1937.

There was a prologue to *The Grapes of Wrath.* Steinbeck wrote *L'Affaire Lettuceberg.* It was thought, by biographer Jay Parini (Parini 248), to have been a trial run for *The Grapes of Wrath,* but told the story differently. Carol typed and retyped the manuscript for weeks, but hated its tone (POM 198). Steinbeck also had doubts, and she told him, 'Burn it,' even though his editor Pat Covici wanted to publish it, sight unseen. Steinbeck felt it was a vicious book, which enabled him to let off steam about the injustice to, and misery of, California's American immigrants from the Dust Bowl.

After they burned all seventy thousand words, the atmosphere must have been strained between them; but had it been published, *The Grapes of Wrath* in its final form might never have existed.

Steinbeck wrote *The Grapes of Wrath* in seven months, between May and December 1938, all two hundred thousand words. He set himself a daily target of two thousand words. Carol was his gatekeeper; she kept visitors at bay, although she relented one warm August day when, unannounced, Charlie Chaplin called and the three of them drank and talked in the afternoon sun. This was rare sunshine in a darkening marriage. Despite Carol's helmsmanship, steering the big book, *The Grapes of Wrath,* home, their relationship was sinking. One observer (Parini 260) said of Carol, 'she found him insolent, arrogant, selfish and self-destructive. He saw her as petty, mean-spirited and bad-tempered.'

Seclusion did not suit them. They needed the commotion, the friends – the activity – to pass the time, unless John was working. Whenever the writing faltered, and Steinbeck had doubts about finishing it, Carol would tell him to stay focused on the detail, and he did. Finished in 1938 and published in April 1939, *The Grapes of Wrath* will forever be one of the permanent fixtures of American literature.

During the summer of 1938, they had moved from their first Los Gatos home, 'The Biddle Place,' which had become noisier and built up, to a more secluded ranch nearby, which had a pool for Carol, for her 'swimming pool set,' according to Steinbeck (Benson 417), and she did most of the house design herself.

Even after publication, the couple hardly celebrated, but squabbled. The book sold 83,000 copies by the end of May 1939, and 430,000 by the end of the year. The more money that John made, the more he resented spending it. Friends stopped coming to see him. Carol found it 'tedious to stay at home and act as a kind of screen for John.' (Parini 277) He couldn't handle success and left the furor with Carol, to go to Hollywood (and Gwen Conger?). Carol's former admirer, Joseph Campbell, who may or may not have done the decent thing years before by walking away from temptation, even at gunpoint, wrote later after Steinbeck's departure from Carol to Gwen, that he was deeply angered. 'I don't happen to have good feelings for men who stay with a wife through the tough years, then, when things begin coming in, they move to another wife.' (Parini 277) Parini himself concluded the parting of John from Carol 'bordered on gross humanity,' and one can but agree.

Sadly, but inevitably, the marriage was slipping away, the couple fighting most of the time. A trip to Hollywood led to a bust-up at a party, and then later in the couple's hotel. A holiday in Oregon and Washington applied a temporary sticking plaster to the relationship. To Steinbeck, money and famous contacts such as Chaplin, Burgess Meredith and Spencer Tracy, were bewildering. He was mesmerized by his sudden fame and could not cope with something that three years earlier he had despised. Change drove him into the arms of a lovely, bright, smart girl who wanted him – and he wanted her.

Carol and John spent more time apart now – Carol alone at Los Gatos with her friends, John away wherever. She may have been unsuspecting of his affair, or not caring; probably glad of the space, but unsure of her future.

The last significant hurrah before the end was the Sea of Cortez mission to the Gulf of California in a chartered boat, a purse seiner, the *Western Flyer*. The purpose was to collect marine samples and write a journal, and Steinbeck and Ed Ricketts had planned it for months. Steinbeck did not want Carol to go, but she insisted, and he consequently did not acknowledge her presence at any point. *The Log from the Sea of Cortez* was published in 1941. This was in complete contrast to the dedication two years earlier in *The*

Grapes of Wrath which said, 'TO CAROL who willed it,' the other part being dedicated to Tom Collins (camp manager), 'TO TOM who lived it.'

On the Cortez trip, John told Carol that she would have to sleep alone in the wheelhouse, but she slept alone in the ship's stateroom. She flirted with a crewman of the charter boat and Ricketts too, for whom, 'she had a yen.' (POM 231) Carol raised a ruckus over the provisioning, and later in the trip jumped overboard in a temper, wearing a valuable watch. The couple could do nothing right as regards each other, although an inland mule ride into the mountains provided a temporary diversion.

After the sailing saga, during the summer of 1940, Steinbeck squired Gwen Conger around Hollywood, probably not caring for Carol's feelings – and she may by now have realized what was happening, if not with whom. She would have known that her marriage was about to end, but would have been mindful of her childlessness and her husband's role in it. She would doubtless have been aghast had she known of Gwen's abortion in 1940, as recorded in her script, and the correspondence from John to Max Wagner, who was acting as a go-between.

Both Carol and John were ill at Christmas 1940. Eleven years on from his concerns about marrying Carol, his indecision returned. He could not decide whether or not to divorce her; there had never previously been a divorce in his family. To buy time, Steinbeck suggested that Carol take a holiday, ostensibly to convalesce. Years before, her sister Idell had had a holiday in Hawaii where, ironically, she had met Joseph Campbell. Carol decided to go there as John said not to think of the money, and that funds for once were not a problem.

As soon as she had gone, John took Gwyn to his sister's seaside cabin, where they spent several weeks. John worked on *Sea of Cortez*, made love to his new lady and awaited the inevitable confrontation with Carol upon her return.

When Carol came back, she certainly knew of an affair. John had said if she was having a good time – why not stay longer! Alarm bells rang. Carol must have felt so let down after all her support. John seemed moody and to drift rudderless – his life was out of control; he even needed backup. Mavis McIntosh knew the score and became a go-between, and in early April 1941 came the day of reckoning.

Gwyn describes that very day in her story. Even so, at the end of it, John vacillated yet again. To Mavis, he wrote, 'My nerves crashed to pieces and I told Carol the whole thing, told her how deeply involved I was and how little was left...Carol acted magnificently. I don't know why in hell anybody would bother with me...And at last, no more whispering is necessary.' (Benson 478)

In the same letter, he said, 'I am staying with Carol as I must,' but a week later they separated – for good. Carol moved to New York, with Steinbeck telling his agents that this put at least the safety of distance – the width of a continent – between them.

In the divorce, Carol put on a brave, no-nonsense front. She received $1,000 a month ($17,000 today), and eventually a substantial final settlement. From Benson we learn that 'despite the cheerful letters Carol managed to send him throughout the separation, the situation was much harder for her to deal with, than for him. She had given her life to him and his work, and now she had neither. She had also not been well, either physically or emotionally. It was the worst possible time for her to cope with such an ordeal and her family blamed Steinbeck for abandoning her when she needed him the most.' (Benson 478)

Carol Steinbeck's divorce was filed in March 1942, the cause of the separation being stated by her as plaintiff, being 'extreme cruelty.' A year later, the divorce became final, on 19 March 1943. John married Gwyn, as she became known, just ten days later, on 29 March in New Orleans.

Characteristically, Carol went to Fort Ord soon after and studied mechanical engineering, winning an award as the best mechanic on her course. There she met her second husband, Loren.

She used her substantial divorce settlement to buy some houses to rent – mainly to the military, selling some at the end of the war for a healthy profit.

In 1943, she married Loren Howard, but the good-looking military 'hunk' was no match for her wit and sharp humor. A womanizer to boot, Carol divorced him on her birthday (also his birthday) in 1947.

Carol married for the third time in 1952. She was then forty-five and her husband Bill six years younger. He was locally well liked, a former hotel manager and insurance agent. He was a sports fanatic, but Carol was his idol. They had met during the war while Loren was overseas in the Philippines.

He brought kindness and stability to her last thirty years, until she died in 1983 aged seventy-six. Flamboyant to the end, she had her ashes scattered, after the wake, by helicopter over the Carmel River.

Carol Henning Steinbeck was a creative, poetic, impulsive, witty, hard-drinking and hard-working lady: never dull, a remarkable person. She almost certainly still loved Steinbeck after his divorce from Gwyn and met him again then, at least once. Susan Shillinglaw's splendid book, *Portrait of a Marriage,* sublimely tells the story of Carol and her life with the master storyteller. Carol was inspirational to Steinbeck, his rock for over a decade. Sadly, she paid a high price for her unique experience and their collaboration, which began that fateful day when she and her sister wandered into the fishery at Lake Tahoe, high in the Sierra Nevada.

Elizabeth Otis (1901-1981)

McIntosh & Otis, literary agents, were formed in 1928 by Mavis McIntosh and Elizabeth Otis and were Steinbeck's only literary agents, placing his first work *The Red Pony* in the *North American Review.*

Steinbeck was recommended to Mavis McIntosh by his friend Carl Wilhelmson, who was already a client. Wilhelmson had been a classmate of Steinbeck at Stanford, winning the short story prize in his final year, the same year that Steinbeck won the essay prize. Three years later, Elizabeth Otis took over the management of Steinbeck's career from her partner, and received many letters from him, part of his warming-up exercise before starting a day's writing. She and Mavis remained close to him throughout both triumph and disaster, and Elizabeth attended his bedside the day he died.

Annie Laurie Williams was associated with the literary agency from the start, and handled Steinbeck's theatre and film rights, the first being the sale of the film rights to *Tortilla Flat* for $4,000 (about $70,000 today), more than Steinbeck's total earnings in his career to date. An unsuccessful introduction to writer John O'Hara about *In Dubious Battle* inspired Steinbeck to think about the theatre as a vehicle for his work. Subsequently, the book *Of Mice and Men* was adapted successfully for the Broadway stage.

Film rights for *The Grapes of Wrath* were also sold by Annie Laurie Williams – who had previously successfully sold the rights to *Gone with the Wind*. Steinbeck was to receive $75,000 and a quarter of the profits. Of *Grapes*, Steinbeck himself wrote: 'Zanuck (Daryll F.) has more than kept his word...it has a hard truthful ring.' (LIL 195) Even critic Edmund Wilson – whom Steinbeck hated with a vengeance, said, *'The Grapes of Wrath* went on the screen as easily as if it had been written in the studio, and was probably the only serious story on record that seemed equally effective as a film and as a book.' At Steinbeck's funeral, Henry Fonda, a long-time friend of Steinbeck and who played Tom Joad in the film, read poetry as a eulogy.

The Grapes of Wrath had in it some very earthy language – a small part of this had to be toned down, with the grudging agreement of Steinbeck. Such were some of the words going over the Western Union telegraph that one of their operators reportedly said to Elizabeth Otis, 'You are not a Christian, Madam.'

The adulation and criticism the book attracted overwhelmed Steinbeck. McIntosh & Otis (and Carol) shielded him from most of this. Over the years Elizabeth Otis received more than five hundred letters from Steinbeck. She became a lifelong confidante in both his personal life and writing development.

Given the early support of the two principals of the agency, Steinbeck remained loyal to them. Their client list included Erskine Caldwell, John Hersey, Sinclair Lewis and Harper Lee. Late in his life, he wrote to Elizabeth about his misgivings over the Vietnam War. Previously he had also written to her about the criticism heaped upon him when he received his much-delayed Nobel Prize in 1962, a few months after the publication of his 1961 book *The Winter of Our Discontent.* Following the award, he gave the agency a percentage of his prize money, but writing to Elizabeth, he said, 'The reviews of *Winter* have depressed me very much. They always do, but this time they have sunk me particularly.' (LIL 698) Steinbeck never wrote another novel.

Elizabeth Otis died aged eighty in New York, where McIntosh & Otis Inc. still represent the Steinbeck estate today, fully justifying their mantra: 'Where literary legends are born.'

Pascal Covici (1885-1964)

Pascal Avram Covici was born in Romania, moved with family to America in 1907 and became John Steinbeck's lifelong publisher and friend. The combined efforts of Covici and McIntosh & Otis, Steinbeck's agents, established Steinbeck's reputation commercially in the harsh economic times of the 1930s. The storyteller remained loyal to both after that. Steinbeck's many letters to Mavis McIntosh, Elizabeth Otis and 'Pat' Covici have provided scholars with a detailed insight into his writing process. Steinbeck loathed the telephone and its intrusiveness.

Starting with a Florida monthly paper, Covici moved on to found a publishing company and bookstore in Chicago. He was controversial in his early years, having two skirmishes with authority over publications deemed obscene.

In 1934, Covici visited a Chicago bookstall by chance and met owner Ben Abramson, a staunch Steinbeck admirer. Abramson had read *The Pastures of Heaven* and *To a God Unknown*, and also *The Red Pony* placed by McIntosh & Otis in *North American Review*.

Covici, having read *Pastures*, contacted McIntosh & Otis and found there were no contractual agreements in place. He made a successful offer for Steinbeck's *Tortilla Flat*, which was 'doing the rounds unsuccessfully,' for publication.

His firm Covici-Friede was struggling, however, and Mavis McIntosh was well aware of this, but Covici offered to reissue Steinbeck's earlier works as well. Thus, he became Steinbeck's publisher and champion for three decades to come. He was, however, surprised by Steinbeck's insistence on no publicity.

Tortilla Flat was Steinbeck's breakthrough with both large book and film rights sales. Steinbeck's gratitude became apparent when, while Covici was away, his office rejected *In Dubious Battle,* due to prejudice against its brutality and political tone, as perceived by one of Covici's colleagues.

On his return, Covici discovered the rejection, fired his colleague and managed to placate McIntosh & Otis. They had meanwhile placed the work elsewhere, but Steinbeck instructed his agents to stay with Covici.

The only further hiccup was the demise of Covici-Friede itself, but Covici persuaded Steinbeck to stay with him when he moved to Viking Press. Viking Press acquired the rights to Steinbeck's work from the previous insolvent business for a modest sum. This turned out to be an astute purchase, given Steinbeck's total book sales running into millions in the years to follow.

Covici influenced him in his writing, for although Steinbeck ceaselessly sought to experiment, Covici urged Steinbeck to write about Monterey again. (Parini 338) *Cannery Row* emerged from this, a decade after *Tortilla Flat*, and later came a third in the Row trilogy, *Sweet Thursday*. When these ensuing 'little books' were not applauded by the critics, Steinbeck is said to have growled about book size and said that he wrote for readers, not reviewers.

Many letters passed between the two men about both business and Steinbeck's personal life. To Covici, Steinbeck wrote of *The Grapes of Wrath* that, 'This will not be a popular book,' (LIL 172) urging caution on the original print run, but the book sold in hundreds of thousands.

Steinbeck also wrote to Covici, 'This book wasn't written for delicate ladies' (LIL 175) – the subsequent furor was enormous. Pat actually asked to have the original manuscript but Steinbeck demurred and gave it to Carol. In a letter to Covici he went on to say, 'No, I want this book to be itself with no history and no writer.'

Covici told Steinbeck that he and Harold Guinzburg, owner of Viking Press, were both 'emotionally exhausted' (LIL 177) after reading *The Grapes of Wrath* before its publication. They then agreed their biggest ever promotional budget, being so convinced of the book's potential.

Covici often had a cranky author to manage, and occasionally his exasperation showed. Years later, after Steinbeck's divorce and final settlement to Gwyn, the writer acted wantonly for a while. He admitted, 'Having had his goddess fall off her pedestal and on to his head, he turned now to the "other kind" of a woman for solace, with what he called a "goat-like lust" reaching out in all directions. It was a kind of revenge for what he now looked back on, as his humiliation at the hands of Gwyn.' (Benson 628) Worried about his client's finances, Covici wrote: 'Indeed I know you are broke. I checked up your February statement and couldn't believe it. You will have to start all over again and you will, and I am sure there is nothing to worry about.' (Benson 629)

Pascal Covici died suddenly in October 1964, and Steinbeck spoke eloquently and kindly of his mentor. Writers Saul Bellow and Arthur Miller also paid tribute. Steinbeck said, 'Pat Covici was more, much more than my friend. He was my editor. Only the writer can understand how a great editor is father, mother, teacher, personal devil and personal God. For thirty years Pat was my collaborator and my conscience. He demanded of me more than I had, and thereby caused me to be more than I should have been without him.' (Parini 552)

It is scarcely surprising that years earlier, Steinbeck had dedicated his other big book, *East of Eden,* to his lifelong friend, including the phrase, 'And on top of these are all the gratitude and love I have for you.'

Ed Ricketts, Marine Biologist (1897-1948)

Edward Flanders Robb Ricketts met Steinbeck early in the same year, 1930, that Steinbeck married Carol Henning. In the thirties, they shared a close, and for Steinbeck, vital friendship, providing him with ideas and inspiration, and providing a refuge for Steinbeck in times of doubt, depression and marital disharmony.

Albeit an outsider, Ricketts's charm, eccentricity, and humanity endeared him to all he met in Monterey. He sported a beard and dressed as he chose, particularly if it was raining, which he hated. 'In the shower, he wore an oilskin sou'wester – a ridiculous sight.' (SC 234)

Five years older than Steinbeck, Ricketts was born in Chicago, and his early life included time in the Army Medical Corps. Moving to California, Ricketts and a college pal set up Pacific Biological Laboratories around 1923, Ed taking sole charge two years later.

The Lab premises were quite extensive, with a showroom of mounted specimens and an office in which lived rattlesnakes. Another room held many white rats and, yet another, apparatus for mounting and baking slides ready for sale. In another were larger preservation tanks. Though gentle by nature, Ricketts was not squeamish and on one occasion butchered a sheep which his friends had somehow acquired.

'He was,' said Steinbeck, 'a great teacher and a great lecher – an immortal who loved women.' (SC 228)

Ed Ricketts married Anna (Nan) and had a son and two daughters, but sadly they parted in 1936, probably due to Ed's consistently amoral behavior.

He told his children to enjoy themselves in life and said, 'We must remember three things. I will tell them to you in the order of their importance. Number one and first in importance, we must have as much fun as we can with what we have. Number two, we must eat as well as we can, because if we don't, we won't have the health and strength to have as much fun as we might. And number three and last in importance, we must keep the house reasonably in order, wash the dishes and such things, but we will not let the last interfere with the first two.' (SC 265)

Steinbeck himself had dabbled in marine biology years earlier, and, as a local living near the Lab, he liked to spend time with Ricketts observing his work, drinking beer, talking about women, literature, music, politics, and life in general.

Ricketts's business sold marine specimens to colleges and medical research companies. An intellectual bohemian, Ricketts spoke German, loved classical music (especially Gregorian chant and Faust), beer and rum, stimulating arguments and women.

Understandably, although admiring Ricketts, Carol Steinbeck must have felt at times her marriage to John was, to use a later phrase, 'a bit crowded.' She had close contact with Ricketts, working for him shortly after her marriage until he could no longer afford to pay her. Ed, a handsome man, with his power to attract women, must have sparked envy in the somewhat less attractive Steinbeck. The writer sometimes considered himself ugly and awkward, especially when he knew Ricketts carried a blanket in the back of his car. 'It was a battle-scarred old blanket, a veteran of many spreadings on hill and beach. Grass seeds and bits of seaweed were pounded and absorbed into the wool itself.' (SC 262)

Many long and riotous parties took place at the Lab, some of which might last for four days, and Ricketts introduced Steinbeck not only to the characters of Cannery Row, but also to its seedy side, which may have caused Steinbeck to shift his view on acceptable behavior. Ricketts's reputation as a ladies' man appears to have been widespread. At one of the Lab parties, Carol met a handsome writer, Joseph Campbell, and their rumored affair festered in Steinbeck's mind for several years.

In 1936, the laboratory and other buildings were destroyed by fire after a power surge, but Ricketts's ecological book *Between Pacific Tides* had happily gone to the publishers. Steinbeck helped Ricketts to rebuild, and after that Steinbeck remained a partner in the enterprise until Ricketts's death. A safe, which survived the fire, happily preserved a pineapple pie, a Gorgonzola cheese and a half-eaten tin of sardines.

The return on Steinbeck's investment was non-monetary, but substantial, as ideas flowed between them, most being from Ricketts to the younger writer. The Lab was not successful financially – Ricketts was more interested in the world than in collecting his debts.

After publication of *The Grapes of Wrath*, Steinbeck spent more of his time in Monterey and at the Lab, while Carol stayed in their Los Gatos property dealing with the publicity storm. The maelstrom increased their marital problems, as Carol was abandoned at home to cope.

Steinbeck and Ricketts planned a 1940 trip to the Gulf of California – which provided the material for *The Log from the Sea of Cortez*. Steinbeck was by this time deeply into an affair with Gwen Conger, as she was then known, and with many commitments his life was chaotic.

Carol wanted to accompany Ed and Steinbeck on the *Cortez* odyssey. Despite John's unwillingness to take her, she insisted. She is never in fact mentioned in the text of the book, even though less than a year earlier, Steinbeck had dedicated *The Grapes of Wrath* to her – 'To Carol who willed it.'

Ricketts's log formed the basis for the *Sea of Cortez* book, but the buying public was indifferent. It was December 1941, the month of the Pearl Harbor attack and the subsequent entry of America into war. The work was also technical in content, with little of Steinbeck's trademark storytelling.

Four months later, Steinbeck found succor at Ricketts's Lab after Carol left him. Ed listened to his troubles and soothed him with classical music. Ricketts himself had by this time acquired a live-in love in Toni Simmons who, with her daughter, Kay, lived with him until 1947, although he was away for a time doing army service as a laboratory technician.

On his return, Ed read *Cannery Row,* and liked it, in which as Doc, he becomes an eccentric and much-loved American literary character, who returns in *Sweet Thursday*. Characters including Friend Ed (*Burning Bright*), Jim Casy (*The Grapes of Wrath*), and Doctor Winter (*The Moon Is Down)* all portray, to a greater or lesser extent, characteristics of Ricketts. Gwyn Steinbeck relates how Ed featured in a Steinbeck fantasy, *Everyman*, written but then destroyed and never completed, after a discussion between her, her husband and publisher Pat Covici. *Everyman* was also an early title for what became *Burning Bright.*

Gwyn herself spoke fondly of Ricketts, remembering how John introduced her to him, seeking Ed's approval of the new relationship. She recalled 'never experiencing anything from Ed except sheer goodness, he opened my mind to philosophy...' and claiming, 'in many ways he was John's offspring: he was the source of the Steinbeck Nile. She recalled how she and John would call Ed on anniversaries, birthdays and at Christmas, but kept in touch otherwise by letter.

Between 1940 and 1947, Ricketts and Steinbeck saw less of each other, as Steinbeck was often in New York or Mexico. There was extensive correspondence from Steinbeck, which sadly he later destroyed – perhaps because of its incriminating contents about Ricketts's love life with Monterey matrons and others.

Ricketts's stepdaughter Kay died in October 1947, and her grieving mother left both Ricketts and California. She remarried in New York a few months later, just before Ricketts's death. He too was not alone for long, meeting another lady, Alice Campbell.

By 1948, Steinbeck's marriage to Gwyn (as she was by then known) was floundering, but an expedition to British Columbia, with Ricketts, was planned. Sadly this never took place. One evening after work, Ricketts was gravely injured. Benson, his biographer, recalls: 'At twilight on May 7, Ed Ricketts got into his old Packard, drove down Cannery Row and then turned on Duke Street to go across the railroad tracks and into town. The old car was noisy, and the crossing blind without any signal. Into his car ran the Del Monte Express, coming in from San Francisco. The train demolished the car and dragged it several hundred feet along the tracks.' (Benson 614) Some suspected it might have been attempted suicide, coming as it did on the birthday of one of Ricketts's former lovers. Suicide would seem improbable, as Ricketts would have had easy access to poison, which would have ensured a more definite and less painful end.

Critically ill, but still conscious, Ricketts was taken to hospital, but died four days later, before Steinbeck, after a chaotic journey from New York, could reach him. On hearing of the accident, Steinbeck said of his muse, 'The greatest man in the world is dying, and there is nothing I can do.' (Benson 615) Later Steinbeck said, 'It wasn't Ed who died but a large and important part of oneself.' (SC 230) Gwyn recalled that after Ed's death, Steinbeck was not a pleasant person.

On reaching Monterey, Steinbeck and many characters of the town attended Ricketts's funeral, and afterward Steinbeck visited the Lab. There, he burned all the private letters, but retained Ricketts's journals with the intention of reviewing and publishing them. John and Ed Ricketts were incredibly close, often writing two letters a week to each other. Steinbeck hated the telephone, even when he could afford it, and the letters between them would have fascinated, but would probably have destroyed many private lives had anyone other than Steinbeck found them.

The second foray into Ed's safe after his death produced little return. It was empty save for a locked inner compartment. A locksmith opened it to reveal a miniature Haig whiskey bottle together with a final note: 'What the hell did you expect to find in here! Here is a drink for your trouble.' (Benson 616)

Strangely, within a fortnight of Ricketts's death, Steinbeck wrote to his lawyer Toby Street asking him about a loan. 'I loaned Ed a thousand dollars fairly recently. I have his correspondence on it...I will have to get it back some how. (LIL 314) In the same letter, he told Street, 'I've got trouble coming and bad trouble...' His second shattering blow of 1948, this time from Gwyn, was on the horizon.

Max Wagner, Character Actor (1901-1975)

Max Wagner was a childhood friend of John Steinbeck, after moving to Salinas in 1911 from Mexico, where he was born and where Revolutionary rebels killed his father.

Spanish-speaking Max had a long career as a bit-part character actor, appearing in some four hundred productions over fifty years, from 1924 to 1973. He appeared in Charlie Chan and Tom Mix films, as well as television series as diverse as *The Cisco Kid*, *Perry Mason* and *Maverick*. He appeared in films with Laurel and Hardy, coached other actors in Spanish, occasionally composed music, and died in California, in 1975.

Known as one of the 'Wagner Boys' in the early twenties in Hollywood, Max had three brothers in the film business and escorted Gwen Conger (Steinbeck) when she was as young as twenty. According to Gwen, they were very close at this time, before she adopted the name form Gwyn in 1941, to avoid confusion with her mother, known as 'Big Gwen.' She read, including some of Steinbeck's early work, and Max introduced her to John in 1939, at a time Steinbeck was exhausted, after his monumental effort in completing *The Grapes of Wrath.*

Max acted as a go-between to Steinbeck and Gwen, until Steinbeck's first wife Carol came to know of the affair. Letters from Steinbeck to Max, such as one in December 1940, refer to the 'secretary' (Gwen). (LIL220)

'Since the secretary is moving and mail is uncertain, I'll make this report through you. Will you tell the secretary that there will be a meeting, under the old rules between the fifth and the tenth (January 1941). And I won't stay at the Garden of Allah. Too many people can find me there. I'll take a small apartment somewhere. Will you tell the secretary that the heat is on the mail?' (LIL 220)

Max Wagner served in North Africa in World War II; was treated by Alcoholics Anonymous in 1950, but recovered to work, mostly in television, until shortly before his death.

A final letter to Max and his brother Jack appears to have marked the end of their friendship as Steinbeck advised them of his wedding to Elaine in December 1950 – albeit not as an invitation. Steinbeck wrote 'You might write us a note of hope or good wishes or something even at the sacrifice of your principles. You were really in on the inception of this good thing.' (LIL 414)

A decade earlier Steinbeck had written, 'Look after Gwyn a little, will you?' (LIL 215) Would not Max have had mixed feelings towards his boyhood friend, John Steinbeck, and of his behavior to Gwyn, Steinbeck's second wife and mother of his children? Max had clearly been devoted to Gwyn for many years.

Burgess Meredith (1907-1997)

Actor, producer and writer, Oliver Burgess Meredith was a close friend and business associate of John Steinbeck from the time they met on set, during the filming of *Of Mice and Men*. In this, Burgess played George and Lon Chaney Jr. played Lennie.

Sometimes known as Buzz or Buzzy, Meredith had an extraordinary and varied career over sixty-five years, and is best known for his film appearance in *The Story of G.I. Joe,* in which he played legendary journalist and war correspondent Ernie Pyle. Following this, Meredith had leading roles as the Penguin in the *Batman* TV series and movie, and as the gravel-voiced trainer and cornerman Mickey Goldmill in Sylvester Stallone's *Rocky* series of films.

In early years, theatre appearances in *Romeo and Juliet, The Barretts of Wimpole Street, The Playboy of the Western World* and *Major Barbara* maintained his high profile. He did everything from the narration of animated characters, such as Puff the Magic Dragon, to adverts for Honda, United Airlines and breakfast cereal, to more weighty roles such as the narrator in *Albert Schweitzer.*

Like Steinbeck, he fell foul of the Un-American Activities investigation, and was blacklisted by Hollywood for several years.

Moving onto television, he appeared in many programs such as *The Twilight Zone, Burke's Law*, and several Western series – *Rawhide, Wagon Train* and *Bonanza.*

Towards the end of Steinbeck and Gwyn's marriage, Meredith was unwillingly involved in the couple's troubles. As the trio were talking and drinking in a New York bar, Gwyn began to whisper to him. 'This is from me to you,' she whispered, taking off her ring and pressing it into his hand, 'I want you to take this for what it means.' Meredith didn't know what the hell it meant since he felt no attraction for Gwyn...but it seemed to be some sort of a message...so he slipped the ring into his pocket...Gwyn later told Steinbeck what she had done, and later told Meredith, 'He never got over my giving you that ring until his dying day.' (Benson 597)

This incident may have colored the relationship between Meredith and Steinbeck.

Meredith said in the aftermath of Steinbeck's dismissal by Gwyn, 'He (John) was like a zombie. The Gwyn crisis did him in.' (Parini 382) However, after Meredith divorced his third wife, Paulette Goddard, he was sanguine about an affair between Steinbeck and his former spouse; this was before Steinbeck met his third wife, Elaine.

Other Steinbeck adaptations in which Meredith was involved besides *Of Mice and Men*, included *The Forgotten Village* (as narrator) and *Cannery Row*. Burgess also encouraged Gwyn and her New York neighbor, Nat Benchley, to bring their joint effort, the fantasy *The Circus of Dr. Lao,* to the cinema screen.

Steinbeck and Meredith saw less of each other in later years and may have fallen out over a costly and abortive expedition to the Bahamas in search of sunken treasure in 1958. Burgess approached John and persuaded him to invest in a venture to recover Spanish gold, and make a film of the search. Steinbeck, often a parsimonious man, felt he had been taken for a fool by Meredith's associate, film producer Kevin McClory. The trip was an abject failure and soured their long friendship. McClory later became the producer of Ian Fleming's *Thunderball*, having bought the rights, which became the fourth and highest-grossing Bond film up to that time.

Burgess Meredith married four times, but his final marriage lasted over forty-five years until his death.

Robert Capa, Photographer (1913-1954)

'For a war correspondent to miss an invasion is like refusing a date with Lana Turner, after completing a five-year stretch at Sing Sing.' (RJ xvi)

So said Robert Capa, whose book with Steinbeck, *A Russian Journal*, was one of the few enjoyable collaborations in which Steinbeck participated, according to the writer himself. Steinbeck sensed the emotion which the photographer captured in his work. It was as though Capa could capture or sense the feelings of his subject. 'He could photograph motion and gaiety and heartbreak. He could photograph thought.' (RJ xviii)

Capa, an acclaimed war photographer, was born Endre Friedmann in Hungary in 1913. He became radical as a student, but being Jewish as Nazism increased, wisely relocated to Paris. He reinvented himself as a wealthy American, charging outrageous prices to newspapers for his pictures and taking extraordinary risks to obtain them. His evocative photographs of the D-Day landing troops on Omaha Beach, and the liberation of Paris, made him world famous. He first met Steinbeck in Italy in 1943.

In Russia, Capa took some 4,000 photos, despite being often thwarted by Russian bureaucracy. His and Steinbeck's efforts enabled Americans to understand ordinary Russian conditions and also the sacrifices Russia had made to ensure victory for the Allies.

The images in the book were without captions, bearing out Steinbeck's promise to tell it 'how it was.' The writer added, 'We would try to do honest reporting, to set down what we saw and heard without editorial comment.' (RJ4) They portrayed the destruction of cities like Stalingrad and the devastation of the male population.

A creative man, Capa described their mission: 'It seemed to us that behind phrases like "Iron Curtain" and "Cold War," thought and humor had finally disappeared. We decided to make an old-fashioned Don Quixote and Sancho Panza quest – to ride behind the "Iron Curtain" and pit our lances (lens?) and pens against the windmills of today.' (RJ xvii)

Apart from Steinbeck's disapproval of Capa's propensity to steal (or 'borrow') books (RJ 50), and occupy the bath for hours at a time (RJ 23), the two men got on well, and the venture was a personal and commercial success. Later there was a spat over the serialization of the journey in a New York magazine, and Capa once enquired of Gwyn why Steinbeck was avoiding him. It blew over. In an action-packed life, Capa played poker with Bogart and squired *Casablanca* movie star, Ingrid Bergman.

Capa was present in New York when Steinbeck met Hemingway, whom Capa had known since they had both covered the Spanish Civil War, which had claimed the life of Capa's lover and fellow photographer, Gerda Taro.

After his collaboration with Steinbeck, in 1947, Capa received the Medal of Freedom from President Eisenhower. In Paris, he then founded Magnum Photos, a central pooling agency for photographers and their work.

After that, Capa covered conflicts in Israel and Indo-China, where, as ever taking a risk, he stepped on the landmine that killed him. He once advised Steinbeck, 'Stay where you are. If they haven't hit you, they haven't seen you.' Coincidentally, Ernie Pyle, Pulitzer Prize-winning journalist, war correspondent and also godfather to Thom Steinbeck, had died on a battlefield a decade earlier. Capa was just forty. Hungary commemorated him on coins and stamps, and Steinbeck, always an emotional man, was badly shaken by Capa's untimely death.

Elaine Anderson Steinbeck (1914-2003)

Letters by Steinbeck after the divorce from Gwyn became final, in 1948, indicated he was determined to put it behind him and play the field. His shyness was largely forgotten, and his fame attracted the fair sex. He wrote of leaving 'his cave and bearskins here' for the gilded haunts of Hollywood.

To friend Bo Beskow, the first person to be told about Gwyn's wish to divorce, he confided, 'I do not think now I will remarry. I think I am not good at it...Two women were turned to hatred and pain by marriage with me. And both of them would probably have been happy mistresses.' (LIL 343) How would this sit with American feminism today, seventy years later? Again to Beskow, Steinbeck mused, 'I think I will try and have no more wives. I am not good for them and they are not good for me. If I marry again I will be really asking for trouble. The difficulty is that I like women. It's only wives I have trouble with.' (LIL 322)

But, little did he know that by December 1950 he would be married again, older and wiser at forty-eight, to a Texan lady who could, and did, manage him and his business affairs for his last eighteen years.

The Texan lady, Elaine Anderson, was from Fort Worth, daughter of an oil pioneer and at one time Texas classmate of Lady Bird Johnson, wife of later President Lyndon Johnson.

At the time she met Steinbeck, Elaine was the wife of film actor Zachary Scott. She had moved with him, following his award of a film contract with Warner Brothers, to Hollywood. She disliked Hollywood, having given up her career in stage management in New York, where she was involved with the staging of the musical *Oklahoma* by Rodgers and Hammerstein.

Their first meeting was fortuitous. John was offered a date with Ava Gardner, then a worldwide movie star, but her plans changed, so he was asked to squire movie actress Ann Sothern, which he did, and she brought along Elaine. In later years, John was frequently prone to raise a glass 'to Ava Gardner!' Ava Gardner married Frank Sinatra in 1951, just a few months after John's marriage to Elaine.

Their relationship developed slowly. Elaine was not yet divorced, although her marriage was over by the time she met John, the final break coming in November 1949. (LIL 389) John also did not want Gwyn to know too much, so they kept a low profile. He worked on *East of Eden* and wrote letters to Elaine, sometimes calling her Belle Hamilton or Bellita.

His first letter to her in June 1949 was delightfully whimsical; Steinbeck at his funny best reading at the beginning: 'Dear Miss West 47th Street. Am a widower with 10,000 acres in Arizona and seven cows, so if you can milk, I will be glad to have you give up that tinsel life of debauchery and sin and come out to God's country where we got purple sage. P.S. Can you bring a little sin and debauchery along? You can get too much purple sage, but you can only just get enough sin.' (LIL 357)

His letter continued in the same vein – there are advantages after all in being a writer. How could a lady resist?

Elaine provided administrative and loyal support during Steinbeck's later years, notably as his health deteriorated. Gwyn says in her script that it was only at Elaine's insistence, too, before their marriage that John recognized his second son, John Jr., whom he had previously largely ignored. Elaine must have had enormous patience to manage John Steinbeck, his writing, his children and his relationship with former wife, Gwyn. Before their marriage, he was a demanding man to live with, but it appears it was third time lucky for him and second time lucky for Elaine in their marriage.

She enjoyed the fruits of his earlier success and *East of Eden* was completed during her watch, albeit work had been done on it previously. *Sweet Thursday* (1954), *The Winter of our Discontent* (1961), and *Travels with Charley* (1962) were his better-known later works, and she shared in his pride and prestige in his 1962 Nobel Prize. She later traveled with her husband to Vietnam in 1966, also to England in search of King Arthur and the Holy Grail, spending what they recalled as their favorite time together in Somerset.

Steinbeck's determination to leave little to his sons was to have recriminations for almost half a century after his death.

The boys Thom and John failed to take proper advice and did not secure the rights they might have expected over their father's literary estate, with Elaine receiving, in their view, more than the lioness's share. Their failure to do so would appear to have soured their relationship with Elaine after Steinbeck's death in 1968 and their mother's death in 1975.

Elaine was companion and nurse to her husband as his health failed. Although they traveled a great deal, they remained in New York City or their secluded cottage at Sag Harbor, Suffolk County, New York, until John Steinbeck died. True to form, the writer had a beach house, perhaps his last 'nest,' at one side of the property. Elaine, as his heiress, ensured his books remained very much in the public eye.

Gwyn Louise Conger Steinbeck (1916-1975)

Gwendolyn was born on 25 October 1916, daughter of Nelson Potter Conger and Grover Gwendolyn Caldwell, who married 5 December 1915. Gwendolyn changed her name to Gwyndoline in 1941. She probably adopted this and the shortened version, Gwyn, to avoid confusion with her mother, known as Big Gwen: 'Bird Eyes' – according to John Steinbeck.

Big Gwen had at least three husbands and a complicated past. Ancestor James Madison Aubrey, a substantial farmer and landowner, acquired thousands of acres of land via grants by President James Polk in the 1840s, just before Wisconsin became the thirtieth state in 1848. Aubrey's son was probably Gwyn's father, though the records are unclear. Gwyn's mother was both a talented musician and music teacher, passing her talent and love of music to her daughter.

Gwyn met John Steinbeck after her friend Max Wagner discovered she had read *The Pastures of Heaven,* an early Steinbeck work. Max, who had known Steinbeck at school, said he was hiding out locally, exhausted from writing *The Grapes of Wrath*. When Max took Gwyn to meet the storyteller and cheer him up with chicken soup, their mutual attraction was immediate.

Gwyn said that she was born in Chicago and was a Wisconsin girl. She also said her grandmother was from Wales, but this is unsubstantiated. In her early life, she was brought up in some style, although her mother's various marriages were unsettling. The first husband squandered most of the inherited wealth so Gwyn, as a mature teenager, had to work. She had moved to California with her mother and grandmother, lured by the pull of the burgeoning movie business. Max Wagner, who spoke Spanish, was also looking for a start in pictures. Gwyn worked as a film extra, even riding a horse, then as a waitress and a nightclub singer.

Gwyn was dynamic, a young woman who knew what she wanted, beautiful and smart. She was also well read. In his Steinbeck biography, Jay Parini describes the first meeting between Gwyn and Steinbeck in a club. The exhausted Steinbeck was dazzled by her silky voice and long legs. Parini also quotes Gwyn's friend, Janet McCall, who said, 'She was pretty too – taller than most of us, with dirty blonde hair and a lovely curl.' (Parini 279) In almost half of the twenty-five poems Steinbeck sent Gwyn in the early months of their affair, he described her as a redhead.

Gwyn was fascinated by this famous man, some of whose books she had read. But after a preliminary affair, they were apart for some months. Then Steinbeck heard Gwyn sing at the CBS Radio Station at the San Francisco Exposition. He called her, and they again got together. After many crises, including an extraordinary meeting between John, his wife Carol and Gwyn, Steinbeck and Carol parted – soon to divorce.

Gwyn and John first lived in Pacific Grove, California, at 425 Eardley Street, then in New York, first at the Hotel Bedford, then at Snedens Landing, sometimes known as 'Hollywood on the Hudson.' They moved to California and then back to New York, before their marriage, a riotous wedding in New Orleans on 29 March 1943. They resided in New York, during John's abrupt departure to be a war correspondent in Britain, North Africa, and Italy, until their first son Thom Steinbeck was born on 2 August 1944.

A combination of smoking, drinking, asthma, and stress increased Gwyn's health problems, with an effect on the marriage. But in early 1945 with a young child of five months, the couple spent time in Mexico, where Gwyn acquired passable Spanish and helped with the music for the film of *The Pearl*. On their return, they bought a new home on East 78th Street, not far from Central Park, where John Steinbeck Jr. was born in 1946. The couple also spent a holiday in Europe, before Steinbeck was decorated by the King of Norway for his book *The Moon Is Down*, an inspiration for Resistance fighters across Europe.

Soon after John Jr.'s birth, Steinbeck wanted to return to California. At first, the couple rented a clifftop house overlooking the sea. Though Gwyn had a nurse to help, she felt isolated, with John away much of the time. She was relieved when Steinbeck bought an old adobe house in Monterey, which he rewired, and she made comfortable, as she did all their residences. The couple occupied the adobe house only briefly before Steinbeck wanted to return to New York yet again.

A short while later Steinbeck was away with Bob Capa on the trip which inspired *The Russian Journal*. Gwyn accompanied the pair as far as Paris, but returned home to her children when Steinbeck and Capa continued to Russia. Months before, she had hosted a drinks party to help negotiate visas for the trip. The Russians did not grant her one; only Steinbeck, and Capa.

During the long hot summer of 1947, Gwyn looked after Thom and John Jr., awaiting Steinbeck's return. For her October birthday, Steinbeck gave her a Hammond organ. For the first time in years, Gwyn happily composed tunes. She also recorded them on a demonstration disk, to the intense annoyance of Steinbeck, who saw her as competing with him. He forbade her to pursue their commercial distribution. Reluctantly, she agreed.

Early in 1948, Steinbeck said he wanted to buy a dairy farm in upstate New York. At this point, the marriage, which had been under considerable strain, fell apart. Gwyn said 'No' to the farm – she was tired of being pushed from place to place. Her husband was hardly at home. To think about his next big book, which became *East of Eden*, he had moved into the Hotel Bedford to escape children, the nurse, and Gwyn.

Prompted by this action, one night, while they were dancing, Gwyn said, 'I want a divorce.' In 1948, she took her sons to Reno, Nevada, there to divorce Steinbeck on the grounds of incompatibility. Gwyn kept the children and received a modest maintenance allowance and a reasonable settlement. Gwyn moved to Palm Springs, where she lived a quiet life, running an art gallery and living in a small apartment, raising her sons.

She continued to speak with her husband, and he would sometimes visit. But over the years they repeatedly argued about Thom and John Jr., of whom Gwyn had custody. They fell out further, in 1964 in New York's family court, following a suit brought by Gwyn's sons against their father for increased maintenance.

The case lasted some days and widened the rift between Gwyn, who never remarried, and her former husband. She felt with the wealth from his writing success, he was deliberately stingy about their ongoing maintenance, although Steinbeck treated his sons to an extensive European trip, taking with them a private tutor, and footed the bills for their education.

After an argument over a scooter accident involving John Jr. and a girlfriend, Gwyn and Steinbeck never spoke to each other again. Gwyn later moved to Boulder, Colorado, where she died in 1975, aged fifty-nine.

Key to References

RJ. A Russian Journal
SC. Sea of Cortez
LIL. Steinbeck – A Life in Letters
Benson. The True Adventures of John Steinbeck - Writer
Parini. John Steinbeck – A Biography
POM. Susan Shillinglaw – Portrait of a Marriage

Bibliography

John Steinbeck

Cup of Gold	Robert M. McBride & Company, 1929
The Pastures of Heaven	Brewer, Warren & Putnam, 1932
To a God Unknown	Robert O. Ballou, 1933
Tortilla Flat	Covici-Friede, 1935
In Dubious Battle	Covici-Friede, 1936
Of Mice and Men	Covici-Friede, 1937
The Red Pony	Covici-Friede, 1937
The Long Valley	Viking, 1938
The Grapes of Wrath	Viking, 1939
Sea of Cortez (co-authored with Ed Ricketts)	Viking, 1941
The Forgotten Village	Viking, 1941
Bombs Away	Viking, 1942
The Moon Is Down	Viking, 1942
Cannery Row	Viking, 1945
The Wayward Bus	Viking, 1947
The Pearl	Viking, 1947
A Russian Journal	Viking, 1948
Burning Bright	Viking, 1950
The Log from the 'Sea of Cortez'	Viking, 1951
East of Eden	Viking, 1952
Sweet Thursday	Viking, 1954
The Short Reign of Pippin IV	Viking, 1957

Once There Was a War	Viking, 1958
The Winter of Our Discontent	Viking, 1961
Travels with Charley: In Search of America	Viking, 1962
America and Americans	Viking, 1966
Journal of a Novel: The 'East of Eden' Letters	Viking, 1969
Viva Zapata!	Viking, 1975
Steinbeck: A Life in Letters Edited by Elaine Steinbeck and Robert Wallsten	Viking, 1975
The Acts of King Arthur and His Noble Knights Edited by Horton Chase	Farrar, Straus & Giroux, 1976
Working Days: The Journal of 'The Grapes of Wrath' Edited by Robert DeMott	Viking, 1989

Jackson J. Benson

The True Adventures of John Steinbeck – Writer	William Heinemann, 1984

Jay Parini

John Steinbeck – A Biography	William Heinemann, 1994

Susan Shillinglaw

Carol and John Steinbeck – Portrait of a Marriage	University of Nevada Press, 2013

PUBLISHERS NOTE

The late Douglas Brown's work, *My Life with John Steinbeck,* came to light in the small Welsh town of Montgomery. He had died prematurely aged 58, while on holiday in England in 1997, and never had time to edit and publish his work. Douglas had dual British and American citizenship having worked as Secretary to the Consul-General in Washington, before becoming editor of the Palm Springs newspaper, *The Desert Sun.* He bequeathed his script to his daughter Candace Brown who gave it to her uncle John Brown of Montgomery, Douglas's brother.

Douglas met Gwyn Steinbeck at Newport Beach, California and later in Palm Springs. She wanted to tell her life story, as the wife of the eminent Nobel prizewinning writer and as the mother of his two sons. Gwyn undoubtedly had asthma and alcohol problems in later life but was with John Steinbeck for over eight years – five of them as his wife. This period included the entire Second World War-an experience in itself.

During their time together Steinbeck was very productive, despite having to deal with sudden fame, following the publication of his best-known work *The Grapes of Wrath.*

Steinbeck, during their time together, became involved in filming some of his works. Nevertheless, he found time to write

Sea of Cortez following his expedition with marine biologist Ed Ricketts, *Bombs Away, The Moon is Down, Cannery Row, The Wayward Bus, The Pearl*, as well as some pre-planning of the vast *East of Eden* saga. During their marriage, he became a war correspondent, and post-war visited Russia with photographer Robert Capa - a collaboration which became *A Russian Journal.*

The publishers believe it would be remiss for Gwyn's story not to be published, although this is but one version as told to Douglas Brown. We have added the Chapter Notes and Dramatis Personae sections to give the general reader more idea of the times and characters that Gwyn encountered. In this, her memoir, she describes the restless nature of the master storyteller and the consequences of their relationship on her; sadly now somewhat forgotten, but who never remarried or stopped loving her former husband.

Lawson Publishing Ltd, Montgomery, Powys, Wales.
August 2018.

CPSIA information can be obtained
at www.ICGtesting.com
Printed in the USA
LVHW02s0240120918
589880LV00010B/354/P